Jim: A Life with AIDS

JUNE CALLWOOD

·

A
Life With
AIDS

LESTER
&ORPEN
DENNYS
PUBLISHERS

FIRST EDITION

Canadian Cataloguing in Publication Data

Callwood, June
  Jim : a life with AIDS

ISBN 0-88619-224-2

1. St. James, James - Health. 2. AIDS (Disease) - Patients - Canada - Biography. 3. AIDS (Disease) - Patients. I. Title.

RC607.A26C34   1988   362.1'969792'00924
                              C88-094008-5

Sonnet xxx of *Fatal Interview* by Edna St. Vincent Millay. From *Collected Sonnets*, Revised and Expanded Edition, Harper & Row, 1988. Copyright © 1931, 1958 by Edna St. Vincent Millay and Norma Millay Ellis. Reprinted by permission.
"The Impossible Dream" copyright © 1965. Words by Joe Darrion and music by Mitch Leigh, from *Man of La Mancha*. Reprinted by permission of Andrew Scott Inc., Helena Music Co. Portions from the lyrics of "Swayin' to the Music (Slow Dancin')" by Jack Tempchin © 1975, 1976 WB Music Corp. All rights reserved. Used by permission.

James St. James gratefully acknowledges the support of the Ontario Arts Council.

Design by David Montle
Printed and bound in Canada by Gagne Ltée

Lester & Orpen Dennys Limited
78 Sullivan Street
Toronto, Canada   M5T 1C1

This book is dedicated to

Jim St. James

and all the PWAs whose suffering is so great.

Introduction

I did not want to write this book. I thought when I first met Jim St. James that he would die in a few months, and I didn't want to watch that happen. Certainly, in the inevitable intimacy that is formed between writer and subject, I would come to care for him, and the pain of his death would be hard to bear.

I met him first, without registering his name, in late summer 1986 at the regular Monday night gathering of PWAs (People with AIDS) that Linda Boyd and Rod McFadzean used to facilitate. Both Linda and Rod were members of a steering committee I chaired that was trying to put together a hospice for people dying of AIDS. On my behalf they asked the group if I could attend in order to write about them for a column I do in the *Globe and Mail*, and the men agreed to it.

Jim arrived late, found no chairs left, and, during the hour or two that I was there, paced restlessly at the end of the room. When he spoke he had a commanding air of authority and optimism.

"I've got AIDS," he declared cheerfully at one point, "but AIDS hasn't got me."

Some weeks later Linda Boyd arrived at a hospice meeting looking distracted. She confided to me, "The strongest person in the PWA group has just made a very serious suicide attempt.

1

It has rattled everyone. If he can't stand the pressure of having AIDS, where does it leave them?"

"That tall dark man who said AIDS didn't have him?" I guessed.

Linda was punctilious about protecting the privacy of people in the PWA group, so she was distressed that I had made the connection. "Yes," she said reluctantly. "That's Jim."

He called me two months later and on a chilly autumn day I met him in the luxurious apartment of his friend Natalie Wexler. They wanted me to work on a book about Jim's life and his two-and-a-half-year struggle against AIDS. Early in his diagnosis and treatment, Jim had fallen into the habit of talking into a tape recorder, they told me, and there was a lot of material with which to begin.

My hunch was that the book was a therapeutic device, probably Natalie's idea, to help Jim handle the pain. The distraction of working on his biography might see him through to the decline that awaited.

I told them that I was already writing a book, due at the publisher's in the spring, and I couldn't consider any other project until then. In truth I was grateful I had a valid excuse. I have had enough of death.

Jim excused himself and bolted from the room. He was gone a long time while Natalie brightly kept up the conversation, her head tilted to listen for what he was doing. When he returned I made a suggestion that Jim begin putting his life story on tape. If he could find a publisher, I would work on the book with him as soon as I was free.

I thought as I waited for the elevator, "That's that."

The following spring the hospice steering committee had raised enough money to purchase a handsome Victorian house on the corner of Huntley and Isabella streets in the heart of Toronto. With the help of the Ontario government, we planned to open the thirteen-bed hospice as soon as renovations and furnishing would allow.

The name, Casey House, was chosen in memory of our twenty-year-old son, Casey Frayne, killed by a drunk driver in April 1982.

Jim lived less than two blocks away and often turned up to see how we were progressing. One day he told me jubilantly that he had found a publisher for "our book". Malcolm Lester of Lester & Orpen Dennys was interested. My reaction was dismay. Did this mean that I was obliged to write the book after all?

Malcolm Lester genially confirmed that the project was on. I like this publisher very much. A book I wrote about the death of my friend Margaret Frazer, *Twelve Weeks in Spring*, had been handled by him with great sensitivity. He was the best possible publisher for the book about Jim St. James, but I had no enthusiasm at all as we entered into discussions of how the proceeds would be split (fifty-fifty) and details of the contract.

I pictured that I would be finishing interviews with Jim in hospital, that he would die before the book was finished. Several times that summer when I left him after hours of taping interviews I would flee to Casey House to weep on the first sympathetic shoulder I could find.

"Promise me you won't die," I told Jim.

He grinned. "Okay, I promise."

Well, he kept his word. In April 1988 the book was finished in time for Jim to celebrate the fourth anniversary of his diagnosis of AIDS.

Here's to Jim.

1

It began in November 1983, when he had a studio portrait taken. He had closed the week before as the star of a production of *Man of La Mancha*, an award-winning performance that brought him standing ovations almost every night. It seemed that at last he was launched on the career in the theatre that he had longed for all his life.

In view of this upward change in his prospects, he decided he needed new publicity photos. He therefore invested in a sitting with a good professional photographer, Ralph Brody.

When the proofs were ready for him to make a selection, he was dismayed to see that the theatrical studio lighting drew attention to a bump on his right temple that he hadn't much noticed before. The hard, dramatic studio lighting the photographer used threw the lump into such relief that it cast a shadow. He stared at it, perplexed, and felt his temple. He had a lump, all right, a small hard swelling, not at all painful, under the skin.

In fact, it was his second such lump. There was another on his scalp, hidden by his hair. A partner had discovered it one night in bed while stroking his head and it was growing larger, painful when his comb scraped it.

His first reaction was annoyance. A man couldn't become a big-time actor—an Oscar, a Tony, the lot—with disfiguring lumps all over him.

At twenty-nine, Jim St. James was older than most people aspiring to a career in the theatre, but his adult life had been dominated by forces that pulled at him and made it difficult for him to focus on a direction. Born James Zanuk into a family of devout Jehovah's Witnesses, he hadn't yet reconciled the inescapable fact of his homosexuality with his devotion to the stern religion of his father and grandfather, a faith that condemned homosexuality as an evil for which "disfellowship", the Witnesses' form of excommunication, was automatic. He swung between extremes, at times a celibate who would immerse himself in his religion, poring over his Bible for hours, going from door to door with the *Watchtower* and *Awake!* to bring God's word to the doomed who belonged to other faiths or had no faith, and at night throwing himself to the floor in despair, prostrate and weeping, to offer frantic prayers to Jehovah God to forgive his homosexuality. This near-hysterical intensity would be followed by periods when he would give up his religion to fling himself into wanton promiscuity, only to collapse months later into another cycle of remorse and prayers.

He still hadn't reconciled the two warring halves of his being, but he had accepted, at last, that he was incontrovertibly a gay man. A few years earlier he had tried to defeat his homosexual yearnings by marrying a beautiful woman to whom he was sexually attracted. He had hoped that the passion he felt for her would enable him to overcome his preference for men so that he could live in harmony with his religion, but the marriage had failed. When he prayed to Jehovah God, he put the question: You created me, and you created me a gay man. How can it be, then, that to be gay offends you so deeply?

Jim didn't do anything about the two lumps right away, caught in the festivities of the Christmas season. He had a new partner, Paul D., a film editor, and together they made the rounds of parties and gay bars. But soon after New Year's, on January 3, 1984, Jim consulted a skin specialist, who said the lumps were sebaceous cysts, little oil deposits under the skin, and nothing to worry about.

"We make a little incision and it pops out like a pea, no problem," he assured Jim. "I'm booked up right now, but call me in a month and we'll make an appointment."

That was fine for the doctor to say, Jim thought, but he had a career to worry about.

He returned to his apartment, brooding about the delay. If the operation was so simple, Jim thought, why didn't he do it himself? He stood in front of his mirror, feeling the lump on his head. The cyst was there all right, hard and round, just under the skin. He picked up a razor and made a tentative, tiny cut with the razor blade.

He was astounded by the gush of blood. His face was covered in blood, blood dripping from his chin, blood soaking the bathroom mat. He touched the incision, trying to feel the cyst, but there was nothing there to pop out. He had to use an ice pack, holding it firmly against the wound for a long time, before the bleeding stopped.

A few days later he was at Paul's apartment. The cyst he had tried to remove had grown to about half an inch across and was protruding from his scalp like a balloon.

Paul was concerned. "It's blowing up," he said.

Jim went to the bathroom to look at it in the mirror and touched the bubble gingerly. Instantly, it exploded in a fountain of blood that drenched his clothes. Without stopping to undress, he stepped into the shower to wash away the blood, which continued to pour down his face. This time it seemed to take for ever to stop.

7

On February 23, he went to another dermatologist.

"You've traumatized that one in your hair," the specialist told him reprovingly, "but your first doctor was right. These are just sebaceous cysts, nothing to worry about."

Jim decided he had no confidence in the man. He'd been told by two doctors that the lumps were only sebaceous cysts that would "pop out like a pea". Well, he had tried it and it didn't pop out like a pea at all. He was convinced that the lumps were something other than sebaceous cysts.

In fact, there seemed to be something generally wrong with his health. His fatigue was extraordinary. On New Year's Eve he was exhausted before midnight and longing for bed. He put it down to getting old. As actors do, he had found a job as a waiter at Chi-Chi's, a Mexican restaurant that had just opened on Toronto's Front Street, but he found himself almost too tired to work. On slow nights, when some of the waiters would be asked to go home, he always requested to be one of them. He thought it must be a lingering flu. Or maybe he was tired from too much partying over Christmas and New Year's.

It grew increasingly difficult to climb out of bed. He woke after ten, twelve, fourteen hours of sleep and wanted to sleep some more. One day he arrived at work already so full of fatigue that he had to lean against the wall to keep from falling. When he asked the supervisor to be allowed to go home, she was annoyed. Jim was their best and most experienced waiter. He returned to his apartment in a state of alarm. This deep exhaustion was much more than too many parties, and it wasn't just a flu bug. Something serious was happening. Was he eating differently? Was it an allergy to something in the environment? Was his digestive system wonky in some way so that he couldn't absorb nutrients?

To add to his perplexity, he had bouts of diarrhoea lasting a day at a time and then mysteriously disappearing. Several times, he felt hot and looked flushed. He would take his temperature to find it wildly elevated, but it soon dropped back to normal. Twice he wakened in a bed that was soaked with sweat.

Fleetingly he wondered if he had acquired immune deficiency syndrome, "this AIDS thing", that was going around New York. Allan D., a man with whom he had been in love, had AIDS, the first case that Jim knew about in Toronto.

The thought of AIDS was in and out of his head in a flash: too impossible. Besides, he looked great, a tall, slim, well-muscled man with the stamp of his Ukrainian heritage on his strong, broad-cheeked face. He was the picture of robust male health, except for being so tired and the other odd symptoms.

Anxious to start making the rounds of casting directors, he decided that the lump on his temple was his most urgent concern. In fact, to his horror, there were more lumps. While combing his hair one morning in front of his brightly lit bathroom mirror, he found another on his scalp. Probing around with his fingers, he discovered four more new ones, making seven in all. In addition he had two purple splotches, like birthmarks, on his left arm.

He was taking voice lessons and he had auditions in the offing. This was no time for his skin to get "funny".

On March 1, he consulted a family physician, Dr. Hal B., who had been recommended by friend and former employer Natalie Wexler. This doctor gave him a thorough examination and said he had nothing to worry about.

"I have to agree with the dermatologists that these are harmless sebaceous cysts."

"But Hal," Jim said, "I have no energy and I'm not feeling well."

"You're probably partying too much," the doctor assured him. "Relax, eat the right food, stay in touch."

Jim wasn't impressed with the diagnosis and neither was Paul D. Jim called a friend who often had spoken of a wonderful doctor, a gay man. He got the name, John W., and called for an appointment.

"I've seen some other doctors and I'm not satisfied with what they tell me," Jim told him. "I'm not feeling well and I'd like you to take a look."

"Why did you call me?" the doctor asked coolly.

Jim felt it indelicate to say that he knew the doctor was gay. Instead he said, "Because I understand you have a large gay clientele and I'm gay. Perhaps there's something different about my condition that you would know about."

The appointment was set for Thursday, April 5, 1984, at 4:45 in the afternoon. Jim was beginning to address the possibility that he had leukemia or some other form of cancer. Or maybe he was a diabetic. AIDS was not on his list of catastrophic diseases; it just wasn't there. Toronto's gay community was aware of AIDS but didn't think of it as an immediate threat. It had hit San Francisco and New York, but in Toronto almost no one had it.

Jim later realized that he had been blocking that fear because he places great stock in maintaining control of his life. He associated AIDS with helplessness, for him a disaster greater than death.

Meanwhile the family physician had referred him to another dermatologist at Sunnybrook Hospital. The appointment was on the morning of Tuesday, April 3, 1984, in Room 1051. This man, the fourth doctor he had consulted, assured him the bumps were harmless but was willing to remove them. First he would need a blood test. Jim awoke the next day with a high fever. Obediently he called Sunnybrook, more certain than ever that something was seriously wrong, and made an appointment for the blood work.

After the phone call he paid a visit to Allan D. Allan was a former university English professor, a handsome, quiet, scholarly man who was working with developmentally handicapped adults. A year earlier Allan had confided in a few people that he had AIDS. Some of them hadn't even heard of the disease, and no one had any idea how it was transmitted. When Jim used Allan's bathroom that day, he avoided touching the soap or towels. He dried his hands on his pants.

When he knocked on Allan's door that cold, bright Saturday in April, his friend answered bare-chested. Allan had been interrupted in a domestic chore, ironing a shirt. To Jim's dismay, Allan's back and chest were covered with hundreds of purple blotches the size of cigarette burns.

When Jim is frightened he makes jokes. He said, "Get me a pen and we'll play connect-the-dots. There's got to be a picture here somewhere."

For some reason he knew the name for them, Kaposi's sarcoma: a kind of skin cancer, previously very rare, that was one of the outcomes of AIDS.

He didn't need to look at his own arm to know that his blotches were identical.

The two men, all passion gone from their relationship, had a long, gentle talk. Jim sat on the floor, as he often prefers to do, and Allan slumped on the couch. Jim thought how pleasant and restful it was to be with Allan, what a beautiful man he was. After a while, he asked if Allan would look at something on his arm. He took off his coat and rolled up his left sleeve.

Allan examined the purple blotches without saying anything, his face indescribably sad.

"Jim, I'm not a doctor," he said slowly, "so I don't really know. It could be anything, but unfortunately it looks like Kaposi's sarcoma to me."

Jim nodded, expecting that answer. He already had braced himself for it. He kept his tone light. In the face of disaster, his preference is to remain controlled, above it all. He told Allan about his other symptoms in a detached, almost disinterested manner. Allan, knowing Jim well, commented slowly, his face full of sorrow.

11

Jim's anxiety slipped out. He said, with a wretched expression, "Allan, what can I do?"

"I don't know how to help you, Jim," Allan replied affectionately, his hand tousling Jim's hair. "I can't help myself even."

It was time for the appointment with Dr. John W. The physician did a complete physical while Jim described his attempts to have his cysts removed. He was using what he describes as his Bay Street manner, all polish and efficiency, as he explained that he was anxious to have new publicity stills taken, it was urgent that he get going on his career, and therefore he wanted his health problems dealt with expeditiously.

Jim discovered that Dr. W. had a habit when making an examination, of murmuring observations. The procedure progressed with accompanying humming sounds of, "You've got some bruises here, I see.... Oh, you've traumatized this one.... Yes, yes, these purple marks." As Jim lay undressed on the examining table, the doctor stooped over something Jim had not yet noticed, two small red bruises on his leg. "Yes, umm, these bruises...."

After Jim had dressed, he sat across from Dr. W., watching as he wrote notes. Finally the doctor looked up.

"Jim," he said, in a neutral tone, "I'm sorry to do this since you've already been to so many doctors, but I have another doctor I want you to see."

"Oh John, come on," Jim protested, grinning, fear flashing through his guts.

The doctor didn't respond. "This is a friend of mine I want you to see. We were in medical school together and she's very good. Her name is Dr. Bernadette Garvey and she's in the haematology clinic at St. Michael's Hospital."

Jim felt with dreadful certainty that he was in mortal danger. With that flooding fear came a strange sense of resolve and dignity. He describes it as "growing up in that moment".

His composure perfectly intact, he said, "If you're sending me
to this Dr. Garvey, you must have something in mind. You've
seen something and you want Dr. Garvey to confirm it and work
with it. Is that correct?"

"Yes, that's correct."

"You must have a very good idea what it is."

The doctor said, "Well, I haven't put it under the microscope,
I haven't seen the tissue...."

"Dr. W., I'm twenty-nine years old and I'm scared. Please tell
me what you think it is. I'm a big boy."

The doctor measured him. "Jim, I think you're in trouble."

Jim asked the question he had hoped would never be necessary. "Is it AIDS?"

"Yes, I think it is."

Jim thanked the doctor warmly and asked briskly when he
would have his appointment with Dr. Garvey. He was told that it
would take place as soon as possible.

"You don't want something like this to linger," the doctor
explained.

Jim nodded that he quite understood. He left the office and
went to the elevator. Waiting, he felt tears sting his eyes and
brushed them away. A jumble of disconnected thoughts went
through his mind: dad, mom, acting career. He took a breath
and steadied himself. The doctor hadn't seen anything under a
microscope, he wasn't sure that it was AIDS, he could be wrong
in thinking it was.

Jim made a plan. He wouldn't think about it, he wouldn't
worry about it, until the diagnosis was certain. He would finish
"the teary thing" at the eleventh floor and leave it there. He got
into the elevator resolved not to allow himself even to consider
AIDS until he had to.

Paul D. was anxious to hear the results of the appointment, so
Jim went to his apartment to report.

Paul answered the door, took one look at his friend's face, and said, "It's AIDS, isn't it?"

"Yes, it's AIDS."

Paul put on some music and lit candles. They sat in silence, listening, their arms around one another. Jim kept his imagination sternly in check. He allowed himself to wonder only briefly what would be changed for him if the diagnosis was true.

Man of La Mancha, in which Jim had starred the previous November, was an amateur theatre production of the Scarborough Music Theatre, a group with a reputation for good-quality professional-class work. *Man of La Mancha* had been the season's highlight and, not unexpectedly, almost everyone connected with it, as well as the production itself, had been nominated for an award in an annual competition called Theo, for Theatre Ontario. Jim was up for Best Actor in a Musical, and the winners were to be announced at a banquet that Saturday, April 7, 1984, in the Toronto Harbour Castle Hilton's hotel ballroom.

Jim was in no mood to go to the banquet, but he lectured himself that he couldn't be cowardly. In the best theatre tradition, he decided, he had to attend as if nothing were the matter. He prepared himself woodenly. It seemed to take for ever to make a simple decision like picking out what he would wear. He selected camel slacks, a fine turtleneck sweater, a blazer, glossy boots.

He got in his car to drive to the hotel but his nerve failed. He went to Paul's apartment instead. Paul held him comfortingly while Jim cried. Hours passed and he knew he had missed the reception and dinner. However, the presentations would just be starting. He'd better show up, he decided, out of respect for the rest of the *Man of La Mancha* team.

He didn't feel steady enough to drive, so Paul called a taxi. Jim hesitated before going into the banquet room, ducking into a men's room to check his face in the mirror. His eyes were a little red, but not noticeably so. He combed his hair again, fixing it to cover the bumps.

As he stepped through the heavy doors, he found the banquet room in semi-darkness. The awards were progressing at a platform bathed in spotlights and fringed with television cameras. He asked a passing waiter where the *Man of La Mancha* table was. The waiter pointed to the back of the room. Jim then inquired if the waiter knew if the award for best actor in a musical had been presented. The waiter thought it had.

Jim threaded his way among the sprawl of chairs pulled away from round tables that were littered with wine bottles, crumpled napkins, and coffee cups. He waved at people he knew, and shook hands. The voice of the adjudicator, John Plank, was booming through the sound system, listing names of productions and performers, but Jim wasn't paying attention. Plank was talking about a production of *Jesus Christ Superstar*. Then he paused. Just as Jim reached the *Man of La Mancha* table, Plank said, "But the most memorable performance I have seen this year and the winner of the best actor in a musical in 1983 iiiiiis *James St. James* for *Man of La Mancha*!"

Dumbfounded, Jim couldn't move. People leaped up to hug him, crying, "You won! You won!" He was surrounded by jubilant cast members as he struggled to collect himself. As people stood to clap, friends pushed him towards the stage.

When he reached the platform, he was blinded by the lights. A stylized chrome statue was pressed into his hands, and John Plank said, "Congratulations. Would you like to say a few words?"

Jim thought, What do I say? I have AIDS and I'm going to die, should I say that? He had a humorous thought, this is Bette Davis in *Dark Victory*. He decided he would behave with dignity.

"Ladies and gentlemen," he began, with what a videotape of the speech shows to be composure and aplomb, "I would like to thank you for honouring me with this award, which indeed is not

15

just an honour for myself but for the whole company. It takes a lot of people pulling together to make a production like *Man of La Mancha*.

"I'd like to thank Mr. Plank for giving me this award, for feeling that my performance merited such an award. I'd like to mention that the reason *Man of La Mancha* succeeded was because, backstage, on the stage, in the front of the house we were men and women, ladies and gentlemen, of the theatre. The actors, the technical crew, the production staff—we worked as a group. I would like to thank all the ladies and gentlemen of the production, who worked with me. I appreciate everything. I wish everyone luck for their futures, and I thank you."

He shook John Plank's hand, tears in his eyes.

Man of La Mancha swept the Theos that year, seven awards in all, among them best production for Herschel Rosen, best director for Blake Heathcote, best set for Bruce Dodds, best lighting for Ian Williamson—and best actor for Jim St. James.

When the awards ended, a dance orchestra started to play. People came across the room to shake Jim's hand and tell him they were thrilled for him. A casting director from the CBC gave Jim his card and asked him to call for an appointment to set up a screen test. Rogers Cable television asked him for an interview. He agreed, and did it in a circle of admiring onlookers. Another person, a director from one of the downtown Toronto professional theatres, said he had a perfect show in mind for Jim, would he call for an audition? A woman stopped him. She had seen the production of *Man of La Mancha*, she said, and he was wonderful. He had a great future. She was connected with a downtown theatre and hoped he would switch to professional theatre. Just give her a call.

He was gracious in his thanks and promised everyone he would get in touch very soon. Handsome, young, laughing, he looked every inch a successful man, on his way at last to a brilliant career.

16

He sat alone in the taxi that took him home. The thought that came into his head was, Well, you got your award and now you're going to die.

Back at his apartment, he put on his tape deck Maurice Ravel's *Pavane pour une infante défunte*, translated variously as *Requiem for a Dying Princess*, *Ode to a Dying Princess*, or, most accurately, *Ode to a Dying Child*. Hugging the teddy bear he had loved from childhood, he listened in the dark to the music. Then, stretched out fully dressed on top of his bed, he cried himself to sleep.

His next medical appointment was on April 10, 1984, when he was supposed to be in Room 948, H Wing, of Sunnybrook Hospital for the blood tests that would precede removal of his cysts. He cancelled that. His appointment with Dr. Bernadette Garvey, chief of haematology at St. Michael's Hospital, was scheduled for the next day, Wednesday, April 11. He was expected at eight-thirty in the morning for blood tests and a chest x-ray.

That day set the stage for what was to become for Bernadette Garvey and Jim St. James a relationship of mutual affection and respect. He glows when he speaks of her. He believes that she is the reason he became one of Canada's longest-surviving persons with AIDS. On her part, she gives much of the credit to his positive, optimistic attitude and to the strong constitution he inherited from his Ukrainian farmer forebears.

Surprisingly, for one who hates to get out of bed in the morning, he was punctual for his first appointment with Dr. Garvey. As a matter of pride, he was dressed as if attending a meeting of a corporate board of directors. He was wearing a perfectly pressed, immaculate, serious suit, a fresh shirt, a handsome silk tie, and glossily polished shoes. He carried an expensive leather briefcase and a morning paper.

Dr. Garvey wasn't in her office. The waiting room was deserted. A woman in a lab coat came running out of a room across the hall and asked, "Are you Jim Zanuk?"

He said he was, and she told him crisply, "We've been waiting for you. We've got to do some blood tests."

She led him into a clinic full of bustling people.

"Are you prone to fainting when you give blood?" she inquired. "We need to draw nineteen vials."

Jim was shocked but maintained an expression of pleasant equanimity. "No, I don't faint," he assured her.

She asked him to take off his jacket, roll up his sleeve, and sit in a chair with his arm braced on a support. While she was busy at a counter with her back to him, he closed his eyes and prayed. They still hadn't done the testing, so maybe he didn't really have AIDS after all. Dr. W. said he thought it was AIDS but he hadn't said he was certain, he could be wrong in his suspicion. It could turn out that Jim had something that was easy to cure. Four doctors had said the cysts were harmless; maybe they were right.

The nurse assembled a tray of vials, each with a different-coloured band, and bent over him to put on a tourniquet. His veins were huge, bulging down his muscled arm. She grinned at him. "I could throw the needle from across the room and I'd still hit a vein," and he chuckled appreciatively. She swabbed a spot, squinted at the needle, held it aloft, and plunged it in. To distract him, she made practised conversation about her sore back.

Jim's façade of detachment was wearing thin. He asked conversationally, "Why do you need so much blood?"

She was businesslike. "You see, Mr. Zanuk," she explained, "in the case of AIDS patients several vials have to go to Western Hospital for testing, several vials have to go to the Hospital for Sick Children for testing, and we do our own testing here."

Jim felt his heart break. He thought: It's real. I have AIDS.

"Where's Dr. Garvey?" he asked.

18

"She's in the clinic," the woman said.

When the tests were done, he rolled down his sleeve, replaced his cuff-link, slipped on his coat, and went to the reception desk. He got directions to the clinic and started through the maze of cream-walled corridors that make up the old hospital. As he neared his destination he saw coming towards him the most efficient-looking woman he had ever seen. She was small, dark-haired, wearing glasses, and on the young side of middle age. Her heels slapping emphatically on the floor and a no-nonsense look on her face, she clearly was in a hurry.

He caught a glimpse of her name on the identification badge pinned to her coat.

"Are you Dr. Garvey?" he asked.

She said, impatiently, that she was.

"I'm Jim Zanuk," he said.

"Well, Mr. Zanuk," she told him severely, "I'm sorry you're late for our appointment at eight but I couldn't wait any longer."

"The appointment was for eight-thirty," he protested. "I was there on time and one of your people took my blood."

Dr. Garvey was startled and annoyed. "That shouldn't happen. The procedure is that I talk to you before tests are done."

"Actually, Dr. Garvey," Jim said, "the nurse told me that I have something serious."

He had intended to say AIDS but found he couldn't get the word out.

The doctor frowned. "That's not the way we run things here. She's not supposed to say anything. That sort of thing shouldn't happen."

Her voice sharp, she went on, "Well, I'm sorry about that, but I can't see you now. I don't have time to see you today, you'll have to make another appointment."

As she started to move away from him, Jim said desperately, "Dr. Garvey, please. You must answer a question." She stopped and gave him a hard look. "I think you can tell me the answer, yes or no. Am I going to die?"

The stiffness went out of her. "Of course I'll talk to you, of course," she said. "I really am completely booked today but I do have to eat lunch. Come to my office at twelve o'clock and we'll talk. This thing has to be handled properly."

Dr. Garvey, as Jim was to learn, has a passion for proper procedure. Nothing could suit his compulsive nature better. He's a man driven to distraction by untidiness, by a finger-smear on his glass coffee table, by towels that aren't folded on the rack. His apartment, like his person, is always spotless and neat. He dotes on formality and the protocols of hospitality.

Jim went to a lunch counter and ordered a breakfast of bacon and eggs. The short-order cook deftly pushed food on the grill with a spatula. Around Jim, people in the diner talked idly and called for more coffee. Outside on the street, pedestrians hurried by, heads down against a chill wind, and traffic splashed dirty water over the curb.

The mundane had become surreal. He was astonished that his pain was invisible. He thought it should be obvious, to look at him, that he was in agony. How could people be so indifferent? Everyone was behaving so ordinarily. It was nothing to them that the man in the dark overcoat, drinking his coffee, had just been given a death sentence.

At noon he reported to Dr. Garvey's office.

"Your doctor, John W., and I are very good friends," she began. "He deals with a large number of gay people and at the moment I'm helping him with problems gay men are encountering of late."

Jim nodded understandingly, as one professional to another.

"We're looking for AIDS in your case," she went on. "You apparently have some bumps, and I'm going to send you up right now to a dermatologist to have one biopsied. We're going to take out a specimen and look at it under the microscope. We're not convinced that anything is a disease until we examine it. Before I tell you that you do or do not have AIDS, I'll have to see the data. Following the biopsy today I'm going to admit you to the hospital for ten days or two weeks. That's for more tests. I need to look inside your stomach, I need to look inside your anus, I need skin tests. The reason for all that testing is that when you have questions to ask me, I'll have the information."

That made eminent sense and Jim was impressed. He liked her logical approach and enjoyed her almost imperious manner. Everything about her cool style and air of efficiency delighted him and made him feel safe.

She rose and said, "There's no point in asking me any questions today because I don't know where we're at."

He thanked her and left. From that meeting, his life would never again be the same.

2

In the years of hospital admissions that were to follow, Jim retained from that first meeting with Bernadette Garvey "a clear idea of how hospitals work", as he puts it. It made sense to him that there should be thorough testing and time-consuming analysis before any treatment began. He was never among those patients who grow restless with delay and a seeming lack of activity. Dr. Garvey and St. Mike's had his complete confidence, without reservation. Her certainty about what she was doing lifted his anxiety. He became, in fact, an ideal patient. No matter how painful the treatment or prolonged the gaps between tests, he never wavered in his belief that everything was proceeding as it should and that Dr. Garvey was working full tilt to help him get well.

"I've learned that patients have to give to the doctors to let them do their job," he explains, "so that the doctors can give to the patients. It's a two-way street. If the patients don't understand the situation they're at the doctors' throats for answers the doctors don't have yet."

He left Dr. Garvey's office that day and went, at her direction, to a dermatologist. Jim had recovered from the shock of the nurse's casual reference to AIDS. His ebullience was restored by Dr. Garvey's unwillingness to confirm the diagnosis, and he was

22

in a mood to believe once more that those who suspected that he had AIDS were making a grievous error.

The dermatologist was a big man whose shoulders were white with dandruff. Jim was amused. He thought such conspicuous display of a scalp problem was a poor advertisement for someone who specialized in afflictions of the skin.

The doctor explained that he would use a local anaesthetic and remove one of the bumps for analysis. Selecting a new one that had just emerged on Jim's left arm, he sterilized the area and inserted the local. Jim didn't want to watch, but on the other hand he couldn't look away. This was his body, and he needed to see what was happening to it.

The doctor removed a little piece of white flesh and sewed the tiny incision. Jim was surprised. He had expected the tumour to be red and bloody. The doctor dropped the specimen into a container and Jim asked to see it.

Keeping his tone light as he studied it, he asked, "What do you suppose it is?"

"Well, I won't be sure until I look at it under the microscope."

Jim commented, with a conspiratorial smile, "You do have a pretty good idea though, don't you?"

"Yes," the doctor nodded. "It's Kaposi's sarcoma, a cancer tumour related to AIDS. It can't be anything else because Kaposi's sarcoma doesn't look like anything else."

"That's what we thought downstairs," Jim said briskly, his heart sinking, "but Dr. Garvey, of course, wanted to confirm it."

Jim put on his shirt, knotted his tie, slipped into his suit jacket, and shrugged to get the hang right as they chatted about the weather. Then Jim thanked the doctor warmly and left. He walked around the block a few times before getting into his car. His mind was empty. He passed a bed of bright tulips, and the thought sprang unbidden that he would never see tulips again. His next thought was that friends might send tulips to his funeral.

23

Then he ordered himself to get a grip. He had to stop thinking that way.

That weekend he phoned his parents and talked about inconsequentials, happy to hear their voices. He hadn't been sure when he dialled that he would tell them he was in trouble, but when pauses came in the conversations he found he didn't want them to know. It wasn't necessary to alarm anyone just yet. It could still be a mistake.

He was to be admitted to hospital on April 18 for more tests. There had been a suggestion of chemotherapy. The word "chemotherapy" had an ugly ring. Allan D., whose body was covered with Kaposi's sarcoma, had received chemotherapy treatments, to no apparent avail.

Jim was aware that somewhere within him was stark terror. He decided to keep a cap on it. Nothing yet was certain. To distract himself, he cleaned his apartment thoroughly, taking satisfaction as always in making it immaculate. He went shopping for new pyjamas and bright jogging suits to wear in the hospital. Everyone he encountered over that weekend remarked on his good mood. He watched his performance approvingly, pleased at how well he was pulling it off.

He reviewed his scant knowledge of AIDS . About a year earlier he had been working out in a New York gymnasium frequented by gay men. As he was leaving he saw a poster about AIDS and stopped to give it a glance. Someone noted his interest and said, "That's something to watch out for."

Jim said, "What's AIDS?" and the man shrugged. "I don't know exactly, but a lot of gays are getting it."

The only other person Jim knew with AIDS was Allan D. AIDS was so unusual in Toronto in 1984 that Dr. W., who had a large number of gay men among his patients, had seen only one or two cases. Though Dr. Garvey was receiving AIDS patients referred by a number of Toronto doctors, Jim was only number eight. In Toronto most gays didn't know the disease had reached Canada and few had any reliable information. People said it seemed to knock out the immune system, but not all of it. There was talk of some curious rare diseases, Kaposi's sarcoma and a strange kind of fungus pneumonia, that meant AIDS. Jim didn't know that Kaposi's sarcoma was cancer until the dermatologist let the information slip.

It was known in the Toronto gay community that a lot of gays were dying of AIDS in San Francisco and New York. The other people being hit with AIDS were drug addicts—underworld people with poor health to begin with. Jim assured himself that the people who were dying must all be frail. It couldn't happen to him because he was in peak condition.

The scariest part was not knowing how the disease was transmitted. Jim hadn't the faintest idea how it was spread, but he assumed it was like catching a cold, you got too close to someone who had a cough. He was worried about possible danger to his friends. For instance, he often shared a bottle of pop with Natalie. Had he put her in danger? What about his contact with Natalie's husband, Bernie, or her twin sons? What about the cast of *Man of La Mancha*? A few times, waiting for his cue to go on stage, he had asked someone standing near the wings with a cup of coffee for a quick sip. Similarly he had shared his coffee or soft drink with someone else. Had he picked up AIDS that way? Or passed it on to some innocent?

His partner, Paul D., had not flinched from sexual intimacy with him, but both were concerned. Though Jim learned that Paul had suspected from the beginning that the bumps and purple blotches meant AIDS, nothing in their intimate relationship changed. Most of the gay community in Toronto believed that the disease somehow was related to the wide use among gays of a drug called poppers. The theory seemed logical because drug-users were the other identifiable group of people with AIDS.

Jim made an effort to learn more about AIDS, but there was no information, only rumours. He decided he could find out more by pumping the doctors at St. Mike's with sly questions.

The tests were exhaustive and Jim was discharged the next day. He would be readmitted after the weekend, he was told. Nothing yet was certain.

That Saturday, April 21, he decided it was time to tell his father. Jim's father, Karl Zanuk, is an interesting man. Ukrainian-born, he's a big, rugged person who bears a very strong resemblance to his son. Jim's father's father, Steve Zanuk, came to Canada from Onoot in the Ukraine, leaving his wife, Dorothy, and their two-year-old son behind. Steve worked for seven years as a labourer in the Steel Company of Canada plant in Hamilton, saving enough from his small wages to buy a two-hundred-acre farm near Brantford, Ontario.

Then Steve sent for his wife and son, Karl, who was nine. During Steve's years of loneliness and self-deprivation he had been drawn by the comradeship offered by the Jehovah's Witness religion. A man of simple, unquestioning faith, he found in Jehovah's Witnesses a great comfort and a way of life that suited his quiet reverential nature. When his wife arrived she obediently became a Jehovah's Witness as well and insisted that their son, Karl, adopt the faith too.

Karl dropped out of high school, as all Jehovah's Witnesses are urged to do, to avoid becoming too "worldly", and embarked on the mission that adult followers undertake to convert their neighbours to the faith in time for Judgement Day. He helped his father on the farm until he was in his twenties, showing an inventive mind and an almost uncanny aptitude with machinery. He married and in rapid succession had four children. Looking to improve his income to support such a large family, he took a job as a salesman with a Brantford company selling aluminum products. Karl Zanuk quickly decided he could make a better product himself. He began producing aluminum storm windows and screens in his father's barn, selling them door to door until the business grew big enough for him to require a sales force. By the time he sold the company, many years later, he was a wealthy man.

As a youth Karl Zanuk married Johanna Marta, a woman he had known since elementary school. She is a passionate member of Jehovah's Witnesses, her conviction far stronger than his. Raised in Alberta, she was one of seven children in a family of Czechoslovakian heritage who moved to the Brantford area when she was still a child. Her schooling ended in grade three, after which she threw herself ardently into studying Scripture and taking the message of Jehovah God from door to door.

In six years Karl and Johanna had four children, Kathryn, Karl Allan, known as Allan, James Steven, known as Jim, and Karen Marie, known as Karen. Though the children were lovingly raised, their parents often were at odds, usually because Johanna felt that Karl spent too much time on his business and not enough attending to his responsibilities as a Jehovah's Witness. After a stormy battle one morning, she left him, taking with her the two youngest, Jim, twelve, and Karen, ten. Jim's parents later were divorced and both remarried.

After that break, Jim's reconciliation with his father had been slow. Much of the effort to mend it came from him, but he was determined to persevere. Jim often endures tirades from his father, usually on the subject of what his father views as Jim's fecklessness. Jim accepts these tongue-lashings meekly, feeling them in good part deserved. He understands what lies beneath his father's bursts of temper. Though he still longs to win his father's respect and approval, he knows that because he is gay he isn't the son his father wanted.

Jim has never ceased trying to impress and please his father, whom he adores. In fact, he loves everyone in his family, his mother perhaps most of all, and he's vulnerable to hurt when they turn from him. When they are cool, or distance themselves entirely, he suffers greatly.

Concerned that his father would be annoyed to hear of his illness indirectly, Jim decided to drive to Brantford to inform him himself. At the back of his mind was his father's reputation for being able to fix anything. Once while the family was driving on a deserted road on the prairies, the car axle broke. Karl Zanuk hopped out and made a temporary repair with a coat hanger. Jim had no illusions that his father could fix AIDS, but it wouldn't have surprised him if he could.

His father and his father's second wife, Eleanor, live in a handsome bungalow built on the original Zanuk farm when the children were small. The family is so clannish and so attached to the land that Jim's brother, Allan, had just purchased a fifteen-room house across the field, not far from the farmhouse where Jim's grandparents once lived.

Jim arrived late that Sunday afternoon in April and found that his father and Eleanor weren't at home. He guessed they were at Allan's new house and drove there.

He was greeted by the sound of voices and hammering upstairs. Nervous of his reception, he climbed the stairs tentatively and found his father, Eleanor, Allan, and Allan's wife, Mary, painting and building cupboards. Since he usually announced his visits in advance, they were surprised to see him but welcomed him warmly. They bubbled with congratulations for his Theo award. Jim had almost forgotten about it. As they chatted, Jim's awkwardness grew.

Eleanor was suspicious. "For a man who just won a big prize, you don't look very happy. What's wrong, Jim?"

Jim said, "I have something important to tell you. If you're not too busy, could you all come over to father's place for a cup of coffee?"

28

They gathered, as always for family discussions, in his father's kitchen, and his father took his accustomed chair at the table. Jim sat on a footstool, not knowing how to begin.

"Well, Jim," prompted his father impatiently, "what's your news?"

Jim had an urge to put his arms around his father and cry, but he stayed where he was.

"You may have noticed I haven't been around for a while," he began slowly. His father nodded, watching him carefully. "The truth is, I haven't been feeling very well. I was in hospital for a bit of testing. They think it's cancer."

Karl Zanuk's face flooded with shock and sorrow, and the others were speechless. Karl recovered first.

"Do you have the test results?" he asked sharply. "Are they certain?"

"I don't know for sure," Jim replied. "I go back into hospital next week. If it's cancer they want to start chemotherapy right away, but I won't know exactly for a little while." Jim saw his father's face change. Concern was replaced by skepticism. Karl has a general view of his son as tending to exaggerate and already had put the news into the category of another of Jim's fantasies.

"Are you sure you're not just being dramatic?" he asked.

Jim grinned. The response was just what he expected. "No Pop," he replied. "I'm not making this up."

The elder Zanuk extracted the name of Jim's doctor and said he was going to check with her. The tone of doubt that he raised sustained them all. No one cried. Allan Zanuk took that moment to announce that Mary was pregnant with their first child. Everyone cheered and hugged. Jim stayed the night and parted from his father and Eleanor the next morning in a congenial mood, promising to keep in touch.

At the last moment, Jim's father silently wrapped his arms around him, which said it all.

AIDS had not been mentioned, but newspapers were beginning to be full of stories about "the gay disease", and Jim knew that his family would suspect that he had it. Nevertheless, he hadn't been able to say the word. Drawing on his own experience of coming to terms gradually with the possibility, he was convinced it was best to give bad news in graduated stages.

Jim worried next about telling his friend Natalie Wexler that he had cancer and probably AIDS. He was trying to work out how to do it. Natalie, however, already knew. The same afternoon that Jim was with his family, a mutual friend had decided that Natalie should be informed and had taken it upon himself to break the news. On his return from Brantford, Jim called her and they met at a restaurant where they ordered a favourite of theirs, "the best German chocolate cake, to die for".

"Look," he told her briskly, "I might have AIDS."

She made a show of being shocked but already she was researching the disease. She had more information than he did. She had discovered that no one yet had seen the AIDS virus. Scientists had not yet isolated it. Doctors knew that something was eating T-cells, which make up a significant part of the body's immune system, but the virus hadn't been found.

She read that AIDS first was recognized as something new in infectious diseases when doctors all over North America noted that their patients weren't responding to the drugs that usually worked to boost the immune system when it was under attack. It was some time before they realized that something unknown was happening to shatter immune systems beyond repair. At that point they gave the still-undetected virus the name human immunodeficiency virus (HIV) and the disease the name acquired immune deficiency syndrome (AIDS).

On the day Jim was to be admitted to hospital, he packed with care and dressed in suit, shirt, and tie. Ready to leave with his briefcase and belongings, he paused and looked in the mirror.

30

He thought, "You look the same, Jim, but it's all different. It's all changed. It's only been a few days, but everything is changed. There's a new set of rules for your life now and you're going to have to figure out how to deal with them from today on. Because if you don't, you'll lose your ever-loving marbles."

His admission to St. Michael's Hospital that April day in 1984 set the tone for almost all his hospitalizations to come. He decided that if the first admission went splendidly, subsequent admissions would be less stressful. He therefore determined to behave with urbanity, civility, and light humour.

Accordingly he packed some accoutrements he thought appropriate for a gentleman of means and taste compelled to endure a less refined environment: a silver tray and two crystal stemware glasses, cinnamon for his breakfast toast, new shirts, a fruit bowl and some perfectly ripened fruit, a colourful bedspread, some books, a tape machine with earphones and a selection of music, a big, many-times-patched teddy bear that has consoled him all his life, and a fine assortment of silk robes, costly pyjamas, elegant slippers, and the new jogging suits. A few days later he augmented this survival gear by returning home for more: two pieces of art to hang on his walls, a guitar, some silverware, monogrammed towels, and a coffee maker.

He grins, "I moved in *in style*."

He was told in the admitting office that he had been assigned to 6A South, the cancer ward.

"Fine," he beamed, concealing his shock at the word "cancer".

He announced himself at the nursing station in the tone of a busy man asking directions to the airport. "Hello," he said. "My name is Jim Zanuk and I'm being admitted today."

Ruth B., the head nurse, surveyed him, unimpressed. Jim liked her on sight and was sure she had seen his kind of performance before, a bluff of being in control while actually frightened out of one's mind.

31

"We were expecting you, Mr. Zanuk," she said warmly, "but your room isn't quite ready. Can I get a lunch tray for you while you're waiting?" She looked for a chair and, finding none, pulled out a wheelchair and pleasantly invited him to use it.

Jim sat in it to eat his lunch. As he waited, visitors passed in the hall, giving him quick looks, their eyes sliding away when they met his. He wondered what they saw—a man with terminal cancer, or a handsome fellow who had made a mistake and was on the wrong floor?

When his room was ready, he began to unpack. Ruth sat on the bed to talk to him. "You'll be here a few days so we'll be seeing a lot of one another," she explained. "Let me introduce myself. I'm Ruth, the head nurse, and I'll be here almost every day. If you don't understand what's being done to you, or things that are happening around you, would you please just ask me. I'd be happy to explain what's going on."

He was reassured by her kindness. As a parade of nurses came to take vital signs, he was in a jovial mood. He announced that he hadn't been treated better in luxury hotels. "This is the St. Michael's Regency," he told everyone, "and I love it."

He received no more food that day but was given a strong laxative to prepare him for a bowel x-ray. A doctor strode in, Dr. P. Jim was to see a good deal of the man and admires him greatly. Like Jim, Dr. P. is of Ukrainian heritage and it amuses them to exchange the fragments of language they have retained from their childhoods. Dr. P. explained that the test the next morning would involve a twenty-inch plastic hose with a camera in one end. It would be inserted into Jim's anus in order to survey the lower bowel. Next they would take a thirty-six inch tube with a camera and insert it down Jim's throat and through his stomach to examine the upper intestines.

In both cases, the doctor assured him, Jim would be under a general anaesthetic and wouldn't even know the procedure had taken place. Though he concealed it, Jim was not reassured. His apprehension and horror returned full force.

The next morning he was given a tranquillizer and was floating in a pleasant haze as he was wheeled into the operating room. People with surgical masks surrounded him, their voices sounding hollow and full of echoes. He maintained his performance of lighthearted cheer, making jokes about the room, the overhead lights, the net that was put on his hair.

Dr. P. appeared and announced that the IV drip would be started. "We want you to count backwards from a hundred. You'll be out in moments."

"Don't fall in," Jim advised him with a wide smile. He heard the doctor chuckling as he began to count: "One hundred, ninety-nine, ninety eiggght, niiiiiine...."

He awakened in his own bed. A nurse, Irene, came in and asked how he felt. He wondered how long he had been unconscious and was told four hours. He was astounded. "It went by like a second!" he gasped.

He often thinks of death, but not with fear. Because he has not a shred of doubt that he will be resurrected on Judgement Day, his only concern is for the interval between dying and being reborn. He has concluded that death will be like an anaesthetic. He simply will drift off into nothingness, to awaken in a second or a thousand years—it won't matter which, since he won't be aware of the passage of time—in a world made beautiful by Jehovah God. He thinks of death as a kindness devised by the Almighty to give rest to bodies broken by mishap, or disease, or age.

Bernadette Garvey left much of the daily contact with Jim to a resident, Dr. André C., a tall man with hair Jim describes as "long and shaggy-dog". Dr. C. came one day when Jim was alone and pulled up a chair beside him. He said he had a lot of respect for Jim, that Jim was an intelligent man, and that he therefore wanted to be frank about Jim's situation.

"I think you're the kind of person who needs to know everything we're doing," he said. "Some of our patients don't want that, but you're the type who is calmer when you have all the facts."

He then laid out what the tests were meant to discover, how they would be done and analysed, and why they were being ordered. Jim interrupted with questions from time to time, his manner serious but under control.

The doctor paused. "I've never met a gay guy like you before," he said impulsively. "You're a regular guy, a really nice guy. I just want to tell you that we're all impressed by the way you're handling this."

Jim was enormously pleased. The man's kindness gave him courage to ask about something that was terrifying him, a tumour growing on the tip of his penis. The doctor assured him that it would probably disappear along with the other tumours when chemotherapy treatment began. On subsequent visits he would draw the curtain around the bed and examine the new tumour carefully. To Jim's relief, the tumour didn't grow over the opening.

Diagnosis of the biopsy specimen taken by the dandruffed dermatologist was completed and the results of the camera explorations were available. Dr. Garvey said she wasn't ready to discuss either. She needed time to assess the information before she was willing to proceed. Her plan was to have Jim discharged the next day, and she made an appointment for him to see her in a week. He held his breath. She hadn't said that he had AIDS.

She looked around the room at his pictures, his bedspread, the silver tray bearing an ice-bucket in which wine and juices were chilling.

"You've redecorated," she said drily.

"I thought it would be fun," he replied with a sunny smile.

He had fallen in love with the nurses on 6A South, *all* of them. Touched by their compassion and good humour, he was awed by their dedication in working on a floor where they were surrounded by pain and death. In turn, they responded to his boyish gallantries and made each medical routine a social occasion rich in merriment. It was just the way he wanted it. When he was ready to cry, however, they were quick to give comfort. They had recognized that he was a desperately frightened man hiding behind jokes and the flamboyance of crystal fruit bowls. One day when he had a temper tantrum, no one seemed surprised or affronted. They calmed him down and left him with assurances of their affection.

That first time in St. Michael's he met a charming and beautiful young woman, Susan, a cancer patient with many admissions to 6A. During his second admission, Susan died. The nurses he loved came into his room with tears streaming down their cheeks, to be consoled by him as best he could.

Some years later when asked when he was last in hospital, without thinking Jim replied, "I haven't been home in a while."

He bought books about cancer. He didn't understand much of the contents, but it seemed apparent that if he had cancer in as many parts of his body as had been tested, he was a dead man. He counted fourteen lumps on his body. They were springing up everywhere, but mostly on his left arm, and growing rapidly. One book, by Linus Pauling, recommended vitamin therapy, so Jim went to health-food stores and examined labels. His friend Allan D. was enthusiastic about vitamin supplements and knowledgeable on the subject. He would check with Allan to learn what he should take for AIDS.

Jim arrived at Dr. Garvey's office for his appointment looking dapper and carefree.

As part of his determination to stay in control of his situation, he had prepared a list of questions: Would he get more lumps on his face? What about his fatigue? What about something new, a sore back? What was the pain in his leg—did it mean that he had cancer there and, like Terry Fox, would have it amputated? He worried about the swollen lumps in his neck: what were they? Did he *really* have AIDS or was it merely a possibility? He was seeing so many doctors; who was the doctor managing the case? What about his previous sex partners—should he make a list of everyone with whom he had been intimate?

He no longer believed that AIDS was related to the "poppers"—amyl nitrate—so popular in the gay community. Everyone had blamed the drug, sold over the counter as room odourizers at six dollars a bottle, that gay men sniffed during intercourse because it dilated blood vessels and enhanced and extended orgasm. Jim decided that if AIDS was caused by poppers, almost every gay man in Toronto would have it.

There had to be another common denominator to explain why AIDS in Canada was hitting primarily the gay community. "It can't be that we have such great apartments," he commented drily during a discussion with friends. "It has to be sexually transmitted."

He was full of anxiety as he drove to his appointment with Dr. Garvey, avid to have the suspense ended. He needed information, but he wasn't willing to pay any price for it. His dignity, for instance, was not on the block. He would put his questions in an academic, detached manner, showing a decent amount of concern but no fear. He planned to insist that he be informed in advance what treatment was being proposed, and why, and what results could be expected.

He scribbled in his date book a line he intended to use in summation: "I'm sick, not mummified."

He also made a note to ask the doctor what he could do to help her. Should he be eating differently? What about vitamins? Should he be avoiding certain activities?

Allan D., after his own diagnosis, had plunged into intensive research about supplements to help boost his immune system. When Jim asked him, Allan outlined his routine. Every day he took one tablet of Vitamin A (5,000 IUs), one tablet of Vitamin D (400 IUs), one tablet of iron (300 mg), Vitamin C (500 mg) two or three times a day, one tablet of selenium, an immune-system booster (50 mg), two tablets of calcium/magnesium (333 mg/167 mg), two or three tablets of Vitamin E (800 IUs) to help detoxify his system, one tablet of B complex, one tablet of zinc (10 mg) to compensate for the zinc lost in diarrhoea, one tablet of Vitamin B6 (25 mg), two tablets of ginseng (518 mg), one or two tablets of desiccated liver (486 mg), and two tablets of garlic.

"Always eat first before taking vitamins," Allan instructed him.

Jim decided to adopt the regimen, unless Dr. Garvey objected. He wouldn't be as severe with it as Allan, who never missed a day, but he would take the pills at least two or three days a week.

He would also continue his habit of drinking copious quantities of apple and grape juice every day. Jim didn't drink orange or grapefruit juice. He read somewhere that people should eat food grown in their own climates, the theory being that orange juice was better suited to people living in tropical climates while apple and grape juice are more in harmony with Canadians' needs.

In addition Jim decided he would eat three or four eggs a day. Research done in Israel suggested that egg yolks contain a natural anti-viral ingredient. To break down the cholesterol in the eggs, he would take two tablets of niacin (500 mg) in the evening every two or three days.

Among the other concerns he intended to raise with Dr. Garvey was, "Is government doing enough?" If she felt that there wasn't sufficient support for AIDS research and treatment, he could offer to write letters of protest and organize others to do the same. Did she need more support for her work from her own hospital? Should he put pressure on her superiors or the hospital board?

Jim cannot tolerate a feeling of helplessness. By casting himself in the role of advocate, he planned to convert the anxiety of his grave situation into energy directed outward. His every impulse was to find an activity that would give him a sense of being in charge of his illness, of turning it to an advantage. The alternative was despair that he felt instinctively would kill him.

Geared as he was for the vigorous presention he had planned, he was still no match for Dr. Garvey, who took the offensive.

"The first thing I want to say is that my phone hasn't stopped ringing for the last two weeks because of you," she began. "Your family keeps calling, your friends keep calling, a woman named Natalie Wexler is on the phone all the time. Would you please appoint a spokesman to handle the information so I won't be bothered with so many calls?"

Jim decided on Natalie Wexler, since his father lived so far from Toronto.

"Fine," Dr. Garvey said, making a note of that. "Well, I think you can handle what I'm about to tell you. I'm going to describe exactly where we stand so that we both understand what's going on and we have our facts straight."

"Do I have AIDS?" he asked steadily.

"Yes," she replied. "We have confirmed that you have AIDS. You have a particular kind of cancer called Kaposi's sarcoma which is generally not found outside of Mediterranean people and older people. In the past two years we've been seeing Kaposi's sarcoma all over North America, occurring mostly in gay men. You're in that high-risk category. We know it's because of a breakdown in the immune system that allows opportunistic infections to develop."

Jim remembered that Linus Pauling had written about "Stage Three" cancer, which he said was the worst. Jim told the doctor about the Pauling book and asked if his cancer was Stage Three. Was he going to die?

She replied that he should stop reading such books. "All they can do is scare you. If you have questions, please ask me instead."

He asked, "Will I get more of these ugly lumps on my face?"

"You could," she nodded. "Kaposi's is a skin cancer and can go anywhere there is skin."

He showed her the list of vitamins he planned to take. She was astonished but listened without comment as he explained that he also would be drinking apple and grape juice and eating several eggs a day.

"Can't hurt," was her economical response.

On the question of his fatigue, she was sympathetic. Exhaustion goes with the territory in cancer, she told him, because fast-breeding tumours consume most of the body's energy. Furthermore, she added, he could expect worse. Chemotherapy would drain him completely.

He rallied to ask his next question, about his sore back. She said she would investigate. The pain in his left leg didn't mean amputation, she assured him. He didn't have the same kind of cancer that Terry Fox did, and Jim's kind of cancer did not usually result in removal of a limb.

The lumps in his neck were more serious, she went on, as he continued down his check-list. If his lymph nodes were infected with cancer, it could get out of control. She would keep a close watch on that situation.

He grinned at her, shook his head admiringly, and continued. Who was the doctor in charge of his case? He was relieved when she said, "I am."

His final question was so difficult he almost lost his nerve. His embarrassment showing, he asked if he should notify previous sex partners that he had AIDS. Dr. Garvey asked how many people that would involve.

"Well," Jim said reluctantly, "actually there are hundreds...."

Her expression didn't change. "I don't think there's any point then," she said, "but I suggest that you co-operate with the epidemiology study that the Toronto General Hospital is doing. There's a doctor there who is trying to chart the spread of AIDS in Toronto." Jim promised to call.

The rest of the news was appalling. All his tumours were malignant. The back of his throat was covered with cancer. Natalie Wexler, looking in his mouth when he complained of pain, announced with horror that she could see the growths. His oesophagus had a tumour the size of a golf ball. His stomach and bowel were full of cancer. In fact, the lining of his stomach was falling apart. There wasn't an inch of it that wasn't covered by cancer tumours. If something wasn't done quickly to reduce them they would eat through his stomach wall and he could haemorrhage to death.

Dr. Garvey's plan was to readmit him on May 10 to St. Michael's for chemotherapy. "Without the treatment," said Dr. Garvey, "you'll be in serious trouble by four weeks."

Jim caught her meaning. He would be dead.

Dr. Garvey described chemotherapy as a monster injection of poisonous drugs, delivered at slightly below a lethal dose. The drugs would attack his entire body, killing not only cancer but healthy tissue as well. When the drugs were stopped, healthy tissue tended to recover quickly, but cancer cells were slow to rebuild and sometimes were knocked out for good.

"It's the heaviest treatment we have on earth today," she told him in her severe manner. "It's the big guns. It will take about six months out of your life while your system recovers. Chemotherapy works for many, many patients, but I must tell you that in some cases it doesn't. We'll know within a month after the treatment whether it has helped you."

His control slipped and his dismay showed. Her tone softened. "Don't worry," she said. "We've been using chemotherapy for many years and we know a lot about it. If it doesn't work for you, I always have something else up my sleeve."

He grinned appreciatively.

"We'll work on this, but it might be advisable for you to see your family and to do whatever papers you need in case this becomes serious."

He realized with a start she was talking about making out his will. He rose and said with composure, "As this goes along, Dr. Garvey, I want you always to tell me the score. I can handle it if I know what's happening. If I don't know what's going on, I'll start to imagine the worst. So please always tell me the truth."

She said, "Jim, I promise."

Jim's affair with Paul D. had waned, but he was in need of comfort from someone close. He went to Paul's apartment with the bad news and was consoled. Then Paul said, offhandedly, "Do you think Dr. Garvey would see me too? Maybe I should find out if there are any problems in this for me."

Jim was grateful for the absence of recrimination. "Of course," he said quickly.

On May 10, 1984, Jim was readmitted to St. Michael's to begin chemotherapy. His father came to see him. Karl Zanuk was blunt. He said, "This is AIDS, isn't it?"

Jim said, "Yes, Dad, it is."

Karl nodded. "I thought so. I don't know much about AIDS."

"I don't either," said Jim with a smile.

"Well then," said the older Zanuk in the in-charge manner that so closely resembled his son's, "we've got to read up on it. I'll see what I can find in the library. Meanwhile, you have nothing to worry about so far as money is concerned. I'll take care of your rent and that sort of thing. You just concentrate on beating this. Your job now is to get a lot of rest, eat well, and not worry about money."

Jim checked into the hospital with a new symptom, a heavy cough. It was decided that his lungs should be examined before the chemotherapy began. He had a bronchoscopomy, a procedure that required another general anaesthetic.

When Jim later regained consciousness in his room, his father was beside his bed. He grinned weakly and then saw that Natalie Wexler and another friend, Bert M., were also in the room. Dr. André C., the resident who worked with Bernadette Garvey on Jim's case, entered carrying a large tray labelled CHEMO—EMERGENCY.

The doctor said, "We're going to give you a small shot of the three chemicals you'll be getting in the chemotherapy treatment. We need to see how you react. If you start to feel funny—have trouble with your breathing, say, or notice your hands swelling—tell me right away. I've got some needles here to neutralize the chemicals."

Jim was still blurred from the anaesthetic, but he recognized that he would be in danger. He saw his father blanch, and Natalie's hands clenched.

He decided to treat the situation with airy amusement, his stock-in-trade for emergencies.

"André," he beamed. "I'm not feeling all that great and I have all these guests here. Why don't we do this tomorrow?"

The doctor shook his head. "You're a little stoned now, so it's a good time. I think we'd better do it right now."

Jim extended his arm languidly for the injection. "Okay," he said. "By the way, Dad, I want you to meet André. He gives me all my drugs and he's a really nice guy."

The doctor smiled and nodded in recognition of the introduction, administered the injection, and left. Everyone waited anxiously, but Jim felt no change. His harsh coughing shattered a heavy silence. Jim's father ran from the room and returned with the doctor, looking concerned. He checked Jim carefully and said the cough wasn't related to the drug. They went back to suspenseful waiting.

An hour passed. The doctor decided Jim was tolerating the chemicals and announced he would administer the first chemotherapy treatment at once. When he lifted the sterile drape on the tray, the needles revealed were gigantic. Jim, no longer under the agreeable haze of the anaesthetic, was horrified.

Everything he had ever heard about chemotherapy indicated that he would have two reactions—one, he would throw up, and, two, his hair would fall out. He couldn't do anything to prevent the latter, but he was damned if he was going to vomit in front of a roomful of people. He braced himself to fight the nausea as he watched the three drugs going into a tube connected to an IV in his arm.

One drug, he noticed, was bright pink. He came to detest that one most of all. As soon as it hit his bloodstream he got an acrid taste like the smell of nail polish in his mouth and felt an intense need to urinate. To his dismay, his urine was bright pink like the drug. The message was that the pink drug had permeated his entire body. For him the worst part of all subsequent chemotherapy treatments was seeing his urine pink with poison. He hated it so much that he would urinate sitting down on the toilet to avoid seeing it.

Dr. André C. was attentive to Jim and always administered the chemotherapy himself. Jim noted that they were the same age. He speculated, though he never broached the subject, that the doctor felt a bond with him and perhaps thought he might have been in Jim's situation had his sexuality been different.

At the same time, having little to lose with a patient in such distress, Dr. Garvey started treatment with the synthetic interferon that she hoped would augment Jim's collapsing immune system. Interferon was first used more than twenty years ago to prolong life in cancer patients and derives its name from its ability, poorly understood, to interfere with viruses. Interferon, a biological treatment that many regard as more humane than chemotherapy or radiation, is an enzyme that the body produces naturally when its immune system is functional.

The regimen that Dr. Garvey proposed was a combination of interferon and chemotherapy. Jim would have two weeks of chemotherapy, followed by a day or two of rest, and then two weeks of interferon. If that seemed to work, it would be repeated after an interval to recover.

Jim learned that interferon creates to an intense degree the conditions that occur when a body fights a serious infection: nausea, diarrhoea, and fever. Interferon, he says, is "like having the worst case of flu in your life."

Interferon, a white liquid, must be injected into muscle tissue. It was decided that the best places on Jim's body were the backs of his once-brawny arms. The amount to be injected each time was so great that six hypodermic syringes were needed to complete each course. To his dismay, Jim learned that he would be given interferon every other day for two weeks, for a total of thirty-six injections.

Though the needles were tiny, the injections were terribly painful. Much worse was to follow. Early in the evening after the injections, Jim would be so feverish that he approached delirium. He would vomit violently and the diarrhoea left him weak. The next morning he would begin to recover, though exhausted by the upheavals of the night. By evening, he would be himself again—then the next morning a nurse would arrive with six more injections.

Jim had expected, from everything he had ever heard about chemotherapy, that he would wake up bald on the morning after the first treatment. He found that's not how it works. Week after week, his hair looked just the same. Then he began noticing a thinning. One day he was in the shower applying shampoo to his head. The foam in his hands felt odd. To his horror, he saw that it was full of hair. He looked at the puddle of water around his feet and there was hair everywhere. When he dried his head, the towel came away full of hair.

In a mirror he saw bald patches. Tears streamed down his face but his resolution returned.

"You're lucky," he told the weeping man in the mirror. "If this is the worst of it, count your blessings. You're behaving like a vain child."

After that he combed his hair no more often than necessary and shampooed lightly, but hair continued to fall out in clumps.

His favourite person on 6A South was a woman he called Jobikins, a pet name given her by her husband, a policeman. She was a sweet woman with a blond pony-tail and an infectious sense of humour. Jobikins was a student on placement from George Brown community college who was assigned to the hospital only briefly. The party mood that Jim liked to maintain in his hospital room suited Jobikins perfectly, and they delighted one another.

Jim was midway through the chemotherapy treatments when Jobikins came to his room to say goodbye, her placement finished.

"I'm going to miss you," she told him.

Jim was touched. "That's really sweet of you to say that," he told her.

She hesitated and then plunged on.

"I've learned more from you than anything I learned at school. Jim, everybody's talking about you. When we heard a gay man was coming in with AIDS, we were scared. You have taught us that you are a real gentleman and a real man, and I want you to know that my experience with you will stay with me for the rest of my life."

She hugged him and fled, leaving him speechless. Only later did it register that she hadn't been wearing a hospital gown and gloves when she touched him. That was significant. On 6A

South, AIDS had lost its mystery and fear had lifted. At the beginning of his first hospitalization only weeks earlier, all staff had worn masks, gloves, and gowns to approach him, but of late the masks and gowns had disappeared entirely and gloves were worn only for such procedures as those requiring needles or that involved touching his sores. Outside his door, next to the warning sign ISOLATION , was a cart stocked with gowns, masks, and gloves, but most people coming into Jim's room ignored it.

In fact, nurses apologized for putting on gloves when they changed his bed linen. Jim would assure them he didn't take offence. Though no one touched his skin with uncovered hands, there was no lack of affectionate contact. Nurses would pat his shoulder or wriggle his toes through the bedclothes.

On the other hand, food servers and cleaners usually were petrified. Information seemed to reach them last. One morning Jim's breakfast didn't arrive. Two hours later a nurse noticed that it had been left outside his door. She brought it in but Jim found it cold and unpalatable. He buzzed to ask for a warm breakfast and the call brought a nurse new to him. She said imperiously that the kitchen was closed and he would have to wait until the lunch trays were delivered.

Jim picked up the breakfast tray, carried it to his door, and threw it down the hall. "Little king performance," he commented disgustedly when reflecting on his behaviour that day.

"I'll have a hot breakfast in fifteen minutes, please," he informed the nurse icily. In a short time, he had warm eggs and toast.

After that outburst, people continued to set his trays outside the door, but they knocked to tell him that the food had arrived.

Jim was one of the first people with AIDS that St. Michael's had seen, though it was quickly to become one of the downtown Toronto teaching hospitals with the largest number of AIDS patients. Stories abounded of staff in other hospitals who went to extremes to gown themselves before approaching someone with AIDS. In some cases staff was hostile and neglectful of AIDS patients.

Of this Jim knew little. With the exception of the reluctant food-service people and some wary cleaners, he was treated with warmth. The precautions taken with him were minimal. St. Michael's staff in general took direction from Phyllis Wyper, a widely-respected expert in infectious diseases, and from Dr. Bernadette Garvey, who always examined Jim with bare hands and simply washed afterwards.

News came that spring from France and the United States almost simultaneously that the virus causing AIDS had been isolated. Each country gave it a different name: HTLV-III in the States, LAV in France. The confusion this caused soon led to agreement on a single name, HIV, for human immunodeficiency virus.

"At least now they can see the little sucker," Jim muttered. There was talk of a vaccine in maybe two years. Maybe more, but it was only a matter of time. Jonas Salk, who discovered the vaccine for polio, said it was inevitable that a vaccine would be found for AIDS.

No one, Jim noted bleakly, was talking about when a cure would be found.

The papers were full of alarm. The number of AIDS cases in the United States had reached 4,000. Britain had its first AIDS death, a man in Scotland. Suddenly the means of transmission became an urgent matter. The experts were saying they had narrowed it down—"blood and semen"—but no one was certain. Some thought it might be airborne, which meant that people could get it from riding in a bus with someone with AIDS.

The media were not helpful as panic built. Stories popped up everywhere that the virus had been found in tears, and in saliva. The stories rarely mentioned that the HIV in such body fluids was either dead or in such weakened condition as to be impotent. Dr. Stanley Read, a Canadian authority on AIDS, was later to say, "You'd have to have three buckets of spit or tears thrown at a wound to get any effect."

The *Toronto Sun* published an article blaming homosexuals for the spread of AIDS, infuriating the gay community. Jim and others read into it poorly concealed homophobia. Allan D. made Jim promise he'd get even with the *Sun* some day.

Dr. Garvey said that Jim could leave the hospital for a while. It would be a few weeks before she would know if the chemotherapy was effective. Meanwhile, he could rest better elsewhere.

Jim heard that Allan D. had also been scheduled for chemotherapy at the same time his was begun. In Allan's case, it had been cancelled because Allan was too frail to tolerate the chemicals. Jim thought: *Allan is dying*.

As Dr. Garvey had warned, Jim was frightfully weak. His appearance was alarming. His hair was gone except for tufts here and there and his pallor was ghastly. His deep-set eyes, the colour of whisky, burned feverishly in the hollows of his gaunt face, and his body had wasted to the bone. His father and Natalie, watching Jim's gallant performance as host with the crystal stemmed glasses and chilled juice, saw a man almost too weak to stand. Who would take care of him while he waited for his therapy to be resumed? Clearly he couldn't return to live alone in his bachelor apartment.

It was agreed that Jim would go to his father's. Karl picked him up on May 13 at the hospital in a van he had outfitted with a mattress and pillows. Making many trips, he carried Jim's belongings and stored them in the vehicle. Then Jim was taken in a wheelchair to an exit on the driveway. His father gently helped him stretch out on the mattress, tucking the blankets around him as he would for a baby.

After two weeks of being tended by Eleanor and his father, Jim was frantic. He missed the camaraderie and support he had known in hospital, when his room was thronged with people who rose to the buoyant mood he imposed and made the room ring with laughter. His father's house was more than an hour's drive from Toronto and, in any case, few of his friends had cars.

Also Jim was fighting with his father, who often channelled his distress at his son's grave illness into anger at his inactivity. Once Jim was so distraught by the rancour that he dragged himself to the highway and hitchhiked to Toronto. His father collected him and brought him back.

A few days later Karl made Jim the splendid present of a new car, a burgundy Ford Mustang, which he said was for Jim's thirtieth birthday a few weeks away. Karl explained that he thought it would spare Jim the stress of taking public transit to hospital and doctor appointments.

"You just concentrate on getting well," the older man gruffly told his grateful son.

Jim confided his loneliness to Natalie Wexler, who offered to approach his father tactfully. She explained to Karl that Jim appreciated his father's support, but missed his friends and needed them to help him through this difficult time. Karl generously offered to pay for a hotel room in Toronto so that Jim could have room service whenever he didn't feel well enough to leave his room to eat. The hotel they selected was the Inn on the Park, which is situated some distance from the heart of the city overlooking a sylvan park. Jim would be able to sit outdoors in quiet, healthful surroundings.

A monthly rate was obtained and Jim was packed into the van again. His exhaustion was profound. It was difficult for him to walk unaided but he was too proud to ask for help. They arrived at the hotel late in the afternoon of a warm summer day. In the hard sunlight, Jim noted compassionately that his father's face was haggard. Eleanor, sensing as she always did tension in the

49

Zanuk family, maintained a light chatter to cover the strain. She and Natalie bustled about, supervising the transfer of Jim's things to the bellman's cart, while Jim watched, keeping a pleasant expression on his face.

When they had settled Jim in his room, there seemed no easy way to part. Natalie suggested they have a drink together. In the lounge, Natalie, Karl, and Eleanor ordered drinks while Jim had a cup of coffee. The mood was heavy with despondency, and people nearby looked at them curiously, seeing in Jim's face the stamp of a deathly illness. What was foremost in Jim's mind was the thought that he would die in that hotel.

Jim was thinking about the next two weeks, wondering how he would know if the chemotherapy had failed. Would he simply black out and die? His weakness was frightening. Did it mean that the cancer was growing again?

For the first time in his life, Karl Zanuk seemed unsure of himself. In the short time since Jim's diagnosis, he had aged. Staring at his drink, moving the glass about absentmindedly, he seemed a crumpled, defeated man. Eleanor and Natalie, usually so skilled at social chat, could think of nothing to say. In the awkwardness, Karl suddenly remembered he had a card from Jim's younger sister, Karen. The distraction came as a relief for them all.

Jim opened it and read it aloud. Karen sent love and said she was praying for Jim. To lighten the tone, she had added what she meant as a playful request to have Jim's teddy bear after he was gone. To his dismay, Jim felt himself about to cry. He said he had to go to the bathroom and might as well go up to his room. A few steps away he remembered he had left the card on the table. When he turned back to get it, he saw that all three were in tears.

He picked up the card and hurried away. The others stayed a long time in the lounge, trying to sort out how they would provide support through the crisis. Karl Zanuk didn't like being so far from his seriously ill son. He said he wanted to speak to Jim privately. In the hotel room, Jim was stretched out on the bed. His father pulled up a chair beside him. He assumed his customary gruff and authoritative style, hands clasped and body leaning forward, and began a speech he apparently had been planning for some time.

Jim recalls that visit in his hotel room as one of the finest, most intimate times he and his father had ever had together. His father's mood, he perceived with amusement, was halfway between despair at Jim's illness and indignation that Jim had brought it on himself by, as Jim put it, "not staying on the farm and eating lots of garlic".

The older man talked earnestly of his own life and the problems he had overcome. This problem of AIDS was a big one for both of them, he went on, but the family had been in fights before and they had always won. They would beat this one too, together.

Karl talked about God, something Jim had not known him to do since Jim's childhood. "We have to rely on God, our creator," Karl said, keeping his eyes fixed fiercely on Jim's face. "There is nothing else we can turn to. You have to keep up your hope and you must keep fighting."

He disposed of practical matters, assuring Jim that he would have no financial worries to cause him any additional stress. Everything Jim needed would be looked after. "Your only job is to stay smiling and stay happy," Karl said, giving his son a strong hug and taking his leave.

Left alone in the room, Jim burst into tears of love and gratitude and despair.

3

James Steven Zanuk was born in the early afternoon of June 24, 1954, at St. Joseph's Hospital in Hamilton, a lively, friendly, bright little boy. He resembled his father, Karl Zanuk, a burly, dark-haired Ukrainian-born farmer with wide cheekbones and a strong body. His mother, Johanna Marta, the daughter of impoverished Czechoslovakian immigrants, is a strong woman, fair and blue-eyed, who was raised in Alberta and who moved while still a child to the Hamilton region, where she met Karl Zanuk at school. They were drawn to each other because they were both Jehovah's Witnesses, and their childhood friendship ripened into marriage when they met again as adults in the same congregation.

Johanna was raised as a Jehovah's Witness, but Karl came to the religion when he was nine years old, after his arrival in Brantford with his mother. Karl's father, Steve, a huge man six and a half feet tall and weighing close to two hundred and fifty pounds, had preceded his family to Canada seven years earlier. Working as a labourer in a Hamilton steel mill, he had saved enough money to purchase a two-hundred-acre farm near Brantford.

During those seven years of frugal living and loneliness, Steve was recruited by a congregation of Jehovah's Witnesses. His wife and son were asked to accept not only a new language and a new country but also a new religion, and neither was ever to adopt it wholeheartedly. Dorothy Zanuk, in fact, never did learn English, and for his part Karl went along with the teachings but failed to develop the zeal that grips most members of the faith.

Many North Americans regard Jehovah's Witnesses as fanatics, best known for their refusal to permit blood transfusions and their rejection of national anthems and the prayers that school children recite. The religion is based on the Christian Bible, however, and has evolved from what once was known as International Bible Students, a world-wide fundamentalist group that takes the Old Testament literally.

Jehovah's Witnesses, as they have called themselves since 1931, believe in the reality of the prophecies of the end of the world that are found in the book of Revelation. Their faith teaches that they stand alone on earth as the only witnesses who understand the true God. All other religions, but especially Roman Catholicism, they believe to be dominated by Satan; all governments and institutions are controlled by the devil. This conviction accounts for their refusal to stand for national anthems, salute flags, observe Christmas or Easter, or take oaths of allegiance. In addition, they are pacifists and are jailed the world over for rejecting conscription.

Jehovah's Witnesses believe that Armageddon is fast approaching, at which time Jehovah God will destroy Satan and all Satan's followers. Accordingly they place a serious burden on all adherents to spread the word, by means of publications such as the *Watchtower* and *Awake!*, so that people now lost to Satan can be redeemed by baptism as Jehovah's Witnesses. At Armageddon, everything evil on earth will be destroyed, and Jehovah will reign over a paradise populated only by those with good hearts, which they hold to be a characteristic of all practising members of the Jehovah's Witness faith. Only people of good heart will be resurrected.

Canada has some 12,010 Jehovah's Witness congregations, most of them small and clannish, meeting to study the Scriptures and discuss their interpretation. The family unit is regarded as the bulwark of the faith. Children are lovingly but strictly raised and are discouraged from associating with children who aren't Jehovah's Witnesses. Divorce is not permitted, except for adultery, and in the past prohibitions against tobacco and alcohol were so severely enforced that a man was excommunicated for smoking a cigarette.

All children of Jehovah's Witnesses are raised to believe that they must devote their lives to missionary work. To remove them from the temptations of mating with non-Jehovah's Witnesses, they are encouraged to leave school early and to make missionary work their principal occupation. To accommodate the demands of days spent distributing the *Watchtower* at bus stops, Jehovah's Witnesses very often take such jobs as night cleaning.

Jehovah's Witnesses worship in simple buildings called Kingdom Halls, holding services on Sundays and prayer meetings Tuesdays and Thursdays in the Kingdom Halls or in one another's homes. On a daily basis they read their Bibles, trying to perfect their understanding of the subtle interpretations open to students of the Scriptures.

Jim's father took from this religious fervour what best fit his nature, which finds poetic expression in his kindness, and his countryman's sense of wonder at the complexities of nature. His first wife, Johanna, however, is a fierce, tense woman of low self-esteem who has immersed herself passionately in the religion and finds in it her strength. Adversity sends her rushing to her Bible for solace. Nothing else in her life has given her the security she finds in her religion, and to shake her adherence would be tantamount to destroying the woman.

Jim's parents had four children in the space of six years. Jim was the third. The oldest, Kathryn, is a beautiful, stormy, popular woman regarded by all as the most intelligent in the family. When she stopped school after grade twelve to become an earnest, full-time Jehovah's Witness missionary, her marks averaged 98.9 per cent. Even so, there was no thought that she should go to university. She had been wistfully inclined towards law before she succumbed to everyone's view that her obligation was to preach.

Today, like many of her contemporaries, she harbours some bitterness for lost opportunities. Armageddon has been delayed, and she and others of her generation find themselves approaching their middle years without the careers they might have achieved. She has left the faith and is an active member of a self-help group that attempts to help former fundamentalist zealots sort out their lives without what once was their centrepole. A divorced woman and the mother of a son, Eric, Kathryn lives in Toronto.

The second child is Karl Allan, called Allan, an easy-going person of independent mind. He was never much impressed with the Jehovah's Witnesses, despite every effort made by his frantic mother and the disapproving elders of his family's congregation. At school Allan's friends were always "worldly" people outside the faith, and he was indifferent at Bible studies. Allan married a woman of Italian origin, a casual adherent of Roman Catholicism, and with her had two daughters, Michelle and Julie-Anne.

A man of enterprising bent like his father, he runs a prosperous disc jockey business in the Brantford area, providing technicians for parties.

Jim is only a year younger than Allan. The youngest child, his sister Karen Marie, is three years younger than he. Karen is an amiable, compliant person and, like her mother, devoted to the faith. She married another ardent Jehovah's Witness, and they spend much of their time in missionary work in and around the small Muskoka town of Gravenhurst, where they are raising two children, Shannon and Benjamin.

Jim was a happy, friendly, adventurous baby, sturdy of build, sound of health, and full of curiosity. One family story concerns a summer day when his mother left the toddler outside in a playpen. Jim climbed out of it and crawled to the middle of the highway that passed their house, seating himself on the centre line the better to observe the traffic. His horrified mother snatched him up and thereafter always confined him in an overturned playpen, like a cage, with bricks on top for good measure.

The family lived in a small, two-bedroom frame house on Steve Zanuk's farm, on land Steve had given as a wedding present to the young couple. As the children came along, the house grew cramped. The parents occupied one bedroom, the daughters the other, and Jim and Allan slept in the den.

Karl Zanuk, like all Jehovah's Witnesses, left school early and at the time of his marriage was working on the farm with his father. He has an astonishing aptitude and ingenuity with machines, and acquired renown in the district for his ability to fix anything and create new tools. As his family grew, it was clear the farm could not provide sufficient income so he got a job as a salesman for a Brantford aluminum company. Quick of mind, he soon decided he could make a better product himself. He set up a small work centre in a corner of his father's barn and began to manufacture and market the aluminum doors and windows that made him a rich man.

Affluence meant the family could build a new home, a wide California-style white brick bungalow with a big picture window, built on the family farm and always known in the family as "the new house". Spacious and well appointed, it contained two big bedrooms for the children, one for the boys and one for the girls, each equipped with built-in furniture, roomy closets, and adjoining bathrooms with twin sinks.

The Zanuks were generous with their children. They were motivated in part by the need to provide entertainment at home to compensate for the restrictions placed on their choice of playmates. The children had loads of toys, and the house teemed with pets. At one time there were nine dogs, as well as fish in an aquarium and budgies in a birdcage. As adolescents, the boys had their own snowmobile. Each child who married was given a house.

Extravagance ended with such indulgences. Karl and Johanna had been raised in poverty, and the parsimonious habits of their childhoods clung to them. Both disapproved of displays of wealth, and were thrifty in such matters as purchasing clothes. For most of his life Karl has driven a pick-up truck, and he is severely disapproving of whatever looks expensive.

The children attended a rural school that accommodated all eight grades in three rooms. The Zanuk children were always immaculate, passing their father's fond inspection as they left the house every morning, and all were honours students. None the less, the first day of school each year was always an ordeal. One or more of them might face a new teacher, who would have to be advised about regulations permitting Jehovah's Witnesses to be excused from prayers and national anthems. The four Zanuks and the three other Jehovah's Witness children in the school would stand in the hall until the rituals were over, slipping back into their seats amid titters of derision.

It was clear to Jim that being a Jehovah's Witness was a position of superiority: he was marked for resurrection, while his teachers and all the other children would be destroyed for their evil beliefs. Even so, some days there was little comfort in such thoughts.

He was a model student, eager to learn, quick to volunteer to help the teacher; his homework assignments were always completed, and he was fastidious to a fault. His first encounter with Plasticine revolted him; he dreaded getting the substance under his fingernails. The teacher insisted he use it, however, and when he followed her instructions the first object he moulded was the figure of a curly-haired woman wearing a long dress.

He hated smudges on his notebooks, or papers that weren't stacked neatly with their edges aligned, or the roughness that marked the play of boys at recess. Big for his age, he was expected to be an athlete, but his inclinations were otherwise. Despite the taunts of other boys, he liked to skip with the girls and was good at it. In fact, he much preferred the company of girls. He found boys too loud, too messy, and too aggressive. Often he was accused of being a sissy. He noticed that his brother, Allan, seemed embarrassed by him. Whenever Jim was the target of bullies, Allan looked the other way.

He had no spirit for fighting back when boys pushed him around, but he wasn't helpless. Aware that most of the children's fathers worked for his father, he would threaten them with firing.

A large teddy bear given him as a baby became for him a kind friend. He slept with his arms around the bear and fell into a lifelong habit of telling the bear his secrets and his sorrows.

When Jim was six he noticed while shinnying up a tree one day that the contact between the tree and his crotch gave him a pleasurable sensation in his penis. He told Allan about this interesting development, that rubbing one's penis felt good, but Allan was indifferent. Jim continued to experiment with the new sensation until his mother one day discovered him rubbing his penis and told him it was wrong and bad.

Jim's favourite objects were things that glittered. Once he retrieved from the garbage a four-strand rhinestone necklace that his mother had discarded. He kept such treasures in a box and liked to stretch out behind a screen of bushes to admire them in the sunlight. Sensual of nature, he also liked rich colours and luxurious textures like silk and satin. Sometimes, when he thought he was safe from detection, he would put on his mother's dresses and jewellery and parade around the room.

One day his father caught him preening before a mirror, a garment of his mother's draped over his shoulders like an evening cape. His father's face clouded with rage but he got control of himself. Instead of striking the boy, as seemed to be his first impulse, he ridiculed him instead.

Jim loved to join his sister Karen when she played with her Barbie dolls. He made dolls' houses for his sisters out of cartons obtained at the supermarket. They were painstakingly fitted with drapes at the windows and silk bed covers. Deft with his fingers, he designed and sewed a wardrobe of dolls' clothes for them, trimming the silk ballgowns with bits of sequin and lace. His father noted this and purchased him a G.I. Joe doll, but its militarism repelled him. Besides, the Scriptures taught that wars and killing are wrong.

His love of theatrics went well with his faith, which required its members to become eloquent public speakers. At the age of seven he held the attention of an entire congregation while, standing behind a lectern so tall that he had to peek around it to be seen, he gave a four-minute analysis of Scripture. He loved the applause. After that he was an indefatigable speech-maker on the subject of the Bible, impressing the elders with his persuasiveness and poise.

He thought of his childhood, at times, as deliriously happy. He loved to awake to the clinky sound the milkman made every morning when he set down the family's eight bottles of milk. He loved the fields of his grandfather's farm, the smell of a good dinner cooking, and running under the black sky of a gathering summer storm. One of his best memories is of Sunday evenings when his father would read *Black Beauty* aloud, the four children curled around him on the living-room rug in front of the fire.

Jim's life was an isolation within an isolation. At school he was a freak, a Jehovah's Witness; at home he was always vaguely aware that something about him disappointed his parents. He escaped into fantasy. He liked to hide in a maple tree in front of his house; he would hang upside down by his knees and daydream of glory. Often he was Jim Zanuk, film star and winner of an Academy Award; or Jim Zanuk, world-famous artist being received at Buckingham Palace. Frequently, he won the Olympics. For a while he took piano lessons on a Heintzman his father purchased for him and during that period he was Jim Zanuk, concert pianist, bowing before a standing ovation in Carnegie Hall.

He was drawn longingly to male strength. He adored his assured, powerful, competent father, whose presence always gave him a sense of protection and comfort. He was thrilled by quiet, fair-minded male authority. His male-dominated religion suited him perfectly. When he attended prayer services at the Kingdom Hall, he loved to watch the elders of the congregation as they conferred and issued pronouncements. He wished such men would hold him in their arms, keeping him safe. It was hard for him to accept that men didn't hug one another, that they could only shake hands.

He had his first crush when he was in grade four. It was on his teacher, a confident, vigorous man.

His personality was shaped by a desire to please. He still feels that anything less than perfection in his behaviour and appearance will result in rejection. This concern maintains a flutter of panic that is constant with him. He is never far from feeling very vulnerable. He believes that his need to be faultless arose from his realization that something intrinsic about him aroused disdain. He therefore worked to be the most cheerful, obedient, neat, polite, and thoughtful boy possible. When he went walking in the fields, he picked wildflowers for his mother. He brought small gifts to his teachers. He was considerate of his elders, devoted to his parents, affectionate with his siblings, protective of animals and small children. He pored over his Bible and memorized whole chunks of Scripture. His hair was always combed.

It was never quite enough.

When he was ten, he and another boy from school took down their pants and examined one another's genitals. The other boy showed him how to masturbate and was full of information about sex. He said that a man's stiff penis went into a girl. The thought had no appeal for Jim. The next day, on a hunch formed from a half-remembered glimpse of his father hiding something in his closet, he searched the closet and found at the back of a shelf a book about sex. He read it avidly, astonished by the positions described. Towards the end he came upon a chapter on homosexuality. It said that men made love to one another and explained how it was done.

At that moment, he knew he was a homosexual.

Stunned by the thought, he pushed it away. Jehovah's Witnesses believe that homosexuality is utterly despised by Jehovah. To be a homosexual and a Jehovah's Witness simply was not possible. Yet both were powerful influences in his life. It might be that he would have to give up one or the other. He began that day to pray to Jehovah to help him.

That summer at a summer cottage he and a cousin masturbated each other. As Witnesses interpret the Old Testament, masturbation is also a sin. Jim prostrated himself on his bed, weeping, and prayed that God would forgive the evil he had done.

His teddy bear was patched and patched again. Eventually his mother threw it in the garbage, from which Jim tearfully rescued it. After that he kept it hidden from her and patched its worn face himself.

He took part in childhood kissing games like Spin the Bottle so that no one would be suspicious of him, but there was no pleasure in kissing a girl. Instead he looked at the lips of boys and dreamed of kissing them. Watching television or movies, he would be attracted to the men, never the women. He had sexual fantasies of men holding him in his arms, after which he would be racked by guilt at the compulsion that was so contrary to his religion.

Allan occasionally raised the subject of homosexuality with Jim and asked about Jim's sexuality, but each time Jim was caught off guard and wasn't ready to discuss it. He had always denied it as convincingly as he could, but he decided that the time had come to be open. He began the discussion with Allan by telling him about his experiments with masturbation, but Allan was indifferent. Then he said, making his voice casual, "You know, Allan, I don't think I like girls all that much. I might like boys better."

Allan looked amused. "You'll get over it," he said, closing the subject.

The Zanuk household appeared idyllic to outsiders, and Jim never fails to describe his childhood as a heaven, but the truth is somewhat different. Johanna Zanuk, a bright, quick woman, was possessed of a flaming temper. The children often were wakened by the sounds of arguments.

Kathy undertook the maternal responsibility of soothing her younger siblings. She would explain that it was only a passing quarrel, that everything would be all right in the morning. Jim came to dread the night, afraid to sleep for fear something appalling would happen. Sometimes after a battle his father would find him huddled in his bed weeping. His father would hold him close and tell him that it was nothing to worry about.

Jim is not sure what caused the arguments. Certainly his mother's sensitive, insecure nature had much to do with it. She had needs her husband did not seem able to meet and, on the surface, the fights were often about his neglect of her for his business interests.

"She wanted something from him that he couldn't give," Jim explains.

Once, soon after Karen's birthday, Johanna was gone from the household for many weeks. The children learned much later that she had been hospitalized during that period for depression.

In the autumn of 1966, when Jim was twelve, the children were having breakfast one morning when an argument broke out between the parents. Eventually calm was restored. Karl Zanuk prepared to go to work and Kathy and Allan, who went to high school some distance away, left with him in the car. As soon as they were gone, Johanna Zanuk, sobbing, ordered Karen and Jim to pack their clothes. When their belongings were collected, Johanna took her children to a neighbour's house.

Late that morning, wanting to retrieve some forgotten things from the house, she sent Jim to see if it was empty. He found the house deserted and was just returning to his mother when he stopped and checked the garage. He found his father there, getting something out of the car. His father behaved as if nothing catastrophic had happened.

"Hi there, Jim," he said cheerfully. "Is lunch ready?"

Jim mumbled that it was and ran.

He has replayed the scene many times in his mind. He regrets bitterly that his mother put him in a situation where he had to be evasive with his beloved father. He imagines his father going into the house, reassured that the quarrel had blown over, to find that his son had deceived him and that everything was for ever changed.

Johanna took the two children to live with relatives, parents of Jim's favourite cousin, Patrick, and a daughter, Susie, who was Karen's age. They stayed about four months, which included Jim's first Christmas away from his father and older siblings. He was devastated but handled his grief by being entertaining. On Christmas day he was the life of the party, telling jokes that kept him at the centre of attention and made the adults laugh.

Jehovah's Witnesses recognize the end of a marriage only when one partner has died or there has been adultery. Neither situation obtained in the Zanuk divorce, for which the grounds were mental cruelty, so in theological terms the divorce didn't exist.

Johanna, Jim, and Karen moved into a small apartment in Hamilton, and the children were enrolled in a new school, Highville, on the mountain. They were awed by its size: two storeys, with classrooms that held only a single grade at a time. The children had to explain all over again that they were Jehovah's Witnesses and endure the curiosity and stares, but both liked the school.

Jim's size marked him for boys' athletics, but his clumsiness in sports put an end to that. Always he was the last one chosen for baseball or basketball. He learned to make jokes when he dropped the ball or failed to catch it. Jim the Clown became an act at which he was adept.

The terms arranged between the parents allowed Karl Zanuk access to his children. Visits took place at his house near Brantford rather than in Hamilton because Johanna was irreconcilable in her bitterness. After each visit she extracted a price from Jim and Karen in tears and recriminations for their disloyalty.

The severe poverty of her childhood enabled her to adjust to her reduced circumstances. By being frugal, she was able to stretch the modest cash settlement and support payments paid for the children over many years.

She allowed herself one excess, a trip to Hawaii for a Jehovah's Witness convention to which she took her sons, Jim and Allan. Jim was part of an odd incident. An old man, a Jehovah's Witness, instigated some horseplay around the pool, hugging Jim in his arms. The embrace went on a shade too long and Jim knew that he and the older man were both aroused. They broke apart and ignored each other afterwards.

One afternoon when the Zanuks were lazing by the hotel pool, Johanna kidded the boys about their interest in the hula dancers who had performed the night before.

"I saw you two staring at them," she teased.

"Not Jim," Allan said quickly. "He's gay."

Johanna said severely, "Don't be silly, Allan."

Jim seized the opportunity. "He's not being silly, mom," he said. "Actually...."

"Stop it," Johanna interrupted, her face flushed. "Stop this nonsense."

Jim never tried to raise the subject with her again.

That year, in what was transparently a war for the affection of the Zanuk sons, Karl took both boys to the Soviet Union for a four-week trip that included motoring through Austria, Germany, and Switzerland.

The high school Jim attended was Clark Road Secondary School, where his home room teacher, Beverley Mathieson, became a catalytic force in his life. She was the first teacher he had known who admired him without reservation. She heaped praise on him and once said with great sincerity, "Jim, it's a pleasure to have you in my class."

Bev Mathieson was the first person to see Jim's potential as an actor. She urged him to take part in the school's drama group. His mother was set against it, pointing out that a Jehovah's Witness had a loftier purpose in life, but Jim couldn't resist joining. Theatre would be only a temporary diversion, he promised.

One exercise was to deliver a dramatic presentation to a tape machine and play it back to gain awareness of how one's own voice sounded. Jim delivered an impassioned poem into the machine and was aghast at the playback. Until then, he had been unaware that his voice was high and light for a male. "I sounded exactly like Donald Duck," he grins. Since that scalding discovery he has made a conscious effort to pitch his voice lower.

He was aware that girls had crushes on him, and he endeavoured to play the swaggering stud. Though he simulated lechery when he talked with other boys about girls, he had no stomach for it. He dated a few girls but always dreaded the moment when he would be expected to kiss them or make a pass. "The nitty-gritty of kissing," as he puts it, chilled him and left a feeling that he had done something wrong. He went along with it in order to be accepted as one of the boys, a regular guy and a member of the pack, but physical contact with girls depressed him.

At the end of grade nine the school drama group presented a variety show, *Up, Up and Away*. For reasons he still cannot fathom, Jim decided to dress in a long gown, high heels, a wig, and jewels and to do a stand-up comedy act as Phyllis Diller. He was a big success in the part, winning applause in each of the three performances, but it was a curious choice. He has never been interested in the drag scene. Effeminate men don't attract him. His preference is for macho-looking males, like himself, and his hangouts tend to be leather bars where classically virile-looking men are to be found.

His grade ten year, following the Phyllis Diller imitation, was a nightmare. He was placed in an all-male technical class. His fellow students, the sons of steelworkers, from the first day baited him mercilessly. They would stroll by him with mincing steps and limp wrists, and coo at him in falsetto voices that he was a queer, a fairy, a faggot. His home-room teacher watched it happen, encouraged the cruelty, and even took his turn at mocking Jim. Once he pinned one of Jim's projects on the class bulletin board. He announced he wanted everyone to see this example of exactly what he didn't want anyone else to do.

Gym classes were the worst. In the change room, boys jostled him, threw his gym bag under the shower, and tried to provoke him to fight. In the gymnasium, they would throw the volleyball directly at him, full force, when he wasn't looking. They tripped him and sent him sprawling. The gym teacher watched impassively, adding to Jim's misery because Jim had a hopeless crush on the man.

Once when he was combing his hair in the change room one of the meanest of his tormentors entered. The boy checked to see that they were alone and then approached Jim.

"Jim," he said, "I know you like to play around with the guys. How about you and I having some fun?"

Jim was horrified, certain that he was being set up for some sadistic game. Later, as an adult, he encountered that person in a gay bar and realized that the offer had been sincere. The boy had taken the lead in vilifying Jim in order to conceal his own homosexuality.

Jim's wretchedness was clearly apparent but his mother pretended to see nothing amiss with her son. Desperate to get her attention, he set a fire in the waste-basket in his bedroom. She slapped him around for doing it but avoided the question of why it had happened. He sent hysterical prayers to Jehovah to stop the pain and fell into exhausted sleep with tears on his face.

He says now, "All the adults around me knew that I was gay—my parents, my teachers, everyone. None offered any compassion, none tried to help me find some self-respect. They just put their heads in the sand and let me suffer."

He got through grade ten thanks to the kindness of Beverley Mathieson, his former teacher. She arranged special access for him to the school auditorium so he could work on the stage by himself on parts he was learning, and she arranged for time out of class so he could read plays. It was a time, too, when he drew great comfort from being a Jehovah's Witness. That made him a special person, he felt. He had Jehovah on his side, so long as he could overcome his homosexuality. The Kingdom Hall his mother attended brought him a sense of peace and place, though he was nagged constantly to stop taking part in theatre. The courtesies of address, Brother So-and-so and Sister So-and-so, soothed him.

Grade eleven was a little better. He was in a different class, away from the taunting classmates of the previous year. He joined the school orchestra, playing the timpani. He had a part in a handsome production of *The Music Man*, winning accolades from teachers and other students. His marks in English were the highest in the school, and his grades in marketing skills won him an award as the best in Ontario.

His mother was bringing heavy pressure on him to stop the drama activities and an art class he had just commenced. He commented of that period, "The Witnesses made me feel that acting was sinful, yet I loved it with every passion I had. There was a real and terrible conflict."

His relationship with his mother was deteriorating. That year Johanna decided that the problem was their proximity to his father and moved herself, Karen, and Jim to London, Ontario.

Johanna promptly joined a small Jehovah's Witness congregation, London Fairmount, which warmly took in the newcomers. A young pioneer missionary couple came once a week to study Bible with Johanna and her children and accompanied Jim and Karen to prayer meetings to help make them comfortable.

The new high school was scarcely an improvement over the one he had left in Hamilton. Once again Jim was reviled for being a sissy and treated with contempt by classmates and teachers alike. Feeling uprooted and fatherless, he sought comfort in the London Fairmount congregation and threw himself into the activities there. His gregarious mother soon made friends, and he immersed himself enthusiastically in religious activities. He particularly enjoyed being assigned after services to a neighbourhood where he would distribute the *Watchtower* and *Awake!* door-to-door. If people invited him in, he would read Scripture and talk about the better world of Jehovah God.

Jim has a great deal of respect for the Jehovah's Witnesses' willingness to preach. He says it's hard work trying to convert people, and he notes that few other faiths take on that responsibility.

Jim's disputes with his mother were increasingly stormy and hurtful. He began to think about living with his father instead. It seemed to him that his problem might be lack of a male role model. Maybe what others saw as effeminacy in him was only the result of being raised by his mother.

One night as he was preparing to go out, Johanna ordered him to stay home. These clashes were becoming commonplace, and he ignored her. As he continued to get into his coat, she said something wounding and he lashed back that he was thinking he'd rather live with his father.

Johanna Zanuk exploded. She picked up a broom, reversed it, and began to beat Jim on the head with the handle. He flared and threw a punch at her, knocking her down, and then ran to his room. She followed him, screaming insults. For hours she went in and out of his room and raged at him. He was genuinely afraid of her wrath and slept that night hidden between his bed and the wall, falling into an exhausted sleep with his shoe in his hand to defend himself.

Towards dawn his mother came quietly into his room and apologized. They agreed Jim should call his father, who invited Jim to live with him. Kathy was gone from the house near Brantford, already married and a dedicated missionary in Toronto, so there was only Allan still at home. Jim moved in with his father and brother, grateful for the peacefulness of his childhood home.

Jim was enrolled with his cousin, Patrick, in a high school in the nearby town of Ancaster. Because of the distance Jim would have to travel, Karl Zanuk bought his son a new car, a Malibu the colour of red wine, and gave him a handsome amount of spending money. The combination of a car and Jim's good looks made him an important person in the school. There was the usual dismay when the coaches discovered that the big, strong youngster couldn't play football, but the school had a serious preoccupation with drama and Jim was in his element there.

Even so, he was uneasy of his welcome in the cafeteria or hangouts near the school. He overheard comments about "the faggot". He took to eating his lunch alone in his car to avoid unpleasantness. He loved to drive that car, cruising the countryside imagining that he was incredibly rich, with a well-connected family.

He tried out for the school production of *Camelot* and listened anxiously as the cast list was announced, beginning with the smallest parts. His name wasn't called. At the end, when only the starring role was left, the director declared, "And now, the final role, the part of King Arthur, goes to the new boy, Jim Zanuk."

He was ecstatic. The role of Lancelot was played by an attractive youth, David Lamont, and Guinevere went to David's girl friend, Toby Hatton. Because the three played many scenes together, they fell into the habit of being a threesome that rapidly extended itself beyond the production. They went everywhere together. They did their homework together and switched classes so they could take courses together.

Toby was in love with David, and so was Jim, though David appeared to have no inkling of Jim's real feelings. David's parents, who made a good guess as to the nature of the relationship, were alarmed. They took exception when the two boys slept overnight at one or the other's place. David was puzzled by his parents' unfriendliness, but since no explanation was given he ignored their complaints. Toby grew suspicious and tried to cut Jim out of their activities, but David was devoted to Jim and wouldn't have him left out.

A new crisis developed in Jim's life. Karl Zanuk had been seeing a pleasant woman, Eleanor Duncan, whom he met at a dance sponsored by Parents without Partners. After a year and a half of dating, they decided to marry. Though five years had elapsed since Karl and Johanna's marriage had fallen apart, the Zanuk divorce still was not recognized by Jehovah's Witnesses. Karl was warned by the elders that he would be excommunicated if he pursued his intention. Excommunication, or disfellowship as Witnesses call it, is a harsh punishment. Offenders are regarded as dead and no one, not even a family member, is permitted to have any contact.

Johanna Zanuk sent word from London that none of her children was to attend the wedding, since their father would automatically be excommunicated as soon as the service was performed. Karen obeyed her without hesitation, and Allan, whose relationship with Eleanor wasn't warm at that time, also agreed to it. That left Jim, who was inclined for the sake of peace with his mother to obey her.

His father asked him to change his mind. He said it would mean the world to him to have Jim as his best man. He had never asked much of his son, he pointed out, and he had always been generous. He reminded Jim of the car, the clothes, the allowance, and pleaded with him to go to the wedding.

Jim yielded. A few days later, Johanna wrote him a letter saying that having him as a son was the worst thing that had ever happened to her in her life. Broken-hearted, he took it to his school guidance teacher who offered comforting advice. The issue really was between Jim's parents, the teacher said. Jim should forget about the letter and get on with his own life.

It was months before his mother would speak to him. His father was immediately excommunicated, which ended all contact with his daughters. In hope of restoring his relationship with his mother, Jim tried to pretend for a time that his father didn't exist, but because they were living in the same house the attempt soon broke down.

Karl Zanuk continued to attend services at the Kingdom Hall that had disfellowshipped him, even though no place was ever made for him and no one would speak to him or even acknowledge that he was there. He endured the abasement humbly and patiently for three years of regular attendance until the elders relented, pronounced him sufficiently repentant, and welcomed him back.

That done, he almost ceased involvement with the Witnesses. His purpose all along had been to repair the breach with his daughters, and when his reinstatement ended that estrangement, he lost interest in religion.

Karl's marriage to Eleanor freed Johanna Zanuk to make a second marriage without risking the penalty of excommunication, since Karl was now viewed by the Witnesses as an adulterer. She made a disastrous marriage with a brutal man who often beat her. Once when Jim was trying to protect her, he and his stepfather had a fist fight on the front lawn. The marriage ended, leaving Johanna with a son Daniel, Jim's half-brother.

Twice a year Jehovah's Witnesses attend a small circuit convention composed of several adjoining congregations, and once a year there is a larger district convention. At one of these Jim had met and fallen in love with a young woman from Lambeth, Nancy Petrov. He was elated to find that he was sexually aroused by her. Since he could love a woman, after all, the major problem of his life was solved.

His explanation of the attachment is that most people have the capacity to be bisexual. Society reinforces the more common tendency, which is for other-sex partners, and isolates those whose preference is for same-sex partners, so people learn to suppress urges within themselves that don't fit the norm.

"Most men sleep with women because that's expected of them," he comments, "but I believe men can have relations with either sex. I know I could. If I met a woman I liked a lot and we began to interest one another sexually, I know I could have an affair with her. It's just that I don't meet women who interest me that way."

Jim was counting on his passion for Nancy to rescue him from homosexuality. Thrilling with adolescent ardour, he drove to Lambeth to see her, preparing speeches of love rich in biblical phraseology—that they would "become one flesh", and so on. He would announce that, as soon as they were old enough, they should be married and would live in Jehovah's love for ever.

The news that awaited him was shocking. Though Nancy, like Jim, was only sixteen, she had decided to marry an older man of some means. Jim begged her to wait and marry him when he finished school but her mind was made up. The horror of his sexuality opened up again for him. She was the only woman he'd ever met who attracted him physically. Without her he was doomed.

When *Camelot* opened in the Ancaster auditorium to tumultuous applause, Jim was acclaimed. His tenor singing voice was true but unremarkable; his dramatic intensity, however, was compelling, and he was a striking, commanding figure on stage. One of his costumes featured a jerkin his new stepmother, Eleanor, had knitted for him and sprayed with silver paint so it resembled chain armour.

Jim got along well with his stepmother, though his brother was slow to accept her, particularly while she was redecorating the house. For his part, Jim appreciated that Eleanor encouraged his acting and was a calming influence in the family.

The celebrations after *Camelot* closed were delirious, made poignant by the sense Jim had that a golden time was ending. He would be leaving school that summer to devote himself to missionary work as a Jehovah's Witness. He saw himself at a crossroads. Either he could choose to be a homosexual and follow that path, which would mean excommunication as a Jehovah's Witness, or he could renounce the sexual part of his nature and remain a life-long celibate. He agonized over the choice between sex and God for months, but it really was no contest. Jehovah God had been the only consistent friend of his life, the one who was always available to listen to his confidences and hear his tearful prayers. He opted to follow God.

4

After the huge success of *Camelot*, Jim, Toby, and David were lionized, a heady experience that made Jim reckless. He and David were sitting in Jim's car late one night after a celebratory party, both exhausted but feeling so elated that they didn't want to go home. Jim found himself in a conversation he had long rehearsed in his mind. He told David that he was gay and said that he was attracted to him. David said he should stop talking nonsense.

"I'm not joking," Jim replied. He put his hand on David's knee. David angrily pushed him away, got out of the car, and slammed the door.

The two didn't meet again until the following Saturday at a graduation party. Jim took David aside and said that they had to talk, that their friendship mattered too much for the issue between them to be left hanging. David hauled back and punched Jim in the eye. A fist fight broke out that ended with David's leaving the party. He went home and gathered up souvenirs and gifts Jim had given him, loaded them into a green garbage bag, returned to the party, and threw the bag in Jim's face. The contents spilled out, and a small cuff-links box, the most valuable of the gifts, was smashed.

His face red with fury, David yelled for all to hear that he wouldn't have a faggot for a friend.

Jim gathered up the gifts, his heart broken. That night he sobbed in his bed, biting the blanket to stifle the sound. He knew that his father and Eleanor, one floor below, could hear him, but no one came to ask what was the matter. He never saw David again.

David was the first close friend of Jim's life. Though Jim was seventeen years old, until David he had never had a pal with whom to go to movies or for a swim. The enormity of his loss plunged him into despair. He spent the next few weeks in prayer, begging Jehovah for help to bear his loneliness and misery. Sometimes he could not prevent himself from masturbating, after which he was tormented with grief and guilt. His conscience was driving him over the edge. He came to the conclusion anew that his salvation was celibacy, and that he would live alone all his life. Grief flooded him at the prospect of never having a mate, but he could not live without his God.

Jehovah, he decided, was his only friend, the one presence in his life who had never betrayed him, who always listened, who could be trusted. Though the choice was painful, he concluded that his only safety lay in following his religion rather than his passions.

He found a job in Hamilton at Simpsons-Sears in the display department and showed a remarkable aptitude for the work. After only a few weeks he was given a raise and more responsibility. At the end of the first year, it was clear he was being groomed to head the department.

He joined a Hamilton Little Theatre group, helping with the props. That gave him access to the theatre, and sometimes he would turn out the lights and stand with his eyes closed in the centre of the stage, imagining that he had just given a performance that had the audience on its feet. The production that year was *Man of La Mancha*, and he found the music deeply thrilling.

One of his older co-workers at Simpsons-Sears showed great interest in him and Jim was flattered. The man suggested that they take in a drive-in movie together and Jim agreed. When Jim picked him up in his car, he was startled to see that the man had dressed in tights, white boots, a cape, and a wig, with rings on every finger. At the movie, protected by darkness and the car's privacy, the man put his hand on Jim's leg, and then on his crotch. Jim, trembling, did not interfere. The man unzipped Jim's pants, took out his erect penis and sucked it. When Jim's orgasm came, he wondered what the man had done with the ejaculation.

"Did you swallow it?" he asked, amazed.

"Certainly," the man replied. "Is this your first time!"

Afterwards Jim was fearful that others where he worked would learn of the encounter and know that he was gay. He went to pains to avoid the co-worker, though the man pursued him everywhere.

The incident convinced him of what he had known since falling in love with Superman—that he truly was a homosexual. He wondered what would become of him. He was trying to gain his father's respect, his mother's love, his own self-esteem and mental stability, and Jehovah God's blessing. The image he had of himself was that of a man being torn to pieces.

Whenever he visited his mother and the Fairmount congregation in London, they urged him to leave his father's household. By living there, he was violating the rules of excommunication. In his new mood of purifying himself, Jim was inclined to agree.

In the summer of 1972 he moved to Toronto, an eighteen-year-old avid for life in a big city, and stayed temporarily with his newly married sister, Kathryn, who with her husband was a busy missionary in the Bendale congregation of Jehovah's Witnesses.

Bendale was an unusual congregation. The Kingdom Halls Jim had known were thronged with families and their grown daughters devoting themselves to missionary work, but the Bendale congregation had a dozen members who were handsome young men of Jim's age. He happily joined them, finding it heaven to be in a group of young men who accepted him and with whom he belonged.

One of the best looking of the group, Tom B., offered to study with him to hasten Jim's return to proper status as a Jehovah's Witness after some years of spotty attendance. Over the next months they spent hours together every week, sipping tea while they studied the Bible. Tom was interested in graphic art, so Jim happily shared that hobby with him. He began to fall in love with Tom.

Jim speculated that Tom was also battling homosexuality, but neither man ever broached the subject. He sensed the other's anguish and fully understood the man's need to stay in the closet in order to continue to serve God. Sometimes they looked at each other longingly, but neither made a move to communicate what each was feeling. Occasionally when they were in a group, the intimacy protected by being public, they would give each other a manly hug. That had to suffice for contact.

It was a time of pure pleasure. Jim went overnight from being an intensely lonely outcast to entering a brotherhood where he fully belonged. He sent grateful prayers to Jehovah God for making his life wonderful. It was wonderful to pray lovingly to God, rather than always begging for forgiveness. He determined to dedicate his life to the glory of God and notified the elders that he wanted to be baptized.

The preparation for baptism as a Jehovah's Witness is arduous, consisting of months of intensive Bible study, followed by a prayer of private declaration to God and a searching interview with the elders. He buckled down to the task joyfully.

He found a job at Eaton's College Street store in the display department. He wasn't aware for a long time that most of his fellow employees were gay. The head of the department and the assistant head each took him to dinner, openly flirting with him, but he innocently missed the message.

To his great relief, he wasn't masturbating as much any more. When it did happen, though, he felt devastated. What he had done was wrong, demonic, bad, evil. He would stretch out on the floor, face in the rug, and pray for forgiveness.

"God, what a thing to do to a human being," he has since reflected.

He saved his money carefully until he could afford a small apartment of his own. Taking pains with every detail, he gradually stocked the kitchen and the linen closet, and bought furniture for the bedroom and living-room. When it was done, he luxuriated in the pride and privacy of being on his own in his first home.

At Eaton's the work load increased with the coming of Christmas. Jehovah's Witnesses believe Christmas to be a pagan festival but Jim kept his views to himself and helped decorate the huge store. At the staff Christmas party, he had too much to drink. Most people, it seemed, were semi-drunk. A fight broke out between two gay men over Jim and some people hustled Jim away and poured him into a taxi. He went home, grinning all the way. It felt wonderful to be wanted. After a heart-breaking year of yearning over David, he now was the object of desire.

The glow was of brief duration, to be replaced by the horrified realization that at Eaton's he was surrounded by homosexual temptation. He quit and took a job driving a delivery truck for an auto parts company owned by a Jehovah's Witness in the Bendale congregation. He was gratified that his working hours gave him more time for missionary activities.

No matter how keenly he flung himself into doing God's work door to door, he could not entirely submerge his gay longings. Handsome men, particularly men in rough work clothes, made his heart thud. He fought against thinking about them and against the release of masturbation. As his mother did, he searched the

Bible for strength. The Scriptures said that if a man lies down with another man as if with a woman it is an abomination in the eyes of God. Was that true? Did God detest him?

He prayed for help in resolving his dilemma. He told Jehovah God that he didn't want to be gay and hadn't chosen it. Was he to be tormented all his life for something that was beyond his power to change? Please help me to be straight, he begged Jehovah God.

He saw his salvation in finding a woman he could love, as he had Nancy. He believed he could overcome being gay if he married. The problem was that he never saw a woman who appealed to him in the slightest, except as a friend.

To give himself more time during the day for missionary work, he took a job as a night cleaner in office buildings. His friend Tom also was a night cleaner and often joined him. The two worked contentedly together, discussing the Scriptures as they dusted desks and wiped floors.

One winter evening he and Tom took a streetcar to Toronto's Sheraton Hotel, across from City Hall, excited at the prospect of attending a Jehovah's Witness convention where important speakers would present revelations of Bible teachings. He has a vivid memory of the gentle snowfall that fell on them like a blessing as they got off the streetcar and of the warmth of the crowd of Jehovah's Witnesses in the convention hall.

As he and Tom descended the escalator, Tom pointed out a striking blonde woman in a sheepskin coat and a tall fur hat. She looked up and waved at Tom. Jim gasped. He had never seen a more beautiful woman.

"She's stunning," he said to Tom. "Who is she?"

"That's untouchable Iris," Tom told him. "Iris Hrabovsky. Want to meet her?"

"Love to."

"You should know that she's Big Money. She drives a fancy car and people think she's a snob. I don't, but that's what people say. She's cold. They call her 'Miss Ice Cube'. She won't date anyone."

They pushed through the crowd but got separated. Jim continued on without Tom and stood in front of the ravishingly pretty woman.

"Good evening, Sister Hrabovsky," he said to her with a wide grin. "My name is Jim Zanuk."

She was amused. "Good evening, Brother Zanuk," she replied. "My name is Iris Hrabovsky."

When Tom caught up with them they were staring at one another admiringly. He said, "I see you two have met."

Iris smiled radiantly. "You have a very charming friend," she told Tom.

Jim felt his heart melt. Here was a woman he could marry, someone blonde and lovely like Nancy. He decided she wasn't cold at all. She just needed someone to show her how to be loving. He was nineteen and she was twenty-one.

He learned that Tom was Iris's usual escort to a weekly Bible study session with an elderly man. Women Jehovah's Witnesses are not allowed to go alone to a Bible study with a man so Tom had been accompanying her. Tom mentioned one night when he and Jim were cleaning an office that he wouldn't be able to take Iris the following week. Jim declared that he would take her instead.

Tom shook his head. "She's very picky, and her family is even pickier. You'll never get to first base."

Jim slapped him on the shoulder and said, "Tom, watch this." He went to the telephone and called her.

A man answered.

"Is that Brother Hrabovsky?" Jim asked.

"Yes," the man replied in a wary tone.

"This is Brother Jim Zanuk," Jim said. "I'd like to talk to Iris if I may, please."

Iris came to the phone. Jim explained that he was free next week and would be happy to go with her to the Bible study if she liked.

"What perfect timing," she cried. "I was wondering what I would do. Thank you, that would be very nice."

Jim put down the receiver and gave Tom a look of triumph.

They met for Bible studies several times and Jim felt his excitement increasing. He adored her delicate politeness, her articulate way of speaking, the look of her. She had a prim, repressed manner, which, by its contrast with the luxurious clothes she wore, aroused him. He grew bold and asked her for a date. She agreed to have lunch with him on a day they would be spending the afternoon at Bible studies.

It was spring of 1974. He was walking on air. Over lunch she invited him to her home for tea. She lived in a Thornhill neighbourhood of huge houses with broad lawns and immaculate flower beds. Jim, ringing the bell, was intimidated by the imposing stone of the Hrabovsky mansion and the four cars in the driveway. Iris, dressed in a long gown, opened the door on an entrance hall from which a grand staircase rose. She showed him through rooms with deep-pile white carpets, silk-covered sofas and chairs, and an amethyst-coloured fireplace; the tour included the indoor swimming pool and a glimpse of her bedroom with its round bed in a sunken pit.

Iris's father was a tall, stately man with a severe manner, and her mother a person of overly elaborate social graces. They had tea together, and Jim left with his head spinning. He felt he had been in the presence of royalty.

The Hrabovskys invited him to attend a party a few days later given by their congregation, where the senior Hrabovsky was an elder. Jim passed this test, and the courtship moved to its next stage, with Jim and Iris permitted to be alone in the Hrabovsky den while they read the Scriptures together. Iris would collect a silver tea tray laid out in the kitchen, set it on the floor before the fire, and daintily pour tea, while Jim drank in the woman and the luxury.

"Brother Zanuk," she said on the first of such evenings. "I think you are becoming romantically inclined towards me." Jim nodded and she went on, "I want you to know that I can't become involved with you because I intend to serve God."

Jim understood the message. She was chaste and did not date anyone because she wanted her first boyfriend to be the one she married. He told her she could do no better than consider him as a marriage partner. He listed his good qualities, among them his devotion to Jehovah God. He drew on his skills as an actor and his confidence as an eloquent nineteen-year-old. After more than an hour of impassioned salesmanship he asked, "Sister Hrabovsky, have I moved you one iota towards continuing our relationship?"

She replied demurely, "Brother Zanuk, you have moved me one percentage point of one percentage point."

He grinned. "That will do." He thought to himself, I'm going to marry you.

He left walking on air. He desired Iris with all his being. The problem of his homosexuality was over. He wouldn't have to fight gay temptations any more. He was like everyone else. If she would marry him, he would be saved.

"I felt very masculine and very relieved," he said of that period.

They went to movies occasionally, but their favourite activity was to study the Bible together to get a better understanding of the Scriptures. The two would sprawl on the floor in the Hrabovsky den, turning the pages of the Bible, discussing the fine points.

A coldness was creeping into the way the rest of the family treated him. Iris had a younger sister, Janet, a teenager, who was not around much, but Iris's mother and, most particularly, her father were usually in the house and would greet Jim with distinct chilliness and then disappear. Once they invited Jim and his cousin Patrick for dinner and Patrick spilled his wine, to Jim's embarrassment. Jim thought the problem might be his manners, so he took great pains to be a perfect gentleman in their presence, to no avail.

A few months later Jim was in bed with flu when he received a call from Roy Hrabovsky. Iris's father wasted no time on preliminaries.

"I have forbidden Iris to see you and I want you to respect my wishes," he said. "I am the head of my household and I don't want her to have any further contact with you."

"What have I done?" Jim asked, stunned.

"I don't have to explain anything," Iris's father replied, and hung up.

Iris called ten minutes later, weeping. They arranged to meet in the parking lot of the Knob Hill shopping mall. Jim got into her car to find her crying. She said she was in pain from her conscience because she was disobeying her father, the family head, which meant she was going against God's wishes as well, but she had to see Jim one last time. *One last time!* Jim begged to know what he had done to offend Iris's father, but she didn't know. She said it had something to do with the fact that she would inherit a great deal of money and Jim wasn't even an elder in his congregation. He was socially beneath the Hrabovskys. She wept that it was sinful of her even to see Jim to say goodbye.

Jim was furious. With Iris he had succeeded in overcoming his homosexuality and he had a chance to end his loneliness. He had done nothing wrong. He couldn't let her go. He insisted that she call him again to set up another meeting time.

The couple continued to see one another at the shopping mall, playing the same scene over and over. Iris would weep that she was defying her father and defying God, that she was among the damned, and Jim would try amid the tears to comfort her. Once she admitted that her father had offered her a huge amount of money if she would stop seeing Jim. She had refused.

Roy Hrabovsky called and said he wanted to see Jim. Jim went to the house and found Iris crying. The discussion with her father took place in the kitchen. The older man was in a rage. "I know you have been seeing Iris," he said. "What kind of a Christian are you to go against my wishes? I want you to promise me that you will accept my decision that you two are never to meet again. Will you do that?"

Jim thought that if he agreed, Roy Hrabovsky might come to realize what a fine, honourable person was courting his daughter. "Yes, I will," he said.

Roy turned to his daughter. "Will you respect my wishes?" he asked.

She replied, "No, Daddy dear, I love Jim."

Jim was ordered out of the house. He was full of remorse that he hadn't been defiant too. What must Iris think of him?

A few weeks went by and Jim could stand it no longer. He called the Hrabovskys and Iris's mother, Jean, answered the phone. She blasted him for calling and hung up. He called back and got Janet, the sister, who was equally indignant. Iris called him back, weeping that she was going against God but couldn't help herself. She loved him.

Jim learned only years later that Roy Hrabovsky had been warned by a Jehovah's Witness that Jim was believed to be a homosexual.

He went to meetings of Iris's congregation because he could be sure of seeing her there. The scene was always the same. At first she would turn her face away from him and not speak, but by sitting near her, his face full of yearning, he could always break her down. Months passed during which Iris continued to be both distraught that she was offending her father and unable to stop seeing Jim.

Roy Hrabovsky made another offer. If Iris would go to Quebec to do missionary work for six months and have no contact with Jim, not even by letter, he might relent.

The couple tearfully agreed. Jim promised there would be no contact of any kind and urged Iris to be strong. If they could survive this trial, surely they would be allowed to marry.

The matter had become a subject of raging controversy in the Jehovah's Witness community. The Bendale congregation was torn by dissension as people took sides; one half supported Jim and the other the rights of a father. The atmosphere became so tense that Jim decided to move back to London, where he found a small apartment at the back of an old house and got a job as a night cleaner. He carried pictures of Iris with him and prayed every night to be allowed to marry her. He slept with his arms around his teddy bear, tears on his face.

His friend Tom from the Bendale congregation wrote that he was dating a girl he thought he would marry. Jim was happy for him, but his bitterness at the unfairness of his own situation increased. Tom was finding a way to cope with his possible homosexuality, but Jim was being denied his only hope.

Four and a half months after their separation, Iris phoned from a phone booth in Toronto. She said she couldn't stand it any longer. She had returned to Toronto in order to get her things together and move out of her father's home. Would he come to the Knob Hill mall the next day and pick her up?

Jim found her seated calmly on top of a pile of her belongings packed in suitcases and green garbage bags. She was reading her Bible. Some distance away, her father was seated behind the wheel of his car, watching with a grim face. Iris cried all the way to London.

Iris immediately picked up her career as a pioneer in the Jehovah's Witnesses, which requires a high level of commitment to missionary work. Her beauty and piety made her an immense hit with the Fairmount congregation in London. A kind sister in the Kingdom Hall made room for Iris in her home, and over the next two months Jim and Iris were happy and inseparable.

It was the summer of 1975. Jim was twenty and Iris twenty-two. One evening, with Iris lovely in yellow chiffon, he bought her yellow roses and drove her to the deserted Fairmount Kingdom Hall. He had the keys and they went inside. He sang "God Is Love" to her, said a prayer, took her hands, and asked her to marry him. She said yes.

Predictably, her parents were furious when she told them her decision. One weekend when Jim was visiting his father, the Hrabovskys drove to London and stormed into the house where Iris was staying. They packed her clothes, forced her into the car, and took her home with them to Toronto. When Jim frantically called, he was subjected to language that shocked him.

"And you call yourself a good Jehovah's Witness!" he shouted at Iris's mother.

It was two weeks before he summoned enough nerve to call. Jean Hrabovsky said pleasantly that Iris had been sent where he would never find her. His letters were returned. Two and a half months later, Iris called from Texas where she had been staying with relatives. She went from there to relatives in Winnipeg and finally back to Toronto. She decided once again to join Jim and called a taxi. Though her mother fought with her, pulling the luggage from her hands, Iris succeeded in reaching the Knob Hill mall and called Jim from a phone booth to come for her.

The couple appealed to a travelling Jehovah's Witness district overseer to reconcile the Hrabovskys so that Iris could have her parents' blessing. A meeting was arranged one cold October evening. Jim and Iris waited nervously in his car outside the Fairmount Kingdom Hall and prayed together. They watched Jean and Roy Hrabovsky drive up and enter. Then the elders arrived, bustling with importance. With everyone assembled, the young couple timidly joined the others.

Jim was confident the misunderstanding was about to be repaired. He wasn't the monstrous person the Hrabovskys seemed to think. A mistake had been made and, at last, it was going to be corrected.

The elders and the Hrabovskys went into the Kingdom Hall study and called Iris to join them. Jim waited apprehensively, offering passionate prayers to Jehovah. He was summoned and found a familiar tableau. Iris was red-eyed from weeping, Jean Hrabovsky was glaring balefully at him, and Roy Hrabovsky, erect with suppressed fury, avoided meeting his eyes.

The district overseer asked Jim to speak. He recited what he had rehearsed in his mind a hundred times—that he was a good person, that he truly loved Iris and wanted to make her happy, and that he was sure the opposition of the Hrabovskys was the result of an error.

"Since all of us in this room love Iris," he pleaded, "can't we do something to take this terrible pressure off her? She shouldn't have to choose between me and her family."

Roy Hrabovsky leaned across the table. "I want you to know that I hate you," he said. At the gasp in the room he amended it, "I don't hate you, I hate what you're doing."

Jim felt tears in his eyes and heard Iris sobbing.

One of the elders said, "Roy, Jim is a fine young man. He's a little young, but he's learning quickly and doing the best he can. I have the greatest respect for him. Most of the congregation does."

Jean Hrabovsky began to cry.

The overseer said, "Roy, this isn't a decision that the elders can make. We're not police, we're just trying to smooth things. Personally I see no reason why Jim and Iris shouldn't marry. I suggest we all say a prayer and hope things work out."

All heads obediently bowed and the overseer offered a sympathetic prayer as Jean Hrabovsky continued to weep loudly. The overseer ended by saying that if Jim and Iris wished to marry it was between them and Jehovah and that no one should cause trouble for them. With that Jean Hrabovsky lost control and flung herself into her husband's arms. Iris tried to comfort her mother, but the expression on Roy Hrabovsky's face was intimidating. Jim pulled her away. They drove to her home in silence and had a cup of tea together.

They set a wedding day, December 13, 1975. The ceremony was held in the London Fairmount congregation's Kingdom Hall. The penniless couple were adopted by the congregations to which they had belonged. Bendale supplied some of the catering costs and helped pay for Iris's gown. Her congregation in Toronto paid the rest, and Jim's father rented the hall.

Before leaving for the wedding, Jim sank to his knees for a long prayer of thanksgiving. The loneliness, the fight with his sexuality, were over. He wept with gratitude throughout the ceremony.

Iris's parents refused to attend, but her sister bravely was there, though she refused to be a bridesmaid for fear she would be disinherited. Jim's brother, Allan, and his friend Tom stood up with him, and there was a reception at which the newlyweds were toasted and loaded with gifts. It seemed to the guests a storybook romance, a Jehovah's Witness version of *Romeo and Juliet*, and they rejoiced at the victory of true love.

In a park a few weeks earlier Jim had given Iris a gentle kiss, her first. She appeared to have had little sexual education. Once she had asked him about necking. She said she had heard it was something men and women did but she couldn't find an explanation in the Bible or in the dictionary. Did people touch necks? Once when he held her in his arms she asked anxiously, "Is this lewd conduct?"

Jim was trembling when they were alone in the apartment he had furnished for them, but Iris seemed calm. He had champagne chilling and two stem glasses on a tray. She went into the bathroom and he heard the sound of the tub filling with water. She turned off the bathroom lights and called to him. He found her immersed in bubbles, a candle lit beside the tub.

He was so nervous he dropped the bottle, but he had a second in reserve. He put down the cover of the toilet seat and sat there while they sipped champagne and talked. The bubbles were disappearing. *I have to make a move*, he thought. He took off his pyjama top and hugged her, stroking her body under the water. She stood up and he dried her. She put on a sheer robe and they moved to a fur rug in the living-room, where he kissed and embraced her. Then they went to bed and made love, Jim awkward but virile and Iris shy but responsive. Both were virgins.

They wakened full of wonder, took the phone off the hook, and opened their wedding gifts. Her family had given nothing, but sentimental Jehovah's Witnesses and Jim's family and friends, knowing they were broke, had been generous.

They were the favourite couple of their congregation, a strikingly good-looking pair who were invited everywhere. Jim had never been happier in his life. He bought a secondhand guitar and sang love songs to Iris. They spent their days in missionary work, and Jim cleaned offices at night. He struggled to keep his sex drive under control. He would have made love to Iris every night but she was reserved, with an edge of disapproval towards his passion.

Iris pined for her family. Janet came to visit her sister frequently, which Jim welcomed at first but came to see as threatening. Janet was full of criticism of Jim and filled Iris with stories of the luxuries that she was missing. His absences in the evenings gave Janet a clear field and, by the end of the first year, Iris was beginning to say that maybe the marriage had been a mistake.

She criticized Jim for not being an elder, like her father, and said if God hadn't seen fit to make Jim an elder, why should anyone respect him? Jim reminded her that at twenty-one he was too young to be an elder, but the resentment continued. Iris complained too that Jim didn't provide for her in the style to which she was accustomed.

Iris announced one day that she was going home for a visit. Her father was thinking of forgiving Jim, she said.

"Forgive me for what?" Jim yelled.

He got himself under control. "Iris, I don't think you should go home alone," he said. "I'm your husband and I think I should go with you."

She persuaded him that this was a peace-making expedition. She would go alone and start the healing. Jim agreed but he had a premonition of disaster.

Iris returned from the visit laden with a fur coat, jewels, and expensive clothes purchased at Creed's and Holt Renfrew. Jim was dejected, taking it as a criticism of his meagre income, but Iris was too elated to notice.

She had more complaints about his behaviour. She ridiculed the prayers Jim wrote and found fault with his opinions. "Why do you act so silly?" she asked often. His grammar came under scrutiny. She said he was immature.

Her weekend visits to her parents in Toronto grew longer. She was gone as long as ten days at a time, and he was forbidden to telephone her while she was in her father's house. When she was with him she immersed herself in the Bible and asked not to be interrupted. Once he asked her to go to a movie with him and she refused. He went alone and the thought struck him that he had married in order never to be alone again. Here he was at a movie alone, as if nothing had changed.

He adopted a stray kitten. When he was alone he played his guitar and practised love songs to the cat.

When he and Iris prayed together, she always asked Jehovah to forgive her for what she had done to her parents.

They argued about her visits to Toronto. She still refused to allow him to go with her. When her sister came, bringing credit cards, the two women would shop most of the day.

Next Iris ridiculed Jim as a lover. She declared that his penis was ugly, a funny-looking thing. She complained of his sexual demands and said that sex once a week was enough. When love-making began, she urged him to be quick about it. He went back to masturbation and sexual fantasy. The partners in his fantasies were always men, who understood his need for sex.

One evening when Iris was in Toronto for a ten-day visit and Jim, alone, was feeling desperately sorry for himself, he went for a walk in a park he knew was frequented by the gay community cruising for sex. He was looking for trouble. He had an illogical idea that if he had a tawdry relationship with a man, Iris and Jehovah would be punished for making him suffer.

Part of him pretended he was only looking for someone to talk to, someone who would understand his struggle to be heterosexual. He met a man who asked him back to his apartment, "for coffee". Jim knew that the man didn't have coffee in mind, but he agreed. Iris be damned, he thought. Thanks a lot, God, for all you've done to help. Thank you, Iris, studying your Bible, being so holy, telling people how to live their lives.

The man put on a pot of coffee and suggested that he and Jim have a shower, since it was a warm night. They stripped and stepped into the shower together.

When the man reached for Jim's penis, Jim started to cry. The man stopped. He consoled Jim and helped him dry off. When they dressed he poured coffee and suggested that Jim tell him his troubles. Jim poured out his whole story, beginning as a child that everyone knew was gay, trying to be straight, trying to fit in with his religion, trying to be married to a woman he loved.

The man listened with total attention and sympathy. At the end of it, he said, "I don't think you're going to solve your problems by being here with me. I think it might even create a few. Why don't you finish your coffee, put on your jacket, and head home?"

The man hugged him and showed Jim to the door. "Before you start meeting strangers and going to their apartments," he suggested kindly, "I think you should sort out your life and make some decisions."

Jim suffered acute shame the next time he and Iris had sex. He sent tormented prayers for forgiveness to the heavens.

One day Jim arrived home to find Iris burning with excitement. Her parents were making her and her sister the present of a trip to Israel. It was something she had long dreamed of, walking where Jesus had walked. Jim asked if the trip included him, knowing it wouldn't. "No," she said. "But is it all right with you if I go?"

"Where does that leave me?" he asked.

She said, "You didn't answer my question."

"Why don't you make the decision," he suggested bitterly.

She went immediately to the phone and called her sister. "Janet," she cried breathlessly, "Jim says I can go."

She calmly sat down to read her *Watchtower* in preparation for the evening's study. When she left, Jim was alone with his devastation. He called a friend, Sam, a fellow Jehovah's Witness with whom he shared hours of Bible study. He was certain Sam was straight because he had girl friends. He asked if he could come over and spend the night, he was lonely. Sam said sure.

The two opened a bottle of liquor and demolished it. Sam said that the bed in the spare bedroom wasn't made up and he had no clean sheets. They would have to share the bed in his room. Sam stripped and climbed into his side of the bed. Jim, self-conscious and attracted to Sam, kept his shorts on. He lay rigidly still, hardly daring to breathe, but Sam appeared to be asleep and finally Jim dropped off too.

He doesn't know who instigated it, but he awoke to find his arms around Sam and Sam's arms around him. Jim began to stroke Sam's body and was flattered that Sam was aroused. There was a moment of hesitation and then the two of them masturbated each other in silence, rolled over back to back, and slept.

In the morning they pretended nothing had happened, but Jim decided it was imperative that he leave London.

Iris's sister, Janet, had moved to Sherbrooke, Quebec, to do missionary work among Roman Catholics, always a prime target for Jehovah's Witnesses. Sherbrooke seemed to Jim a likely move for him. Iris would be far from her parents but would still have her sister. He could perhaps woo her from her parents. Janet's boyfriend in the Sherbrooke group of Jehovah's Witnesses was starting a small business that would employ Jim as a night cleaner. Iris agreed to it. The relationship between them was improving. Iris had been touched by an elaborate surprise party Jim had arranged for their first wedding anniversary. In a renewed mood of romanticism, she spoke of making a new start. Moreover, the Jehovah's Witness group in Sherbrooke was known to be active and keen.

Jim felt that Jehovah, after long neglect, finally had dropped a gift on him.

They stayed first in a small apartment in Sherbrooke. Their relationship was growing prickly again. One evening they had a wild argument about Jim's cat, which was missing. Jim blamed Iris for being careless and went into the bedroom, throwing himself on the bed. Iris came and sat beside him in miserable silence. He collected his courage.

"Iris," he began, "I've got to be honest with you. This marriage is falling apart. I'm lonely and unhappy, and I'm sorry for what you're going through with your family. I hate to see you in turmoil. I hate it that you enjoy being with your family more than you do with me."

She didn't reply. "Perhaps it's my fault," he continued with difficulty. "I want to tell you why I need you to be close to me, to stay with me. I have gay tendencies. I fooled around as a kid.

93

I know that the Bible says it's wrong and I've anguished over it, but that's what's true."

She was tender with him. She said she had suspected it all along. In fact, an elder Jim trusted had advised Iris's father that there was talk in the congregation that Jim was gay. She said she'd like to think about what he had said and they would discuss it again. They never did.

The couple found a three-storey house to rent and plunged into decorating it, a project that absorbed them and drew them together. The respite was brief. A few months later, the visits to Toronto began again. Then Iris had news that her father was driving to Sherbrooke with a load of kitchen appliances for Janet and some for her. The best part of it, she told Jim, was that he was willing to have Jim stay in the house when he came to visit. Jim, stung by the condescension, flared at her.

Roy Hrabovsky arrived in a Cadillac with a trailer containing a stove, refrigerator, and dishwasher. He inspected the house, gave his daughter some money, and prepared to leave.

Jim extended his hand. "Brother Hrabovsky, thank you for the things you brought," he said. "I appreciate you coming to our home."

His father-in-law shook hands curtly and said, "Not at all."

When the door closed behind him, Iris burst into tears of joy. "He shook your hand," she exclaimed. "*He shook your hand.*"

"What do you mean, he shook my hand, as if that's a big deal," Jim retorted. "He was rude. I'm your husband and this is our second year of marriage and he's acting like a child."

A sore point between them was that Iris didn't want children. Jim adores children and longed to be a father but she was repulsed by the idea. Jim hadn't expected that, because she had seemed affectionate with the children of the congregation in London.

One month she missed a period and thought she was pregnant. She was furious and didn't speak to him for a week. When finally she did speak, it was to rage against him for what he had done to her. The pregnancy would ruin her career as a missionary. She complained of his "insatiable sex drive".

When it developed that she wasn't pregnant, both were relieved.

Their nerves remained ragged. One day when Iris had her head in the *Watchtower*, Jim snatched it out of her hands and yelled, "Pay attention to me, damn it! *Look at me*."

She looked at him coldly. "You're getting between me and my God," she told him.

Once when they were having an argument, she told him he wasn't the man her father was, that he wasn't nearly as intelligent.

He slapped her hard enough to cause her nose to bruise and swell.

They had sex rarely. One night during intercourse she tapped him on the back and asked him to hurry. She had a busy schedule the next day.

One evening when he was having a disconsolate cup of coffee in a restaurant, a man at a nearby table caught Jim's eye. They exchanged knowing looks and the man invited him to his apartment. Jim went but when both were undressed his nerve failed. He pulled on his clothes and fled.

Jim came to the realization that the marriage would never work. Unless the situation changed, he couldn't imagine twenty-five years of living with Iris, and he came to the conclusion that there would be no improvement. He decided they should divorce.

He and Iris had an anguished conversation. She was shocked at his decision and pleaded with him to reconsider. What seemed to be paramount in her mind was the position it would put her in with the Jehovah's Witnesses. He said, "I'm a human being too, Iris, and I can't stand the way you're treating me."

They decided they needed a break to think matters over. He packed his things while Iris wept. He drove to his father's place in utter misery. His father, who had always thought Iris was snobbish, said he hadn't expected the marriage to last.

One night on an impulse, Jim drove to Toronto and went to the only gay bar he'd heard of, the St. Charles Tavern on Yonge Street. He proceeded to get drunk. What he had in mind was another confused plan to punish Iris and God by drinking himself unconscious. He was weaving when he got back into his car to return to his father's.

He returned to Sherbrooke and told Iris wearily that the marriage was ended. While Iris wept, he packed his possessions in a trailer hitched to his car. "You can't do this," she wailed. "It's going to look so *bad*."

"Iris, something has to be for me. Your sister is moving in with you. You'll be happy to have Janet on my side of the bed. You won't have to have sex with her, as far as I know. You'll have your daddy's money, so you'll be well provided for. You're a little saintly girl, what do you need me for? You never needed me."

He left his belongings at his father's place and dropped off his luggage with his cousin Patrick in Toronto, where he had arranged to stay. With a hurried excuse to Patrick, he went straight to the St. Charles Tavern to get drunk again. On his first visit he had kept his eyes resolutely fixed on objects, shaking off the interest he aroused in a clientele mainly interested in a sexual pickup. This time he looked around boldly. A group of men were sitting, laughing and relaxed, at a nearby table. They were older than he, all of them in their late thirties and early forties.

One noticed Jim's attention, approached him, and introduced himself as Charlie G. He sat down at Jim's table and bought him a beer.

"You look as though you've lost every friend in the world," he said.

Jim laughed. "You're close. I'm not in the best of moods."

"Come and join us," the other man said. "We're having a good time and maybe we can cheer you up."

Jim accepted and that night went bar-hopping with his new friends, expanding his repertoire of gay haunts. For the first time, he saw men dancing together. Charlie asked him for a dance. Jim was shocked.

"I've never danced like that," he said.

"You'll like it," Charlie promised him. He loved it. He loved having a man's arms around him, holding him close, and he loved that the man seemed sincerely to care about him.

Charlie took him next to a bath house and rented a cubicle. He undressed and Jim followed his example. Both wrapped towels around their waists and Charlie kissed him. They talked cosily, both a little drunk, and then Charlie fell asleep on the cot. Jim sat beside him on the floor, dazed and happy. He waited a while and then slipped away, glowing with delight, to return to his cousin's. He saw Charlie's interest in him as the dawn of a wonderful friendship and maybe true love.

He called Charlie the next morning to thank him. Charlie invited Jim to live with him, and Jim accepted gladly. He was stiff from an uncomfortable night on Patrick's couch. They arranged that Jim would move on the following Monday, after a trip to Sherbrooke. Iris was closing the house to return to Toronto and wanted him to take some of the furnishings.

He and Iris visited a lawyer to begin working out the divorce agreement. Then she left with her sister. Jim wandered sadly through the big vacant house for a final farewell and then on Sunday morning drove to his father's place with the rest of his belongings. Though he wasn't expected until the next day, he was anxious to see Charlie, so around ten that night he drove to Charlie's apartment.

Charlie wasn't home. Jim sat on the front steps to wait. Around two in the morning, Charlie appeared with a young man in tow.

When he attempted to introduce Jim, he didn't know the man's name. Jim guessed that the man was a prostitute.

With all the dignity he could muster, Jim said, "I just stopped off, Charlie. I'm on my way to my cousin's tonight but I wanted to say hello."

"Please stay," Charlie urged him. "You can sleep on the couch and we'll talk tomorrow."

Jim, deeply distressed, kept his tone light. "No, thanks. I'll just drop off my suitcase, and I'll see you tomorrow."

It was too late to go to Patrick's. Jim parked his car by the lake in the Beaches area and stared at the dark water. Life as a gay man was no less cruel than marriage had been.

He decided that Charlie should be allowed one indiscretion. Undoubtedly, it wouldn't happen again once he moved in. The next night he returned to Charlie, who apologized profusely and took him to bed. It was Jim's first experience with penetration and it left him achingly sore for a day or two.

Jim was in love. It was delirious to be wanted physically. They went out to dinner and to movies together. Jim threw himself into contributing to the relationship, keeping the apartment shining and the laundry done. At the end of two weeks Charlie briskly asked him to move out.

"What have I done wrong?" Jim gasped.

"You've been fun," Charlie assured him, "but you'll have to learn about gay life. You can be taken advantage of. I'm sorry about this, but I have a lover and he comes home tomorrow, so you'll have to get out."

Jim stayed with Patrick for the next two weeks. His father called him there. He wanted to see him about an important matter. When Jim arrived at his father's house, a car was parked outside and he found Iris in the living-room.

Karl looked from one to the other earnestly. "You two have had some difficulties but I think you can sort them out. Why don't you try?"

"I would like Jim back as my husband," Iris said.

Karl Zanuk turned to his son. "Jim, what's the problem here? See, she wants you back."

Jim said, "Dad, ask her why she wants me back."

Karl gave Iris an inquiring look and she responded, "The reason is that if we break up it will be bad for our reputations. It would look bad for our God and our religion, and bad for my father's name."

"See," said Karl, beaming, "she wants you back."

Jim exploded. "Why can't she say she wants us to stay together because she fucking loves me?" he yelled. "Do you think I want to settle for this crap! What ever happened to love in a marriage?"

Iris sat with her head down, saying nothing.

Jim steadied. "Do you love me, Iris? Because that's the only way this marriage will stay together."

She said quietly, "No, Jim, I don't think I love you any more."

He got back in his car and drove to Toronto.

The next week they met with a lawyer selected by Roy Hrabovsky. Iris asked Jim to make the grounds adultery so that the divorce would be recognized by Jehovah's Witnesses. He didn't object.

They had few possessions and no children. The lawyer said it wouldn't take long.

His cousin Patrick was a devoted Jehovah's Witness. Horrified at Jim's lack of interest in prayer meetings and services, he told him he no longer was welcome. He didn't approve of Jim associating with "worldly persons". Jim had nowhere to turn but his father's.

He moped for months, living in his father's trailer parked near the house. His father was sympathetic, assuming that his son's depression was caused by the marital breakup. Jim wandered the fields of his childhood, shocked to think of the shambles his life had become at only twenty-one. He had left his God, or his

God had left him, and he had failed at both heterosexuality and homosexuality. Even his cousin didn't want him.

He found a job on the front desk of the Skyline Hotel near Toronto's airport. A male airline attendant invited him to his room, but Jim played a cruel game of tease. When they had stripped and the man was ready for sex, Jim put on his clothes and left. His mood was savage. He cruised the gay bars wearing tight blue jeans, flirting with men who bought him drinks, and then walking out. He was aware that he was hurting people out of revenge, but it felt sweet.

He started to meet men he liked. The first was Bert M., a hairdresser, big and macho, who introduced him around. He went for drinks on Friday nights with Bert's gang and Jim gradually confided his anger at the betrayals of his life, to be comforted by their understanding and sympathy.

His car was falling apart. With no money to repair or replace it, he switched jobs and became a chauffeur for the Deer Park livery, a company that rented limousines. The world of Toronto's wealthiest opened to him. A charming and handsome man, he was much in demand. He drove judges and tycoons and celebrities—among them Lee Remick, Christopher Plummer, Helen Reddy, and Dinah Shore.

The judges were interested in his divorce and one volunteered to examine the papers the lawyer had drawn up. He became Jim's adviser on condition that Jim never reveal that he had helped. "Don't worry," the judge said. "This is a simple case."

Iris, looking ravishingly beautiful, met Jim at the courthouse on the day the divorce was to be heard.

Jim took her hands. "Iris, we can stop this. If you think we could leave our families and live our own lives, if you can love me, we can make a good life together."

She said, "I love you Jim, but as a brother. I don't love you as a husband."

Ninety days later, on June 20, 1979, Jim received the final decree. He and Iris signed some papers and he inquired politely if she needed a ride. Yes she did. She was meeting her mother at Holt Renfrew. He dropped her off. As she was getting out of the car she removed her gold wedding band and gave it to him. "Goodbye, Jim," she said, with a wave.

He watched her walk away, his heart breaking. On a side street, he parked by a culvert and dropped the wedding band into the sewer.

He spent a long bitter time alone, living in his father's trailer, talking to his teddy bear. He hadn't meant to slap Iris. He hated being a homosexual. What was to become of him? Who the hell wanted him?

He found a small apartment on Lakeshore Boulevard in Mimico and joined a Mimico congregation of Jehovah's Witnesses. He went back to driving limousines and tried earnestly to become a dutiful adherent of his faith, but the effort failed. He stopped going to meetings, but he read the *Watchtower* and *Awake!* regularly and spent long hours praying. For the first time in his life, at age twenty-four, he was on his own with no rudder of school, family, or religion.

He drifted into the gay community and embraced its extremes with the same driven dedication he had once given his religious observance. He began a life of abandoned sex, hanging out in the city's leather bars, attracted to roughly dressed men in leather and chains who made those bars their hangouts. He developed a taste for sado-masochistic sex, beating up his partners as part of the relationship. He was the aggressive one, the one who did the whipping and slapping. He's no psychiatrist, but he suspected that he was in some way taking on the role of his tormentors in the Hamilton high school.

What followed in 1979 was a wild period. Over about a year and a half, he estimates that he had between five and six

101

hundred sexual partners. He has varying explanations for the extraordinary promiscuity of so many newly uncloseted young gay men during the seventies. One is loneliness. Jim explains that gay men usually live alone and feel the absence of a mate or family acutely. Before AIDS it was normal for many of them to fill the emptiness of their lives by hanging out in gay bars and restaurants, looking for impersonal sex.

He admits that part of the motivation is also to gratify lust. Since sex between men does not involve the risk of pregnancy, it was thought to be harmless and guilt-free. A man could sample as many partners as he pleased without having to pretend that romance was involved.

The mood of freedom and licence took a number of gay men to the edge in their search for thrills and novelty. Gay men, isolated from childhood from the mainstream, had nothing more to lose and some became as reckless as outlaws. Feeling rejected by society, their revenge was outrageous behaviour.

"You'd have sex first and get the name later," Jim says of the era. It wasn't unusual for him to have three men in one night. He would go out, looking to meet someone, and meet an attractive man who would ask him back to his apartment. They would have sex immediately, after which Jim would settle down to talk; but the man would be finished with him and ask him to leave. Jim would return to the bar, pick up another man and go to his place, where the same sequence would occur. Around one in the morning, desperate to find someone with whom to spend the whole night, he would find a third man and this time insist on a contract that the man would stay all night. That made three sexual partners.

Three was far from a record. On one Saturday he and a buddy had a contest to see how many men they could sleep with between noon and midnight. Jim scored nine and beat his adversary, who slept with only seven.

Jim says that this was not abnormal behaviour in the gay community of that period. He says of himself that he was searching for something more than sex, and he thinks that probably was true of many others. He longed for permanence but felt too worthless to deserve it. He didn't really give a damn what happened to him, what men wanted to do to him, what he did to another man. None of it mattered. Life was the pits.

He was quite an acquisition for a cruising gay male of means. Young, handsome, comical, and articulate, he had the muscled build of a stevedore from his regular routine of weight-lifting. Given his good looks and habitual cheerfulness, he was in demand among older and well-to-do gay men. One of his admirers, a waiter in the executive suite of the Toronto-Dominion Bank, took Jim to New York and dazzled him with the gay life there. The Jehovah's Witness boy from Ontario, raised on a farm, was having a great time.

5

Natalie Kaufman came into Jim's life in January 1979, while he was driving limousines. They met through Jim's friend Johnny, who also worked for Deer Park limousines on a part-time basis. Johnny raved to Jim about the beauty and charm of a wealthy woman for whom he was a regular driver, a Mrs. Kaufman. One night when Johnny's commitments overlapped, Jim agreed to substitute for him and drive Mrs. Kaufman to a bar mitzvah.

On the appointed evening he went to a handsome townhouse in North York. The door was answered by a boy of about twelve, who politely invited him in. A moment later, Mrs. Kaufman, wearing a sparkly evening dress with a mink coat slung over her shoulder, came regally down the stairs of the entrance hall. She was a small, stunning woman, gracious and superbly groomed— and blonde. Jim always had been drawn to beautiful blonde women, and he was entranced.

She explained that one of her two sons, the twin to the boy who answered the door, wasn't feeling well. Probably she wouldn't be staying long at the reception. Jim was touched that such an exotic woman could show such maternal consideration. Awed and deferential, he helped Mrs. Kaufman and her elderly mother into the limousine.

On their return, Mrs. Kaufman asked Jim for his telephone number and said she might have work for him in the future. She called three months later.

"I have a job offer for you if you'd like to come around to my home to discuss it," she said.

He drove to her house thinking he would turn it down because he didn't want to be someone's private chauffeur. He was enjoying the variety his job with the livery service provided. It turned out Mrs. Kaufman had something else in mind. She had been investigating him, she said, and she found he was held in high esteem by his associates. She was an interior designer, she said, with her own company, Natalie Kaufman Interiors.

"I have to meet with suppliers and contractors a lot and some of them get the idea that I'm available to have dinner with them, or whatever. It's a nuisance for a woman in business to deal with passes all the time so I like to have a man with me. Also, I need someone to help me keep track of the orders and look after details. Besides, I think you would be good at it. You're quick and intelligent and I'd be happy to teach you something about business."

Jim was flattered but said he wanted to think it over.

A few days later he called and said, "Mrs. Kaufman, you have a deal."

For whatever reasons, Mrs. Kaufman immediately cast herself in the role of Pygmalion in Jim's life. She found him an awkward country boy, desperately anxious to please and coltish in his devotion to her. He absorbed the rudiments of fine table manners and the graces of hospitality thirstily. Mrs. Kaufman fed him praise for his potential and many fine qualities, while also helping him to improve himself. She took him shopping and introduced him to the splendours of silk and fine leather and cashmere. She quickly developed a knack for seeing through the fabrications with which he protected his privacy and, to his amazement and delight, would reprimand him with mock severity. It was exactly the kind of firm hand he craved in his life.

One day, when he was several weeks into his new job, she invited him to have a drink with her in a bar in the Park Plaza Hotel. They proceeded, as Jim put it, "to get hammered". She had decided to take him into her confidence. She told him, in uproarious detail, about her marriages. She said, giving him a significant look, that she was sure he had much to tell her about himself too.

He knew at once that she was aware that he was gay but he was timid at first to confide. Instead he poured out the story of his marriage. She seemed startled, not so much by the fact that he had married as by the evidence that he still was deeply in love with Iris.

Inspired by the alcohol and her sympathy, he eventually was able to tell her he was gay. He was grateful that she accepted the information without distaste and was supportive and kind. Drained by the confidences and more than a little drunk, they were too unsteady to manage their transportation home. She called a friend, Bernie Wexler, a big friendly man who obligingly collected them and delivered them to their doors.

Yielding to pressure from his mother and his sister Karen, who were scandalized that he had dropped away from Jehovah's Witnesses, Jim renewed his connection with his religion and rejoined the Mimico congregation, where he was welcomed warmly as a lost sheep returned to the fold. Caught as always by the familiar raptures of the charismatic faith, he plunged into Bible studies and the long discussions over interpretations of Scripture with his old fervour.

Nights when he wasn't occupied with Jehovah's Witness responsibilities, he put on tight jeans and went to leather bars. His double life severely tested his actor's ability to dissemble. At prayer meetings he was impeccably dressed and devout; at midnight he was in gay bars, looking for someone who would enjoy sex with a pummelling.

He discovered what he called "a gimmick" to keep his sanity. When thoughts of his shattered life and estrangement from God threatened to overwhelm him, he turned off his mind and went out looking for sex. It was a technique that sustained him for many years.

In his busy social life in the gay community, he frequently encountered serious-minded men who were sincerely interested in him. They made overtures, inviting him to dinner and to spend weekends with them. He never allowed those relationships to develop. If he had a permanent partner, how could he take that person to meet his mother? His father? How long would it be before the Mimico congregation discovered that he was living with a man? He couldn't risk it.

Natalie Kaufman was a woman with an entrepreneurial nature. Out of the growing craze for health food, she hit on the idea of establishing a new business selling dried fruit and nuts and thought up the catchy name "From Fruit to Nuts". In the summer of 1979, with Jim as her assistant, she selected her first location, a shopping mall in Oakville just west of Toronto, and rented space to establish a kiosk.

She designed the kiosk herself and also the outfits her sales staff would wear. She and Jim hustled all over the city to arrange for cash machines and counters and a range of dried fruit and nuts. By this time, Jim was completely taken with Mrs. Kaufman. He loved her gorgeous clothes, her firm opinions, her frankness, her canniness in business, her sophistication. Her interest in him also deepened. They became companions, bustling about the city by day to order supplies and spending many evenings together as well. She would invite him to her home for dinner and instruct him on social protocol. Despite the developing intimacy, she had a dignified way about her and they were not on a first-name basis.

During the frantic weeks leading up to the opening of the kiosk in Oakville, Jim and Mrs. Kaufman grew even closer. Her zaniness delighted him, and they shared a taste for imaginative pranks. They ate in fine restaurants and went shopping together, something they both loved to do. He was aghast when she spent $500 on a shirt and $400 on boots but she explained to him the pleasures of quality. He began to dress better, paying more attention to fit and fine cloth.

Out of curiosity, she went with him to his favourite gay bars and severely disapproved of the rough ones. Under her instruction, he cleaned up the slang in his language and improved his grammar.

The From Fruit to Nuts kiosk was ready for business in August 1979. A staff of eight people was hired, with Jim on salary as the kiosk manager. The week before the opening, Jim moved into Mrs. Kaufman's house in order to simplify transportation. Jim and Mrs. Kaufman decided to give themselves the fun of working on opening day. They dressed in the outfits she had selected for her staff: white pants and shirts with wild check vests trimmed with brass buttons. The kiosk was such a huge success they got no rest. That night at Mrs. Kaufman's, exhausted and exhilarated, they took the cash from the day's sales and threw it in the air, giggling together under a shower of money.

Over the next few weeks business continued to be good. Mrs. Kaufman stopped supervising and left Jim to run the business. He was spending more time at her house, enjoying formal dinners where he sat on her left and candlelight sparkled on crystal and real silver. He had become like an older brother to her sons, Rodney and Jeff. He played with them on their skate boards and once got into an uproarious water fight that drenched Mrs. Kaufman's bedroom.

The domestic bliss at the Kaufmans' only increased his grief at the loss of his marriage, his only hope of normality. He brooded over it in long talks with Mrs. Kaufman. He was convinced that he and Iris would have been happy if her parents hadn't intervened, but Mrs. Kaufman argued that Iris was no fool. If she had loved Jim, her parents would not have been able to influence her.

Mrs. Kaufman offered to talk to Iris, who confirmed her theory. Iris said that she could see that she and Jim were going in different directions and that the marriage would not last. She was pushed by her parents, she admitted, but the final decision had been hers.

Jim was despondent to hear it. He began to wonder if he and Iris would have married at all if they had not been driven together by her father's opposition. A normal, unchallenged courtship, he suspected, would have revealed to them both their fundamental differences.

About seven months after From Fruits to Nuts opened, the novelty had worn off for Jim and Mrs. Kaufman. In February 1980 she welcomed an opportunity to sell the operation at a good profit and revived her former business of interior decorating. Jim proved invaluable to her, especially in antique shops, where his lively imagination invested grubby objects with the potential to be treasures. Even so, the business generated wasn't enough to sustain an employee, and Mrs. Kaufman and Jim decided to end their formal business association. That done, she informed him that they would remain friends as before and he could call her Natalie. He was elated.

He was having trouble paying the rent on his bachelor apartment in Mimico. Hunting through the want ads, he came across a position as manager of a Consumers Distributing outlet in Stouffville, a fair distance from Toronto but near enough to commute. In April 1980 he moved to a dingy apartment in Stouffville and plunged into a job he came to loathe. The more unhappy and lonely he grew, the more he sparkled with good humour. He was a great success.

109

When he could get back to Toronto, he and Natalie often went to discothèques together. She and Jim made an eye-catching couple and once they danced until dawn.

Jim was in a gay bar one evening in October 1980 when he ran into Allan D. They had met some months earlier and Jim was attracted to the older man, but Allan was part of a couple then. Allan and his lover had picked Jim up at a party and taken him home with them for a threesome that Jim found memorable. After that he and Allan danced together when they happened to be at the same party and occasionally, when Jim could get to town from Stouffville, they had lunch.

Allan, then in his mid-thirties, was exceptionally handsome, blond and superbly built. When he and Jim encountered each other that night in October, Allan's relationship had just ended. He was free to explore his interest in Jim. Jim was attracted and flattered by Allan's attention because Allan was an intellectual, a former English professor at the University of Western Ontario. He had left his position and his home in London in order to write a novel, towards which he had received a grant.

Allan appeared to be in love. That evening he took Jim to his apartment and made him coffee.

"I know you're rough," he said, "but I would prefer not to be rough. Let's not have sex at all tonight. I'd like us to get to know one another."

He asked Jim about his life, listened attentively, and refused Jim's suggestion that they go to bed. Jim was intrigued. It felt wonderful to be cared for as a person, not just a sexual partner. They made love the next time they were together but it was different from the savage matings that Jim had been experiencing. At Allan's insistence the sex between them was passionate but gentle. Jim sank gratefully into the comforts and beauty of monogamy. He was more than content to have sex with the same person and no one else, knowing what to expect and what pleased, the heightened intimacies of familiarity.

Allan courted him, giving him flowers, wine, and small surprise gifts of knick-knacks. On weekends they slept in Allan's huge bed, snuggled under the duvet. For the first time in his life, Jim felt safe enough to sleep without a night light. He stopped going to bars, except with Allan. In the evenings the two played soft music and Allan talked about literature and theatre. Sometimes they watched Sherlock Holmes movies and shared bowls of popcorn.

Allan was outraged that Jim was wasting himself on the job in Stouffville. He urged him to quit and move in with him. Allan had a well-paid position as an assessor in a program to help mentally retarded adults enter the labour force. He had ample income to support them both, he said, and he wanted Jim to begin to pursue seriously a career on the stage, before it was too late.

Jim accepted gladly. Though Allan's apartment was small, the move proved a mere matter of rearranging the closets.

Jim made the rounds of a few auditions but his lack of experience or professional training was a problem. He quickly became too discouraged to face the humiliating rejections. Instead he revelled in being the homemaker in Allan's apartment. Housework appealed to his passion for tidiness and polish, so the apartment gleamed. Evenings when Allan returned from work, Jim would have a drink ready, the table set for dinner, and a warm scented bath run.

They spent their evenings cosily in long philosophical discussions. Allan drew out from Jim accounts of the rough sex experiences of the past year and was dismayed. His analysis of it was that Jim was taking out his bitterness on other people. That was unworthy of him, Allan said. Jim was too fine a person to let himself sink so low.

Jim sank into blissful domesticity without a regret for the wild times after the leather bars closed. The message Allan was trying

111

to convey was that it was all right to be gay, but not all right to be promiscuous.

Some of their most tense discussions were about religion. Allan, raised a Roman Catholic, had studied for the priesthood with the Jesuits and understood how Jim was haunted by longings to fit in with Jehovah's Witness teachings. Allan, however, was embittered with religion and said he hated God, a blasphemy that shocked Jim. To Allan's disgust, Jim insisted on trying to restore Allan's faith and preached to him about Jehovah God.

Jim was slow to realize that it was as painful for Allan to reopen the wounds of his faith as it was for Jim to close his.

Jim maintained his ties with the Mimico congregation of Jehovah's Witnesses. He didn't want to let Allan go and he didn't want to let his religion go. Sometimes he thought that what would go was his sanity.

The relationship, with Allan in the breadwinner role and Jim the housekeeper, felt to Jim like a real marriage. He wanted it to seem more legitimate and his imagination turned to wedding services. He broached to Allan the idea that they should have some sort of wedding ceremony during which they would make a commitment to one another that the relationship was permanent. He talked wistfully about a symbolic rite attended by their friends, where they would exchange vows and wedding bands. Allan didn't take Jim's suggestions seriously.

This was disappointing and sometimes alarming, but Jim was ecstatically in love with Allan and the older man adored him. They had lovers' names for one another, Jimbo and Bear. When Jim awoke, usually after Allan had left for work, he found tender notes: "Hi! When you have some food in your stomach, take your vitamins. I love you."

Allan left lines of poetry with the pet name inserted:

Slow dancing
No one else in the whole wide world
Just you and me. We just flow together
When the lights are low
Just me and my Jimbo
Don't ever let me go. So much love in this heart of mine
Hold me tight
You're the one I thought I'd never find

Love you Jimmy,
Allan

And:

How cozy to see
Your lovely sleeping self.
I wait on your beauty
My day begins
With You

Love, Allan Bear

Jim saved them all.

Jim proudly introduced Natalie Kaufman to Allan. To Jim's acute distress, Allan loathed her on sight. Jim was bewildered when Allan refused to go with him to dinner at Mrs. Kaufman's. He came to accept that any attempt to resolve the animosity was hopeless and resigned himself to keeping the two most important people in his life apart.

When Jim reported to Allan on his outings with Mrs. Kaufman, Allan would fume. Allan blamed Mrs. Kaufman for the hostility that grew between the two men, but Jim always denied that it was her fault. His relationship with Allan certainly changed. For some perverse reason, he started to be unfaithful. His explanation is that Allan misunderstood how important it was to him to have the symbolic wedding service. For Jim it represented safety and a measure of purity; Allan thought it a preposterous idea.

One night, restless and alone because Allan was at a meeting, Jim slipped out to a leather bar to see his old friends. He wound up in someone's apartment with a whip in his hand. After that he went to the bars frequently, making transparent excuses, and ended up doing one-night stands in other men's apartments.

Allan discovered almost at once that Jim was unfaithful. They talked about it, fought about it, wept about it. Some bank of rage in Jim kept him going, despite Allan's entreaties. He suspected he wanted either to test Allan's love or to break Allan's hold on him because it made him feel vulnerable.

Jim spent occasional weekends visiting his family and one night he returned to Allan's apartment a day earlier than expected. He found the living-room littered with beer bottles and a man in the pullout bed with Allan. He prepared disconsolately to sleep on the couch but, as he went about finding extra blankets and pillows, his anger at what he experienced as another rejection began to boil. This was his home, he told himself. It was insulting that someone else was sleeping in his place.

He hurled an empty beer bottle at the wall above the bed where the men were sleeping. It exploded like a bomb as Allan sat up groggily and turned on the light. Jim picked up another and threw it, and another. Back in the living-room, he up-ended the coffee table with its mirror top and smashed it. That was followed by a lamp, which he threw at an oil painting.

In a few minutes he had devastated the apartment and was gasping for breath. Allan looked around at the ruin and wept. Jim stalked out, pushing the protesting Allan aside roughly and punching three prints that hung in the hallway. Then he drove the square of the Don Valley Parkway, Highway 401, Highway 27, and the Gardiner Expressway before returning to the apartment.

Allan was alone, cleaning up the mess. He poured Jim a glass of white wine and Jim threw it at the wall. He thought to himself, that's enough. His anger drained and, without speaking, he pitched in to help Allan straighten the room and pick up the broken glass that was strewn everywhere. When they had some order restored it was nearly dawn. They went silently to bed. Allan wakened only long enough to call his employer to say that he wouldn't be at work. They wakened in mid-afternoon, made love, and had a reconciliation.

In the weeks that followed Jim returned to the bars. He had a rationalization this time: Allan didn't really love him after all. As soon as Jim's back was turned, he had taken someone else into his bed. At the same time, he was distressed to realize his love for Allan was growing. If he came to the point where he couldn't live without Allan, what chance did he have of ever being a whole-hearted Jehovah's Witness, with nothing to fear from his God's wrath?

The arguments between Jim and Allan were becoming more painful than either could bear. Much of the time together they were sad and frightened. The main issue, as Jim saw it, was Allan's refusal to consider the commitment ceremony that Jim wanted. Allan's point was that it would have no meaning. They loved one another and that was commitment enough. Jim began to feel increasingly that it wasn't. His need for security fastened on the importance of the exchange of vows and he railed against Allan's reluctance.

In turn, Allan accused Jim of being influenced against him by Natalie Kaufman, a charge Jim hotly and loyally denied.

In the spring of 1981 Jim made several visits to New York with men he met in bars. He loved the wildness of the gay lifestyle in that city. His rationalization for wanting to live there was that he could get started in theatre, but the real reason, he well knew, was that he needed to separate from Allan D. and his reproachful silences. He decided in June 1981 that he would move to New York and seek his fortune on Broadway. At the back of his mind was the hope that in his absence Allan would change his mind about the commitment ceremony.

Allan was horrified by Jim's decision and begged him not to leave, but also he understood Jim well enough to know that the parting was necessary.

Jim went to say goodbye to Natalie Kaufman and found her weeping. Her twin sons, Rod and Jeff, now fourteen, had tears in their eyes. Jim had grown close to them; as for the boys, he was the most constant male in their lives.

On one of his previous visits to New York Jim had met a man, Steve, with whom he'd had a brief sexual fling. He'd kept Steve's phone number and, when he got off the train at New York's Grand Central Station on June 1, 1981, he called. Steve invited him to stay with him in his huge loft for a few days while he got settled.

Steve told him that in New York the big problem for a newcomer was finding a place to live. Jim should look for an apartment first and then find a job. Jim thought that was crazy advice. He needed income, so the job came first. Steve said jobs were scarce too. He was doubtful that Jim would find either. Jim said with a grin, "Give me a day."

He went to Greenwich Village, walked into the first good-looking restaurant he saw, Trilogy, and applied for a job. He was hired on the spot to start that night as a bus boy, though he admitted he had no experience.

"We'll teach you how to work in a restaurant," the manager assured him. "Do you have a place to stay?"

Jim said he didn't. The manager suggested that he put his name on the restaurant bulletin board, stating that he was looking for shared accommodation. That night, David Burchette, a waiter at

Trilogy, approached Jim and said he was looking for a roommate. Was Jim interested?

He returned to Steve triumphant. On his first day in New York he had found both a job and a place to live. Two weeks later he was promoted. The restaurant made him a sort of late-night host, with responsibility to make customers feel welcome, and his income improved sharply.

New York presented him with sexual depravity beyond anything he had ever known, even in Toronto's roughest S & M community. He visited the infamous Mine Shaft and several other places like it—the Anvil, the I Scream Parlor. In huge, ramshackle rooms, anything that can be done physically to a male body was done with an appreciative audience grouped around.

Jim's theory about the horror and degradation he witnessed is much the same as his explanation for promiscuity in the gay community. He speaks of the loneliness and social isolation of men who grow up gay. Some are driven by rage and frustration to test the outer limits of sexuality, including such aberrations as "fisting". Fisting is a perilous practice that began with dildoes inserted in rectums. For thrills, the dildoes became increasingly large and strangely shaped and their use a spectator sport. From dildoes men moved to putting fists in another man's anus. Then the fist was inserted up to mid-arm. Sometimes two fists were inserted; for a time the rage was for a foot and part of a leg to be inserted. Jim heard in the Mine Shaft that one time a bald man put his head into an anus.

He also sought out the leather bars, which celebrated a masculine look. To that end men dressed in scruffy jeans with wide studded belts. In some places they stripped to a leather jock strap and carried whips. It's a fantasy trip, Jim explains. It draws men who have sexual dreams of rape and brutish couplings. They play out their fancies on the stages of dark bars where the floors are covered with sawdust. Patrons undress at the door, check

117

their street clothes, and costume themselves in leather and chains according to the dictates of fervid imaginations.

At the Mine Shaft one night he saw a young blond man tied hand and foot to scaffolding, with a line of men waiting their turn to have sex with him. It was what the gay community calls a master and slave scene. If the "slave" youth protested, his "master" slapped him viciously.

Through a trapdoor in the floor, down a dark stairway, in the basement, he saw worse.

Jim reacted with disgust, and fear, and a measure of titillation. His only concern was that the practices could be life-threatening. Because the participants almost invariably were deeply stoned on drugs, there was always the risk that their judgement would fail and they would go too far. He heard rumours of orgies that slipped over the edge into such sadistic depravity that people were seriously injured—or killed. It was too crazy and dangerous for him, but it aroused him to seek out sexual partners, anyone attractive, and have sex right there on the floor of the bar. It happened several times, in fact, but only in the normal sex of gay men.

He has discussed the depravities of the Mine Shaft with other gay men who were as puzzled as he. Some had indulged in the brutalities and reported that the release of orgasm was stupendous but that afterwards they felt totally worthless. Jim finds that a confirmation of his belief that gay men find a measure of therapy in behaving loathsomely. Burdened by feelings of self-hatred, they give themselves permission to abandon themselves wantonly and welcome the subsequent remorse as fair punishment.

"Being called 'animals' and 'perverts' takes its toll," he says. "A few of us decide if we're going to be given such names we might as well have the game too."

In the wake of the AIDS tragedy, the gay lifestyle of the seventies has been subjected to serious analysis, which has yielded theories not far from Jim's own. Gay men, excluded from and reviled by mainstream society, established bars and bath houses of their own in which festering indignation and rage were converted into maniacal invention. Gays took over the macho image of heterosexual males, particularly the cowboy-in-leather stereotype, and sent it up mockingly. With that release, what also came out of Pandora's box were rage and cruelty.

On the brighter side were such imaginative and luxurious discos as the Saint, with its planetarium ceiling of stars and a magnificent mirror bar crowned with huge flower arrangements. Jim loved the opulence and lowered himself into it joyfully, accepting at the same time that New York gays used drugs with abandon. Drugs had been a source of argument between Jim and Allan D. because Jim disapproved of Allan's enthusiastic use of soft drugs. Allan was especially fond of the drug amyl nitrate, called poppers, and sold under such names as Rush and Locker Room, which enhanced orgasm by dilating blood vessels. New York gays had a wider and wilder assortment of drugs than Jim had ever seen.

While Jim's wages and tips didn't go far in such a fast-paced community, he had no lack of escorts willing to buy him drinks and drugs and take him to dinner. None the less, in comparison with Toronto, his sexual life was demure. He estimates about forty sexual partners in the six weeks he lived in New York.

"No wonder AIDS spread through the gay community so rapidly," he reflects. "Everyone slept with everyone else. In Toronto it was common to go to a party and find that everyone there had been your sexual partner at least once."

Allan D. called every week and wrote frequently, pouring out his loneliness and love. Jim kept one letter: "My dear Jimbo, I love you and miss you when you are not here. You have all my heart. I trust you implicitly. I wait for you. I want you with me always. You are my better half. You make me whole. You are the joy of my life. I love you. I love you. I love you."

After six weeks Jim missed Allan and his intellectual and principled approach to life. On Sunday, July 12, 1981, when Allan said he was ready to have the ceremony Jim wanted, Jim promptly replied that he was coming home.

In any case, his expectations of becoming a Broadway star had been dashed by reality. He discovered that New York was full of handsome young men from all over the world who were aspiring to theatre careers. Most of them had training in acting school, which he did not. His closest association with the theatre had been reading *Variety*, which he could do in Toronto. If he was to get training and experience on the stage, he reasoned, it would be in Toronto.

Just before leaving New York he went for a final workout in the Sheridan Square Health Spa. In the steam room he fell into a conversation with a man who spotted him as a Canadian by his "ehs" at the end of sentences. "If you're a stranger in New York you should watch out for this AIDS thing that's going around."

"What's that?" Jim asked.

"It seems to be something dangerous. There's a poster about it on the back of the door over there," the man replied.

Jim read the poster, a warning about something called AIDS. He scanned it without much interest. AIDS was a contagious disease that was going around, it said. Gay men and drug addicts were particularly vulnerable. The symptoms were weight loss, night sweats, persistent cough, a coating of the tongue and throat called thrush, and purple marks on the skin.

The poor guys, he thought. It didn't have anything to do with him. He had just been checked out at the Bellevue Hospital VD clinic.

Jim didn't finish reading about AIDS. He was meeting someone in a bar for a farewell drink.

It was July 22, 1981, when he moved back into Allan's apartment for a tearful reunion, with promises on both sides that the relationship would last for ever. Jim began excited plans for the ceremony, too pleased with the arrangements to notice at first Allan's lack of enthusiasm. On August 6 Allan admitted that he felt the project a foolish one. He urged Jim to drop the idea and there was a terrible fight.

Jim thinks now that Allan was embarrassed at the idea of a formal exchange of vows in front of their friends. At the time he saw it only as another betrayal, like the crash of his hopes with Iris. In an unpleasant scene he greatly regrets, he called Allan a coward and a liar and moved out.

In August 1981, Natalie Kaufman married again. Her husband, an old friend, was Sidney W. and the couple realized almost at once that the marriage was a mistake. After a month they separated and filed for divorce. To expedite matters, they decided to use the grounds of adultery and Jim was named as correspondent, to his huge amusement.

While the divorce was proceeding, Jim happened to meet Natalie's friend Bernie Wexler. Bernie inquired about Natalie and was startled to be informed that her marriage had ended. A week later, Bernie Wexler was squiring Natalie around town, and they soon announced their impending marriage. Jim felt like Cupid.

He had been working as a waiter in the New York Café and then at Rhodes restaurant on Yonge Street. In November 1981 he found a job at a bustling, trendy Mr. Greenjeans restaurant on Adelaide Street East, and then at the Nuts and Bolts restaurant. He slept often at Allan's or wherever friends had room.

Jim was growing discontented. He was out of touch with Jehovah's Witnesses, which left a hollowness in his life that tormented him, and his estrangement from Allan resulted in more loneliness and despair than he had known since leaving Iris. He lectured himself sternly. He needed more purpose in his life. His

121

boyhood dreams of fame pulled on his imagination still. He was twenty-six years old and he decided it was time for him to stop wasting his life. He would make a serious effort to become an actor.

In June 1982 he got a job as manager of a Golden Griddle Pancake House on Carlton Street and found a small one-bedroom apartment on the fourth floor of a Sherbourne Street building. Though he missed Allan acutely, he managed to remain furious with him. For months the two men made sporadic attempts to repair the relationship. Jim now blames himself entirely for the breach, and realizes that he loved Allan deeply and owes him a great debt. It was Allan who introduced him to dignity and constancy within the gay lifestyle, the first he had known, and Allan who saved him from the crudeness and bitterness that eventually would have consumed and destroyed him.

In their regular attempts to patch things up, he continued to find fault with Allan. He fastened on such justifications as the smallness of Allan's apartment, or the fact that Allan supported him at the cost of Jim's self-respect, or his objections to Allan's extensive use of drugs. Jim eventually was worn out with the arguments and declared the relationship over.

He has preserved one of Allan's letters marking the end of their efforts at reconciliation. Written in a spirit of gentle reproachfulness, it says, in part:

> I was cheered by your speech last night explaining why we are not compatible. Cheered because I do not believe it is accurate—for reasons well rehearsed before, small space, unemployment, drugs, etc. I must look elsewhere to understand how we have moved from September's marriage plans to March's divorce.... You and I were bound to have difficulties. A gay relationship is easy prey.... I look forward to knowing you in some degree at a calmer time. If

I can help you I will. Keep this letter as a gift. Be good as always. Live and enjoy. Your friend Allan.

Jim's sex life deteriorated again to S & M. In his encounters he was always the aggressor, the one who applied the whips and beatings. He avoided analysing what was happening to him but it was all too plain that the punishment and degradation had a great deal to do with his self-loathing.

On a fine summer evening, July 9, 1982, Jim went to a gay outing on a boat cruise and had far too much to drink. Looking for sex, he found a small, rough-looking, comical man, Bruce C., who worked for a union. They found a dark corner where they could neck. When the boat docked at midnight they staggered off the gangplank arm in arm and hitched a ride to Jim's apartment.

The sex was good, but what held Jim was Bruce C.'s sweet, generous, loving nature. Bruce was an uncomplicated person who bought his clothes haphazardly, was serious about his running shoes, and rode his bicycle to work. Jim later declared that Bruce was "the love of my life". They began an affair that lasted that winter of 1982 and into 1983. Jim lost all interest in promiscuity. In a few weeks, he gave up his own apartment and moved into Bruce's apartment in St. James Town.

Jim was falling deeply in love with Bruce and their relationship settled into domesticity. Their favourite evenings were spent making huge amounts of spaghetti, which they ate sprawled in front of the television. Jim wasn't interested in sports, but he even liked the companionable afternoons they spent together watching football.

As his love for Bruce grew, so did his panic. A loving relationship with a man seemed a greater sin than impersonal homosexual sex. If he settled into a permanent relationship with a man, he was incontrovertibly gay and would not be resurrected after Armageddon. As he had also sometimes felt with Allan, he worried that commitment to a long-term relationship would jeopardize his acceptance back into his faith. Jehovah might overlook casual gay sex, but not homosexual love. He was being pulled apart: everything in his being screamed for permanency, but the price was God's wrath.

Some evenings he was so edgy and restless that everything irritated him. He found a measure of control by reading *Awake!* and the *Watchtower* and his Bible, shutting Bruce out. Afterwards he criticized Bruce meanly, finding fault with everything Bruce did. He returned over and over to the Bible's stern warning, "Neither...men kept for unnatural purposes nor men who lie with men...will inherit God's kingdom."

He picked fights with Bruce, fabricating issues the nature of which he now forgets, and in February of 1983 moved out abruptly, after staging a stormy scene. "I made a big thing about why the relationship wouldn't work," Jim says of that day. "It was all a crock. The truth was that I couldn't get my conscience together."

Bruce helped him pack.

Natalie Wexler helped console Bruce, who was heart-broken, explaining to him Jim's conflict between being gay and being a Jehovah's Witness. Bruce gamely tried to understand and forgive.

Bruce wrote tender notes, sometimes on the paper placemats of the Golden Griddle where Jim was working as manager.

"You are not ready for the kind of relationship with me that I would like," Bruce wrote sadly. "Perhaps I am better off with another person as I do not feel you have the maturity at this point to handle what I am prepared to give. When I am involved with another person I give unquestioningly of myself. It has been abused in the past, and will be in the future, but my conscience can rest because I know how to give and why I do."

Another time Bruce wrote, "It is still kind of hard to accept all this. I guess it's just that I hate to start all over again. I'll be

33 soon and I just do not feel very attractive about myself.... I feel I know you and your sensitivity more than most people and I would like to know that it would be me that you turn to in times of crisis. I would very much like to remain involved in your life, but this is up to you.... I hope also that you know I want only the best in what life brings you. God bless, all my love, Bruce."

Jim began to feel smothered by the contradictions in his life in Toronto. He longed for something simpler, closer to his roots. He talked to his father about buying him a house, as Karl Zanuk had done for his other children when they married. Karl reluctantly agreed that it was only fair. In February 1983 Jim found a handsome century-old house on Oak Street in Cambridge, Ontario, a safe distance, he hoped, from the temptations of Toronto, and his father supplied the money for the down payment. Jim had an idea he would settle there for the rest of his life, celibate and devout, running a restaurant, perhaps, or maybe raising Irish setters.

Instead, after a fine spree of fixing up and furnishing the house, he started a business of selling framed posters. He would make a buying trip to Toronto to pick out posters, work all week cutting glass and mats to frame them artistically, and then return to Toronto where he had persuaded restaurant owners to hang his posters for sale on consignment. During the week while working on the pictures, he was Jim Zanuk, a businessman with a fledgling company, J.Z. Interiors, and a devout member of the local Jehovah's Witness congregation. Weekends he was Jim Zanuk, a gay man in jeans who loved parties. In Toronto he stayed with Bruce and they made love, after which he hurried back to Cambridge on Sundays in time for congregational meetings.

He took stock and decided his life was ludicrous. To the annoyance of his father, in July 1983 he sold the house, returned the money, and moved back to Toronto to live with Bruce again. He was gay, he decided, and no amount of hiding or running away would change it. It stood as a fact. He could not change his sexual orientation any more than a black man could change the colour of his skin. He made a resolution to stop trying to be part of a Jehovah's Witness congregation, to stop running around gay bars, and to begin a serious attempt to find a career in theatre.

Bruce had moved to an apartment on Church Street, number 601, and the irony was that Allan D. lived next door, in 603. Allan had a new partner, Eric G. After the initial awkwardness, Jim and Allan established that their relationship was now a comfortable, warm friendship.

One afternoon late that summer Allan invited Jim for a cup of coffee. They sat on the balcony, enjoying a fine day, and talked idly. Jim noticed two small freshly sutured incisions on the inside of Allan's left arm.

"What's that?" he asked, pointing to it.

"Actually," Allan replied, "that's what I want to tell you about. I had a little lump there and they've done a biopsy. It's a cancer that's related to AIDS. I have AIDS. It's a disease that has knocked out my immune system, and the cancer is spreading in my body. They can't stop it. There is no cure. It's fatal."

Jim was stunned. His first thought was that Allan was exaggerating. He couldn't believe that doctors couldn't stop the cancer from spreading. It was ridiculous. He got away with a hasty excuse about getting Bruce's dinner ready.

The more he thought about it, the more angry he grew. It wasn't fair. Allan D. didn't deserve such an illness. He had never hurt anyone in his life. When he told Bruce that Allan had AIDS, Bruce was baffled. Neither of them had ever known anyone with AIDS. They had believed that only gays in San Francisco and New York got it. They decided they'd better find out if it could be spread by sex. If that was true, they were really in trouble. Both had known hundreds of sex partners. They vowed they would do some research but neither got around to it.

Jim mentioned on his next visit to his father that Allan D. had AIDS. That opened a conversation about the period Jim had spent living with Allan. Karl Zanuk was curious about that. Why didn't Jim live with women?

"I know what you're asking, Dad," Jim replied. "Have you ever thought that I might be gay?"

"Yes," his father replied promptly. "I've thought that for a long time."

Both were calm. "Well, I am," Jim said. "Could we have a talk?"

They went into his father's office in the basement and shut the door. Jim said he had known early in his life, as far back as he could remember, that he was attracted to men and not often to women. It wasn't something that he liked in himself. He had fought it to the best of his ability and the marriage to Iris was part of that struggle, but it was true without any doubt that he was homosexual.

"Gay people don't have a choice," he told his father earnestly. "The worst thing people do is reject gay people. It isn't their fault."

His father protested that it was unnatural. "Animals aren't homosexual," he said.

"It's not that unnatural," Jim told him. "Please don't tell me it's a disease that I could get over, or tell me to see a psychiatrist to cure me. It isn't like that. If I was black you wouldn't send me somewhere to get my skin washed. It could not be done. This is the same thing."

The conversation lasted two hours and Jim's anguish touched Karl Zanuk. He said with compassion in his voice that he only wished they had talked about this sooner. He might have been able to help when Jim was having such a miserable time in high school.

"You went through hell then and I'm sorry I wasn't understanding. Whatever happens," Karl said emotionally, "you're my

127

son and I will always love you. I'll stand by you. But I want you to know that if you rethink this business of being gay, I'll help you change."

Jim grinned his rueful thanks and they embraced.

A high school in New York has an enrolment that is exclusively homosexual. Jim believes that if Canada had such facilities where adolescent gays could get their education without the merciless insults they now encounter, it might be possible for them to appreciate who they are and acquire a sense of worth and dignity.

Some friends of Allan D. decided to give an old-fashioned lobster party in Allan's apartment. Jim hadn't seen Allan for a while, but the last time they had met Allan had looked well. Nevertheless Jim felt uneasy being near him. Newspapers were full of stories about the AIDS virus appearing in tears, in saliva. Did it mean that being near Allan put him at risk?

When the six guests arrived in Allan's apartment Jim noticed that Allan had more of the purple blotches. They were showing above his collar on his neck. Jim cringed. The others appeared to be as worried as Jim felt. They found that Allan had anticipated their concern. He served the lobsters on paper plates and provided plastic utensils and plastic wine glasses. Jim used Allan's bathroom and was terrified to touch the toilet.

He was ashamed of himself, and also saddened. Allan wasn't his beloved friend any more. He was something alien and alarming. He was a man with AIDS, and no one knew how AIDS was transmitted.

In October 1983 Jim and Bruce parted for a second time. Jim wanted some space to try to reconcile the turmoil of his divided life. In order to put distance between himself and the gay community, he took an apartment on Dunfield, near Yonge and

Eglinton. Feeling virtuous and firm of purpose, he enrolled in acting classes and got a job as waiter at Chi-Chi's Mexican Restaurante. Being an actor was the work he was born for, he decided, and he started resolutely going to auditions.

6

One of the casting calls Jim heard about was for *Man of La Mancha*. A friend, Gary C., urged him to try for a part, but Jim was distracted and forgot. A week later he saw Gary in their favourite bar, the Barn, and Gary said that every part was cast except for the lead, Don Quixote. Jim would be right for that part, he insisted. He badgered Jim into making a phone call to the director, who set a time during Sunday morning's opening rehearsal for Jim to audition.

That Saturday night Jim partied too heavily and wakened the next morning with a sickening hangover. His first impulse was to go back to sleep, but his conscience intervened. Squinting to reduce the pain of a splitting headache, he arrived only a few minutes late at the Scarborough Village Theatre on Kingston Road in the east end of Toronto.

He introduced himself as James St. James. He'd been toying half his life with possible stage names. Zanuk, he thought, didn't work for a marquee. At his Hamilton high school a teacher whose last name was James had been involved in the theatre group. For a while Jim was intrigued with the notion of calling himself James James, but when he tried signing his name that way it wasn't quite right. He put his middle initial into it, James S.

James, and it looked better. James St. James, which came to him in a flash one day, seemed perfect.

He arrived during a break in the rehearsal. The producer, Herschel Rosen, a heavy-set man with a beatific smile, was waiting for him with the director, Blake Heathcote. They asked first that he sing for them. A piano player, Bruce McGregor, shuffled the sheet music for *Man of La Mancha*. Jim stood beside the piano, took a breath, and belted out the opening song.

The rest of the cast, chatting over their coffee break at the back of the theatre, stopped and stared. He sang another song and then another.

"Do you have a monologue?" the director asked.

He did, and delivered it.

Blake Heathcote turned to Herschel Rosen and said briefly, "Okay, I can work with him."

"Welcome to the cast, Mr. St. James," the producer said. "Glad to have you aboard."

Jim prepared to leave to take care of his hangover.

"If it's not too inconvenient, Mr. St. James," Heathcote said, "we'll be rehearsing until six."

That evening Jim went home exhausted and walking on air. He thought about the responsibility he had assumed as the lead in a show with a large cast. In his view, the lead must be quick, bright, aware, always at his or her best. It lets down the cast if the lead is dragging during rehearsal, he feels. He vowed he would cut out parties until the show closed.

It was the beginning of one of the best times of his life. He was doing what he has always felt he can do best and what he wanted most in the world to do. He had never felt so alive. He worked hard all day at rehearsals and costume fittings and at night went to Bruce's apartment, where he rehearsed his lines until even the tolerant Bruce's patience wore thin.

His earlier experience in *Man of La Mancha* was a help to him. In that school production he had the minor role of a prison guard, from which perspective he had some critical views of the actor playing the lead. As he saw it, the man was *playing* Don Quixote; Jim thought the right way to do the part was to *be* Don Quixote, and that's what he set out to do.

He reasoned that if he loved the double character of Cervantes and Don Quixote enough, if he could care deeply about them as people, he would be able to make an audience appreciate them too.

It wasn't difficult for him to have a strong affinity for Don Quixote. The man's poignant search for a better world had haunting overtones for someone raised a Jehovah's Witness. "How to ponder the problem?" Cervantes says. "How to ponder a world where evil brings profit and virtue none at all?" Jim had heard the same yearning in every Kingdom Hall he'd ever known.

The work did not proceed without pain. He had difficulty with one crucial scene when the slut Aldonza, played by Suzanne Bennett, shrieks at Quixote while the man of La Mancha sits meekly under the tirade. They spent a morning working on it, going over it a dozen times, but Jim was unable to satisfy the director, who grew more and more exasperated.

At the end of the session, Blake Heathcote got up and glared at Jim. "You're the worst goddamned actor I ever met in my life," he roared, and strode from the room, slamming the door behind him.

Jim was stunned. He and Suzanne stared speechlessly at each other.

Blake came back into the room.

"Now Jim," he said briskly. "Did you notice what you did when I yelled at you? See if you can do the same thing when Suzanne yells."

As opening night approached in November 1983, Jim's tension grew. While *Man of La Mancha* was an amateur production, the Scarborough Music Theatre had a good reputation in the theatre community. It was well regarded by theatrical producers and directors, many of whom attended productions, and for a number of aspiring actors it had been an entry into professional theatre.

Jim's acting technique depended on erasing James St. James, and he began the process during the half hour it required to drive to the theatre. The frame of mind he wanted was a suspension of reality. He wanted to float out of the contemporary, troubled man he was and make space in his whole being for a battered old sixteenth-century knight. At the theatre he was quiet and remote to hold off chatterers and tried to relax by taking deep breaths. He poured himself a coffee and pensively put on his stage make-up. He kept his flutters of panic out of sight. His theory is that nervousness is contagious backstage. As the lead, he had a duty to the others in the cast to appear calm.

On opening night he found in his dressing-room an enormous presentation bouquet of flowers from the Wexlers, a "masculine" arrangement, as he put it, of branches and orange tiger lilies. Director Blake Heathcote came backstage to beam confidence on his cast. With the heartiness directors reserve for such occasions, he told everyone to have fun and not worry if something went wrong, it didn't matter. Actors smiled back with panic in their eyes.

About five minutes before curtain, Jim found a quiet, dark corner backstage and conjured up the spirit of Miguel de Cervantes, to whom he offered a prayer, promising to honour the character of Don Quixote that the Spanish writer had created. He tried to absorb Cervantes into his being, the man who had known imprisonment, poverty, and despair and out of it had written a soaring classic to the questing spirit. With a minute to the overture, he wanted to feel himself totally a sixteenth-century Spaniard about to descend into a prison dungeon. He calls it "walking into the character".

The lights went down. The babble of audience sounds grew still and the first chords of the overture were heard. It can be a petrifying moment for an actor; there is no turning back. Jim's heart pounded. He drew in two deep breaths, held them, and exhaled slowly.

The set for *Man of La Mancha* is a dusty, cobwebbed prison dungeon dominated by a staircase that can be raised or lowered. The show opens with the young writer, Cervantes, being led down the stairs by guards and left among a rabble of mean-looking wretches. As the curtain rose, Jim took his place high on the platform at the top of the stairs. He picked up one side of a wooden trunk, and Gerry Smith, playing the role of Sancho Panza, picked up the other. On cue, they descended the stairs in an eerie blue spotlight.

The first scene shows Cervantes pleading with the prisoners, who want to burn the manuscript they find in his trunk. He offers to demonstrate what the manuscript is about. They agree that if they like the story, they won't burn it. With that Cervantes turns his back to the audience, takes out a make-up kit, and quickly does a transformation that makes him an old man, Don Quixote, a dishevelled knight who longs for a perfect world. The moment when the actor spins around, having swiftly aged his face, is always marked by a gasp from the audience. When Jim heard that reaction, he was flooded with a sense of the power of the theatre. He felt absolutely marvellous. Then he swung into the opening song, "I, Don Quixote", at full belt.

The *Scarborough Mirror* reviewed the show. The opening paragraphs were in a Fact-Truth format borrowed from one of the lines in the play:

Fact—Scarborough Music Theatre is an amateur theatre group.
Truth—The actors perform professionally.
Fact—James St. James, who plays Miguel de Cervantes in body and Don Quixote in mind, has not applied grease paint to his face in more than a decade.
Truth—St. James appears as if he's never left the stage....
A must see...a flawless performance.

Jim's mother came, despite her reservations about a Jehovah's Witness being in theatre. His father and Eleanor came early in the two-week run. Karl Zanuk said he was impressed. Jim had been waiting all his life to hear that. The Wexlers came three times. Bruce came and cheered. Five audiences gave the show standing ovations. Jim had never been happier.

After the show the cast had to reach the shower rooms by way of a corridor used by the departing audience. Jim, like the others, preferred to wait for the crowd to disperse, but one night he found that two elderly women had out-waited him.

They had tears in their eyes. "Mr. St. James," one said, "we want to tell you this wasn't just a show, it was a religious experience. We are very touched."

He hated the approach of the closing night. When it came he drove to the theatre fighting with a sense of great loss. It wasn't just the end of being in the spotlight and hearing applause, the glory he had craved all his life. He had fallen in love with the character he was playing. The witless old man, Don Quixote, searching for love and truth, appealed to his deepest self; indeed, was himself.

During that final performance, he had an unreal sense of floating. Each line he spoke was a farewell to that moment, each song he sang the last time he would sing that song. When he sang "The Impossible Dream", with its lyrics rich in spiritual aspiration, his grief at leaving the show almost choked him.

The final line of the play is delivered as Cervantes mounts the staircase on his way to face the Inquisition. Someone says to him that he thinks Cervantes and Don Quixote have much in common. Cervantes replies, "God help us, we are both men of La Mancha." Jim got the line out but found that he was weeping.

Two weeks later he found the lump on his head. A few months after that, he was in St. Michael's Hospital listening to a doctor tell him he had AIDS. That summer, the first chemotherapy and interferon treatments completed, he stretched out on a bed in the artificial stillness of a hotel room sealed against the elements and thought, "I could be dead in two weeks. I'm dying. This is what dying is."

The words of "The Impossible Dream", the most-loved song in *Man of La Mancha*, came to him:

To dream the impossible dream,
To fight the unbeatable foe,
To bear with unbearable sorrow,
To run where the brave dare not go,

To right the unrightable wrong,
To love, pure and chaste from afar,
To try, when your arms are too weary,
To reach the unreachable star.

This is my Quest, to follow that star,
No matter how hopeless, no matter how far.
To fight for the right without question or pause,
To be willing to march into hell for a heavenly cause.

And I know, if I'll only be true to this glorious quest,
That my heart will lie peaceful and calm

when I'm laid to my rest,

And the world will be better for this
That one man, scorned and covered with scars,
Still strove with his last ounce of courage,
To reach the unreachable stars.

He slept.

7

Acquired immune deficiency syndrome (AIDS) is caused by the complicated and tricky human immunodeficiency virus (HIV), which is so minute it can be seen only by advanced microscopic technology and can be detected only by an expensive and not always reliable antigen test. HIV is a retrovirus, a peculiar organism that works backwards to program a healthy cell to produce myriad replicas of the AIDS virus. HIV feeds primarily on a specific protein, NF kappa B, which is the genetic material of the T-4 cells, the white blood cells that are the body's chief defence against disease. The virus tricks this protein into producing proteins identical to it, all of them containing the AIDS virus.

Until the technology is available and more affordable, the presence of the virus is determined by the havoc it wreaks on T-4 cells. However, the T-4 cell is not the only target of the HIV. The AIDS virus has also been seen to attack brain cells directly, and there has been evidence that HIV has found hosts in rectums and the intestines.

In the United States it is estimated that 1.5 million people are infected with HIV; in Canada in the summer of 1988, the estimate of those infected was 50,000. Most of these have not been tested; their state of health appears untroubled by anything out of the ordinary. Because immune systems may cope with the virus for a decade or more, infected people experience only occasional fatigue, a bit of fever, something that feels like flu—the familiar, unalarming symptoms of mild illness.

In 1988 the World Health Organization (WHO) estimated that ten million people in seventy-four countries the world over are carrying the AIDS virus; it issued the appalling statement that one hundred million people could be infected with the AIDS virus by 1991. In November 1986 Dr. Halfdan Mahler, head of the WHO, said that he doubted if any other world epidemic, smallpox included, has ever reached such proportions.

In the spring of 1988, scientists began to say that everyone carrying the AIDS virus will develop AIDS. Dr. Roy Schwarz, assistant vice-president of the American Medical Association, told a conference in Washington, "If you are infected, you are dead. It's just a matter of time."

At the beginning of the AIDS epidemic, epidemiologists predicted optimistically that only 5 per cent of all those infected by the virus would develop full-blown AIDS, but they were unaware that the virus can sleep for as long as ten years before erupting. As casualty lists mounted, the figure was revised to 10 per cent, then 30 per cent. The number has continued to climb as people succumb to the disease as many as fifteen years after being infected.

The best available data on AIDS comes from a group of three hundred and fifty-nine gay men in San Francisco who volunteered for a hepatitis study in 1978. Their blood specimens were saved, and since 1985 the blood has been tested regularly for HIV antibodies, providing researchers with a profile of AIDS development. Five years after being infected with HIV, 15 per cent had AIDS; after six years, 24 per cent had AIDS; after seven years, it was 33 per cent; at eight years, 36 per cent had AIDS.

Another study of the same blood samples involved sixty-three men who had been infected with the virus for six years: only 22 per cent were symptom-free.

"The longer one is infected, the higher are the chances of developing AIDS ," said Dr. George Rutherford of the San Francisco Health Department to *New York Times* medical writer Lawrence K. Altman.

Privately, many experts speculate that in two decades everyone with the virus will have developed AIDS and died.

Only time will tell if this dreadful prediction is true; meanwhile insurance companies are monitoring the changing statistics carefully. In the autumn of 1987, the National Centers for Disease Control in Atlanta issued a report that of one thousand thirty-four-year-old males testing positive for the presence of AIDS, at least two hundred would be dead of the disease in seven years. By contrast, actuarial tables show that of one thousand thirty-four-year-old men in standard health, 7.5 will die in seven years. The risk difference is 2,666 per cent.

The disease is transmitted very specifically. The transmission is through the exchange of semen and blood, which occurs when sexual penetration causes tearing of tissue. It is also transmitted during intercourse if the uninfected partner has a lesion in the orifice receiving infected semen. Some believe a woman is more susceptible to HIV infection if she is menstruating while having intercourse with an infected man.

Intravenous drug users, for reasons of economy, share needles. This practice makes them so vulnerable to the spread of AIDS that some health units in the United States are offering addicts free needles. In New York, as elsewhere, the incidence of HIV infection is dropping among gay men but continues to rise among drug addicts.

Another identifiable group of victims is haemophiliacs, whose use of pooled blood, sourced from a hundred donors, made them highly susceptible during the early 1980s before blood was screened for the AIDS virus. It has been estimated that more than half the twenty thousand haemophiliacs in the United States have been infected with the AIDS virus. Of the group of Americans whose haemophilia is severe, 70 to 90 per cent are infected. Fortunately, the virus appears to be weak in haemophiliacs. In the States, only 3 per cent of haemophiliacs who test positive for the virus have so far developed AIDS. Furthermore, sexual partners of haemophiliacs rarely become infected with the virus.

A final and most tragic group are babies born to women with AIDS. Their life expectancy averages less than a year, and the damage to their bodies is appalling.

There are no documented cases where AIDS has been spread through human bites or telephones or whirlpool tubs, or by tears, sweat, saliva, urine, vomit, or a bleeding sore.

As the World Health Organization states: "AIDS is not spread by daily and routine activities such as sitting next to someone or shaking hands, or working with people. Nor is it spread by insects or insect bites. And AIDS is not spread by swimming pools, public transportation, food, cups, glasses, plates, toilets, water, air, touching or hugging, coughing or sneezing."

Of the more than fifty thousand cases of AIDS reported worldwide, not one has been caused by simple kissing. According to a pamphlet prepared by the Ontario Ministry of Health, "Kissing is okay, but don't bite. It's blood you have to worry about, not saliva."

No cases of AIDS have been transmitted through food preparation or food handling. No personal service workers, such as hairdressers, barbers, and manicurists, have become infected with AIDS because of their occupations. Extensive studies of families of persons with AIDS have not found one case where the disease was contracted through sharing bathrooms, kitchenware, or clothes.

The AIDS virus is found in low concentration in blood and semen, which must come into immediate contact with a point of entry in another person, such as a lesion, in order for transmission to occur.

The director of New York's Bellevue Hospital clinic once observed, "The more you know about the virus which causes AIDS, the more you realize how difficult it is to transmit it."

The United States regularly studies AIDS patients who appear to have become infected from unknown sources to discover if a new pathway is occurring. In 1988, when 2,059 such patients were followed by the Centers for Disease Control in Atlanta, the familiar risks were identified: homosexual intercourse, intravenous drug use, sex with partners at high risk of AIDS infection, or the receipt of contaminated blood products.

As evidence of the weakness of the AIDS virus, the Centers for Disease Control have not one reported case of a family member, friend, or lover who contracted the virus while providing home care to a person dying of AIDS. Since people with AIDS may have open lesions on their bodies and often suffer acute spells of diarrhoea, it would seem that relatives, lovers, and friends might be at acute risk, but this has not proved the case. Neither have health professionals been shown to be in great danger.

A woman health-care worker in Toronto who accidentally spiked herself with a contaminated needle subsequently tested positive for the presence of the virus, creating panic among nurses and lab technicians, but the test result later was found to be false.

To date, twelve health professionals in the United States, France, and Martinique have become infected with the virus and report no other high-risk contact except at their place of employment. This may be true, but there is also a possibility that at least some of them would rather blame the work-place than admit to an activity that would be an embarrassment.

Whether they develop AIDS or not, people with the virus are carriers of the disease and can infect others.

The early symptoms of AIDS include inexplicable bouts of severe diarrhoea, night sweats, weight loss, persistent fever, swollen lymph glands, and devastating fatigue. Certain illnesses that were once extremely rare have come to be associated with the onset of AIDS. One of these is Kaposi's sarcoma, a tumour of the blood vessel walls that appears as a purple lesion on the skin; and another is pneumocystis carinii pneumonia, known as PCP, a form of pneumonia caused by a parasite. Blood tests taken of people suffering from these disorders will show a decline in the count of T-lymphocytes, or T-4 cells, the white blood cells which make up the foundation of the human body's immune system.

Scientists don't see a cure for AIDS in this century. The problem is that antiviral drugs aimed at killing the HIV will also kill the T-4 cells in which the virus is living. The "cure" will be no better than the disease.

People with AIDS—PWA s, they call themselves—monitor the progress of their illness by watching their T-4 cell count. In normal blood, T-4 cells appear in the range of 800 to 1,000 per cubic centimetre. The danger threshold is 200 T-4 cells per cubic centimetre, an indicator that the person's immune system is seriously crippled.

For reasons scientists would dearly love to understand, many people—perhaps even most people—who are exposed to AIDS will reject the virus. Laboratory workers who have stabbed themselves accidentally with AIDS-contaminated needles will test negative even years later. By the summer of 1987, 120 health-care workers in Canada had accidentally exposed themselves to the disease through needles or through splashing their eyes, open wounds, or scalpel cuts with contaminated blood; none became infected.

Even unprotected sex with someone carrying the virus is not likely to transmit the infection. Estimates are that this will happen in less than 1 per cent of all exposures.

Seventy sexually active people with the AIDS virus were studied over a five-year period. Despite the fact that some were having sex once a day and none of them took any precautions to protect their partners against the virus, the incidence of infection among their partners was astonishingly low. Of the twenty men married to infected women in the study, only one was infected; of the fifty women having regular, unsafe sex with infected men, only eight got the virus.

HIV antibodies do not form immediately after the virus has entered the bloodstream. In some cases, antibodies have not shown themselves until eight months after the infection occurred. This time lag is one of the most important reasons why mandatory testing for AIDS would have little value. Infected people do test negative even while microscopic examination of the blood reveals the presence of the virus.

At some point, in some people, the virus attacking the immune system asserts itself with such authority that antibodies form. When this process has begun, a blood test will reveal the presence of the HIV antibodies and confirm the existence of the invisible attack. Unfortunately, the test, known as ELISA, is imperfect. The most careful ELISA tests are conducted by the United States on military recruits and embassy staff proceeding overseas, with a margin error of 0.005 per cent, or one in twenty thousand. When the ELISA test is given to the general population, however, the error rate can run as high as twenty per thousand. One series of tests on a low-risk group, women blood donors, produced one false positive in every three positives.

False positives are far from uncommon, even when experienced people conduct the test. People have committed suicide in despair over what eventually proved to be a false HIV-positive report.

Because of the widely recognized failures of ELISA, a more time-consuming test called Western Blot is always done when ELISA turns up a sero-positive result. Western Blot has only a very small margin of error but is very expensive. In Canada ELISA costs $5, not including overhead costs, which are borne by the health-care system, and Western Blot costs $100.

Finally, a laboratory culture is examined to isolate the virus under a microscope.

Sometimes the virus lies almost dormant for years, but people can develop full-blown AIDS in a matter of weeks after becoming infected. Among the most vulnerable are infants, women, and drug users. Those with the best life-expectancy are gay men in whom the onset of AIDS was marked by Kaposi's sarcoma. Of the 15 per cent of people with AIDS who live five years or more, almost all are in this latter category.

At present the mean life expectancy in Canada of someone with AIDS is about two years from diagnosis. This is an improvement brought about by better treatment for PCP, the pneumonia associated with AIDS. In 1985, the life expectancy was ten months.

Death occurs very quickly in drug addicts, probably because their physical condition already is deplorable. In New York, a drug user with AIDS dies within an average of 318 days; women addicts die more quickly than men, in an average of 298 days. Gay men, by contrast, have an average life expectancy after diagnosis of 400 days.

In the early history of AIDS in North America, most people died of the form of pneumonia, called PCP, that is peculiar to AIDS. Treatment of PCP improved rapidly, however. A highly toxic drug, azidothymidine, known as AZT, which blocks the ability of the AIDS virus to multiply, has been demonstrated to prolong life in some PWAs. Another drug, AL-721, derived from egg lecithin, is believed by some to interfere with the AIDS virus. The antibiotic pentamidine, when administered by aerosol spray, has also been shown effective against PCP.

With improved treatment came new disasters. People with AIDS began to show such conditions as cytomegalovirus infection of the retinas, which made them blind, or invasion of their brains, causing disorientation or such neurological complications as encephalitis and dementia.

In February 1988, doctors attending a medical conference in Toronto on AIDS reported signs of dementia in 87 per cent of AIDS patients and 44 per cent of people who had tested sero-positive but had no other symptoms of disease.

"This disorder has become scarier to patients than death itself," Dr. Jonathan Hunter, chief psychiatric resident at Mount Sinai Hospital in Toronto, told delegates.

Among the signs that HIV is attacking brain cells are loss of fine motor control, loss of balance, weakness, impaired memory, mental slowness, difficulty in concentrating, apathy, and social withdrawal. The doctor added that the dementia "often masks itself as depression".

In the latter stages of AIDS, sufferers become emaciated, the wasting syndrome known as the "slim disease" in Africa. A major cause of the weight loss is a protozoan parasite, cryptosporidium, which causes severe, uncontrollable diarrhoea, leading to malnutrition and dehydration.

The New York–based Social Science Research Council noted in December 1987 that world epidemics such as smallpox, cholera, tuberculosis, polio, and the bubonic plague cause profound changes in behaviour, popular beliefs, health services, and government policies. The impact of AIDS to date has raised serious implications both for civil rights and for health costs, quite apart from the human tragedy of what has been described as the foremost catastrophe of modern history.

No one expects that either a cure for AIDS or a vaccine to protect against the virus will be found in the next decade. The National Academy of Sciences and the Institute of Medicine in the States have acknowledged that "neither vaccines nor satisfactory drug therapies for HIV or AIDS are likely to be available in the near future." "Once you've got the virus," said Dr. Douglas Dietrich of the New York University School of Medicine, "you've got it for ever."

Prevention of AIDS therefore is the only hope for containing the destruction. Fortunately, the AIDS virus is fragile and dies when it leaves the body. While it can be recovered from dried material at room temperature for up to three days, and wet material for up to a week, the vigour of the virus is severely depleted and its power to infect has decreased significantly.

If AIDS were as readily transmitted as such airborne infections as the common cold and influenza, or if it could be contracted without penetration, like most sexually transmitted diseases, or if it were as virulent as hepatitis-B, millions of people already would have died.

Sensible precautions to take against AIDS include avoidance of sexual intercourse with intravenous drug users, prostitutes (male or female), and others who have multiple sex partners. Use of latex condoms greatly reduces but does not eliminate the risk of infection. People should avoid non-sterile needles and syringes. Blood-screening practices in most countries are now adequate, which reduces the danger of contracting the virus during surgery. Diabetics travelling abroad should take a sufficient supply of syringes and needles.

Dr. C. Everett Koop, the Surgeon General of the United States, repeatedly has endorsed condoms as the "best line of defence"— next to monogamy or celibacy. Condoms, however, allow *safer* sex, not sex that is entirely safe. Condoms in conjunction with spermicidal foam containing the ingredient nonoxynol-9 provide the best protection, since evidence is growing that spermicides seem to weaken the AIDS virus.

When used as a contraceptive, however, condoms have been shown to have a high failure rate. Out of every ten couples using condoms regularly for a year, one woman will become pregnant.

"Even if you use condoms," comments Dr. Katherine Stone, an epidemiologist in the Division of Sexually Transmitted Diseases in Atlanta, "it doesn't mean that you can sleep with a new person every day without risk. Nothing in life is one hundred per cent effective."

Latex condoms are believed to be the safest of the types available, although they tend to deteriorate rapidly when exposed to heat, light, or oil-based lubricants such as petroleum jelly. The AIDS virus passes with ease through "natural" condoms made of lambs' intestines.

A University of Miami study of twelve AIDS patients and their uninfected heterosexual partners, all using condoms, found that two of the partners became infected. The sampling, however, is small and suspect. The two partners could have been infected by some other means than intercourse or by some other sexual partner.

AIDS Vancouver prepared a pamphlet entitled, *Revised Safer Sex Guidelines for Gay Men*, which describes the proper use of condoms: DO put on when penis is erect; DO squeeze air out of tip; DO use water-based lube (Astroglide, KY, Probe, Foreplay); DO hold on to condom when pulling out; DO use a new condom every time; DON'T unroll condom before putting on; DON'T use the same condom more than once; DON'T use petroleum-based lube (Crisco, Lube, Performance).

By far the majority of sufferers from AIDS in Canada have been gay men. Typically, in them the onset of AIDS is often signalled by Kaposi's sarcoma, a once-rare kind of skin cancer that occurs almost exclusively in gay men. AIDS is only beginning to move into the relatively small group of addicts in Canada who use needles.

The complexity of the virus is demonstrated by the variety of damage it inflicts. AIDS follows a very different pattern when drug users are infected. They tend to develop infections of the valve on the right side of the heart or abcesses in the brain— conditions almost never seen in the rest of the population. In Haiti, the disease takes yet another course: diarrhoea is the most common manifestation, along with gastroenteritis, fungal infections of the oesophagus, and tuberculosis.

Obviously there are many strains of the virus. Microbiologists are labouring over the puzzling differences in symptoms and in individual resistance. As with most infectious diseases, there are several critical factors, only one of which is an invasion of the virus. Nutrition, general health, and a variety of environmental factors also contribute to its victory, but no one yet knows how, or to what extent.

So far, many different strains of HIV have been identified, and there are enormous differences in their potency. One is so weak that it causes only temporary damage to the cell it invades. Some strains lurk in the cell in a sort of trance, neither destroying the cell nor disappearing. People with this form of virus have become known as "healthy" carriers; they have no symptoms of disease, but they can infect others. The AIDS virus lying dormant in human cells probably can be activated by a wide variety of other infections, some of them as minor as a cold.

Other strains are killers. They multiply rapidly, quickly destroy T-4 cells, and race for other prey. Scientists speculate that some types mutate and become more virulent as they change.

Until very recently it was believed that eventually everyone with full-blown AIDS would die of it. Scientists no longer are certain. In North America it isn't uncommon to find people who, like Jim St. James, have lived a long time after diagnosis—four years, six years, one person lived nine years. In New York, for instance, reports are that 15 per cent of people with AIDS were alive five years after diagnosis.

In the spring of 1988, New York City researchers were looking for two men, known to be alive, whose AIDS was diagnosed in 1977 and 1978. However, these figures have been disputed by one investigator, Ann Hardy, who was unable to find most of the survivors listed in the New York study. Her estimate, after a vain search for long-term survivors, is that only 2 to 5 per cent of people with AIDS survive for more than three years.

Long-term AIDS survivors, however scarce, have much in common: they are almost invariably gay men who are young and fit and whose disease began with Kaposi's sarcoma but who did not develop some of the other grievous maladies, such as pneumocystis carinii pneumonia.

Studies of such survivors "provides some light, some hope", commented Dr. Richard Rothenberg of the Centers for Disease Control in Atlanta. Scientists disagree on the reason some people seem more resistant to the AIDS virus than others. One study by Laurence Badgeley seems to demonstrate that a change of attitude and lifestyle contributes to what seems almost a miracle.

Dr. Robert Gallo of the National Cancer Institute in Bethesda, Maryland, much honoured for his work with Dr. Luc Montagnier of the Pasteur Institute in Paris in identifying and isolating the virus, believes that three factors contribute to susceptibility. One is that the person has just experienced an infection and therefore the body has manufactured an increase in T-4 cells and macrophages to fight the invader. If the AIDS virus arrives on the scene during this time of elevated numbers of antibodies, the HIV will have a feast.

Should the person pick up another infection while the HIV is hunting for its preferred food—T-4 cells—the body will produce a hospitable supply for the HIV to flourish.

Another factor is the link scientists are finding between hepatitis and, possibly, herpes, which have a gene that appears to activate the AIDS virus. Interferon, a substance produced naturally by the human immune system, has been duplicated artificially and used as a treatment for both AIDS and hepatitis.

A third factor is very likely the variation in strength among different strains of the virus itself.

The first known case of AIDS in North America was a fifteen-year-old boy whose death in 1969 of bronchial pneumonia had some aspects that baffled his doctors at a Washington University hospital in St. Louis, Missouri. Puzzled, they decided to freeze his tissue for later study. When the tissue was put under a microscope in 1987, the AIDS virus was present.

This discovery followed very quickly the report in Randy Shilts' book, *And the Band Played On: Politics, People and the AIDS Epidemic*. Patient Zero—"the man who brought AIDS to North America"—was described as an Air Canada flight attendant, Gaetan Dugas, who picked up AIDS in France some time in the late 1970s. Scientists tracking the disease discovered that Dugas, a promiscuous man who had sex in bath houses across the continent and bragged that he averaged 250 sexual liaisons a year, is known to have transmitted the virus to 40 of the first 248 homosexual men diagnosed with AIDS by April 1982. Dugas died of AIDS in 1984.

Dugas certainly contributed to the spread of AIDS, but it is doubtful that he was Patient Zero. As Catherine Hankins, director of the Montreal Sexually Transmitted Diseases Control Program, told *Maclean's* magazine in October 1987, some people who died before 1981, ostensibly of pneumonia or skin cancer, may actually have been victims of AIDS.

The origin of AIDS probably never will be known. Like all the parasitical diseases to which the human body is prone, the human immunodeficiency virus undoubtedly has a long history of attempting to find a vulnerable cell. The second step in the evolutionary process that will convert a random parasite into a world-wide epidemic is means of transmission. The long adaptation of the HIV to become its present menace may well have been accomplished over a century, or more.

The theory most accepted is that the virus was transmitted from a green monkey to a man in West Africa in the 1950s. Chimpanzees, the only animal known to become infected with the AIDS virus, do not develop the disease but can be carriers.

By 1980 AIDS was prevalent in Uganda, where a group of male smugglers in a small isolated fishing village on Lake Victoria spread the disease to their wives. Carriers moved to other towns, infecting populations there, and long-distance truckers carried it across Africa to the sea. The virus spread, incubating silently and lethally, until people all over Africa, France, and the Caribbean were showing the symptoms and dying. The virus is believed to have been brought to North America in 1976 by people attending New York's celebration of the U.S. Bicentennial.

As Dr. Robert C. Gallo of the U.S. National Cancer Institute has noted: "The AIDS virus didn't come in at one time." Most likely, several sexually active people or drug abusers carried the virus, infecting only a few people—or none. As Dr. Robert May, a Princeton University mathematician who has studied the spread of AIDS, commented: "It wouldn't be surprising if AIDS appeared once, twice, three times before it finally took."

Eventually pockets of people with AIDS emerged in major cities, alerting doctors very slowly to the realization that the increase in deaths from Kaposi's sarcoma and pneumocystis carinii pneumonia was not a medical curiosity but a sign of the arrival of a disaster.

The first known case in Canada occurred in 1979. Three years later, medical statistics showed ten cases. By spring of 1988, there were 1,760 cases of full-blown AIDS and 10,000 Canadians whose blood had been tested positive for the virus. There is regional disparity in the target population of the disease. In Africa, for instance, 75 per cent of people with AIDS are heterosexual. In the United States, 70 per cent of people with AIDS are homosexual, and the next largest identifiable group in New York City, fast approaching equal numbers with homosexuals, are users of intravenous drugs. In Canada, which has a relatively small problem with drug addiction, close to 90 per cent of people with AIDS are homosexual.

One of those was Tim Jocelyn, a brilliant young Toronto textile designer. At Expo 86 in Vancouver there were pictures of him beneath a sculpture he was commissioned to do, chatting with Prince Charles and Lady Di and Prime Minister Brian Mulroney and Mila. A few months later, he was dead from AIDS. Among the people who wept at the elegant wake his family gave in a studio loft were several notable artists whose faces bore the haunted look of AIDS.

Someone said, "This is not just a personal tragedy. It is a national disaster."

In February 1988, with the epidemic in North America eight years old, a pattern began to emerge. The rate on new cases of HIV-positive tests in the gay population had slowed significantly. Clearly, education was working and people were taking preventive measures. The spread into the heterosexual population hadn't occurred in the great numbers expected. In fact it was confined for the most part to black and Hispanic women who were partners of intravenous drug users or were intravenous drug users themselves.

While these trends gave some encouragement, the worst is still to come as people who are now symptom-free but HIV-positive slip into full-blown AIDS. On February 14, 1988, the *New York Times* estimated that "a huge part" of the gay population in San Francisco will be wiped out. In New York, where addicts and their sexual partners and babies are hard hit, the health costs of responding to AIDS are expected to be $1 billion a year in 1991.

"In the 25- to 40-year age group," said Dr. June Osborn, dean of the school of public health at the University of Michigan, "everybody is going to know somebody suffering from AIDS."

8

In July 1984, four days after Jim had settled himself at the Inn on the Park to wait for signs that the chemotherapy and interferon treatments were working—or not working—he was gripped by a raging fever of 103 degrees. At midnight he called Dr. Garvey in a panic and she ordered him to hospital immediately.

This, his third admission to St. Mike's, arose so suddenly that there were no beds available for him on 6A, the cancer ward he knew so well. Instead, after a very long delay, he was wheeled to another floor and settled in a private room. He noted that the door to his bathroom was taped shut and bore a hand-lettered sign, DO NOT USE. He assumed something was wrong with the plumbing.

The next morning, he was feeling better but his skin was sticky from the fever. As he prepared to leave the room to find a shower, a nurse stopped him. She said he must stay inside. He explained that his washroom was out of order and he had to find a facility somewhere else. She said that the washroom actually wasn't out of order. The staff just didn't want him to use it.

Jim felt his temper start to rise and tried to check it. He told himself that the people on the new floor weren't trained in AIDS, they didn't have the experience that staff on 6A had, and he couldn't expect them to be comfortable with him. *Be nice*, he ordered himself.

He called the head nurse, who turned out to be a pleasant person, and asked her courteously if he could leave the room to shower and use a toilet. "I'm sorry," she said, "but we can't allow you out of this room."

"Watch this," Jim said with a tight smile.

He got out of bed and strode to the door. The hall outside was bustling with doctors, nurses, and orderlies hurrying on various chores. When they saw him standing outside his door in his bathrobe, they froze like figures in a child's game of Simon Says. Every face turned to him wore an expression of sheer panic.

His indignation vanished. For the first time in his life, he was causing fear and revulsion. He was aghast. Their reaction made an absurdity of his ambition to be a warm and likeable ambassador for the gay community. He turned and went quietly back to his room.

He spent a long day alone with bleak thoughts. The prospect of dying had been painful enough, but now it appeared that he was very likely to die among people who loathed him on sight and dreaded to be near him.

The next morning a young nurse pushed open his door and stood trembling on the threshold with a blood-pressure cuff in her hands. She was an astonishing sight. Her hair was covered by the cotton cap that surgeons wear and a mask hid all of her face except her terrified eyes. She had surgical gloves on her hands, a long gown over her uniform and paper boots wrapped over her shoes.

In a quivering, muffled voice she said she had come to take his blood pressure. She took a step into the room and stopped. Then she stepped back and stood frozen, unable to make herself enter. Immediately, she had Jim's sympathy.

"That's all right," he told her, being careful not to move in her direction, "you don't have to do it. It's not fair to make you do it, and I understand."

He called Phyllis Wyper, St. Michael's Hospital's expert on infection control and the person responsible for the relaxed tone on 6A. "I think you need to do some staff training," he told her drily.

Phyllis moved quickly. By mid-morning the seals were off Jim's bathroom and he was having a shower.

Jim was pleased with himself for his behaviour with the frightened nurse. Despite his own desolation, he had been a gentleman. It gave him satisfaction that he had pulled off a difficult situation without making a scene.

It was his first such experience, but he knew it wasn't an uncommon event for staff to refuse to come near an AIDS patient. People with AIDS were still rare in Toronto hospitals and were so dreaded that it wasn't unusual for cleaners or food service workers to refuse to enter the room, or for nurses and doctors to avoid touching the patient or coming near the bed. In one case, a hospital chaplain who was asked to visit a man dying of AIDS arrived in a surgical gown, mask, cap, shoe covers, and gloves.

Jim observed, "The cleaning staff are always the last to be informed. They see nurses going in and out of an AIDS patient's room wearing nothing but their uniforms, but the person who mops the floor will come in with a mask, gloves, hair-covering, and gown."

People with AIDS generally have one of two reactions to irrational fear. Because they are already distraught at the gravity of their fatal illness, they are especially vulnerable to slights. The sturdiest and least sick respond with rage, the others simply roll over and weep.

Jim was pleased to have kept his head, but he thinks he was helped by the memory of his own reaction when he heard that Allan D. had AIDS. He had been terrified to use Allan's bathroom. He had flinched from touching the handle of the toilet to flush, and nothing would have induced him to use the soap or towels. His fearfulness had been no less unreasonable than that of the young nurse.

Moreover, his calm had been effective. He had straightened out the mess caused by ignorance and, in a word he likes, he had been a "gentleman" while doing it.

In this crisis of his lifetime, he was finding the style with which he would see the illness through. He would be light-hearted, civilized, and a charmer in the Cary Grant and David Niven manner. If he was dying, and it looked very much as if he was, he would be remembered for laughter and for his dignity.

The performance was a natural for him because it drew on the qualities of consideration and sophistication that he had been cultivating since childhood. Best of all, an air of nonchalance would protect his privacy. He would be spared pity, which he never wanted or courted. A laughing man is not a candidate for charity. Instead he might achieve the aspiration of his life— admiration, approval, love. Ironically, the possibility that he was dying was providing him with an opportunity to be more fully alive and useful than he had ever been.

The nurse called Jobikins had unwittingly played a major role in shaping his style when she said that his behaviour had changed her mind about homosexuals. Jim saw in that comment his opportunity to escape the horror of helplessness. With the self-assigned task of creating goodwill for gays, he was once more in command of the situation. He was an ambassador, a gay man who challenged the stereotype of silliness. He had a job to do. While being open about his sexuality, he would behave with intelligence and courage. He could help dissolve prejudices—a project worthy of Don Quixote.

This, his third stay in St. Michael's Hospital, lasted about a week. He was to be hospitalized for the mysterious fever five times over the next year and a half. No explanation was ever found for the blasts of temperature. While fevers indicate the presence of infection, exhaustive tests of blood, saliva, urine, and faeces could find no organism to explain them.

Jim's almost unfailing optimism enabled him to find good news in the fevers. He sees them as a function akin to that of self-cleaning ovens. When his temperature soars, he pictures his body fighting with such intensity that it is burning out the infections. He tells other people with AIDS not to worry about their inexplicable, alarming fevers. They should rejoice, he tells them cheerfully. He sees the fevers as evidence that his immune system isn't completely gone—a few antibodies are still kicking in bravely to help his body get well.

Jim is a firm believer in the adage that fear kills. He gives some credit for his longevity in the face of AIDS to the fact that he doesn't allow himself to be frightened—at least not for long. When a new lump grows, or he suffers a severe headache, or diarrhoea, or days of nausea, or the Kaposi's sarcoma spreads to a new area, he fights down the paralysing thought, "Maybe this is *it*, the end of the road, the luck has run out." Instead, his pose is, "This is interesting. Wonder what it means? Better ask Dr. Garvey."

He once announced proudly to a room full of PWAs, "I've got AIDS, but AIDS hasn't got me."

He was approaching his thirtieth birthday, June 24, 1984, and it happened that he was between treatments, his strength gradually returning. He spent most of his time resting in his apartment. He went nowhere. He was too tired, for one reason. Also, he didn't like what he saw in the mirror. The handsome man who had starred in *La Mancha* half a year earlier was now scrawny and aged by illness and pain, his hair almost gone.

He was spending his time in gloomy reflection. Alone with his melancholy, no longer obliged to sustain the performance of

158

cheerfulness, he listened to *Requiem to a Dying Princess* over and over.

He cleaned his apartment, leaving nothing in it that would embarrass him if he should die in hospital. He gathered his stack of male love magazines and clippings about gay love and put them in the incinerator.

Back in the apartment, he took out copies of *Watchtower* and *Awake!* and studied writings about the Scriptures. That evening he started to write letters to his closest friends. He told them that if he died they should look for comfort in the Bible, and he identified passages where they could find words of solace. His heart was full of yearning for everyone to find the peace he had in being certain of resurrection. He described the coming of a government of God and explained how his friends could find answers to their questions about life after death.

The two hardest farewell letters were to Natalie Wexler and to his mother. He rewrote the one to his mother a dozen times, throwing away draft after draft, and eventually gave up trying to tell her of the love he felt for her. He couldn't even begin the letter to Natalie; what could he say to someone who had given him so much friendship?

Allan D. sent him a poem about love and death. He memorized it, effortlessly. People told him that Allan was very sick and often in hospital. He and Allan did not communicate. Each felt the other's struggle, but they seemed to have reached a mutual conclusion that contact could only be seen as a cry for comfort and would place an unfair burden on each other's resources, already stretched to the utmost.

He expected that Natalie would do something very special for his birthday; she always did. They had a friendly competition about birthdays, each trying to surprise the other with something delightful. Her first birthday gift to him had been a cross; at the time she had not understood that for a Jehovah's Witness the Christian cross is a pagan symbol. He gave it back to her

159

and explained that his belief didn't permit him to wear it. That impressed her. The next year, she gave him a solid silver egg.

He always tried to reciprocate imaginatively, and one of her birthdays, about five years before he got AIDS, had marked a significant time for him. The birthday itself occurred after months of accelerating drug use that had begun at a Hallowe'en party where Jim was introduced to a white powder he was told was MDA.

"What does it do?" he asked.

"It makes you dance hard and have a really good time," he was informed.

That sounded all right, so Jim ate some. A little while later the same person, Ken, a striking-looking man in his early forties, observed that Jim wasn't yet high enough and urged him to have more. Jim, carefree and careless, took another hit from a plastic envelope. In total that night he had five hits of MDA.

He began to have trouble seeing, so Ken drove him to his home. In the shower, Jim had an attack of claustrophobia and was grateful that Ken was there to calm him. After that Jim adjusted to MDA and became a regular user at weekend parties in the group of about ten men, all heavy drug users, who surrounded Ken. Some he had a good sexual time with and some he didn't like much, but with the drug it didn't matter.

At first he could return to his normal self on Mondays, but after several weeks this no longer was possible. His drug use became continuous. His friends noticed a change in his personality. He had become silly and irrational, his ability to concentrate gone. By the time of Natalie's birthday on December 13, he was stoned most of the time and seriously disoriented all of the time.

When dressing to meet her for lunch, he looked for a pair of socks a long time before noticing that he had them in his hand, and he at first couldn't find his shirt, then realized he was already wearing it.

160

He had flowers for her and remembered to present them, but the rest of the meal was a blur. He was aware that his head kept switching position of its own volition. She inquired about his father and he tried to answer but couldn't remember the question.

"Aren't you going to eat your salad?" she asked.

"I don't like cabbage," he explained.

"It's not cabbage," she told him. "It's lettuce."

He stared at it. It still looked like cabbage.

Natalie Wexler devised a plan she hoped would bring Jim to his senses. She invited him for dinner on a Sunday evening and informed him she was also asking a gay couple, Ken and Robert. Jim didn't like either man. He thinks of them as "fruit flies", that is, conspicuously gay. His preference is for men who appear to be heterosexual.

He found Natalie dressed in a black velvet *peignoir* and dripping with diamonds. She served cocktails in the living-room in front of an open fire and, to his dismay, directed her attention exclusively to Ken and Robert. Sitting between them on the couch, she showed them family photograph albums and chatted entertainingly about her life and loves. She excluded Jim totally from the conversation.

At one point she said coolly, "We're not hearing much from you, Jim." Jim thought, she knows what's going on; this is deliberate. Why?

He wasn't prepared to find that he wasn't sitting at his accustomed place on her right at the dining-room table. Instead he was at the other end, next to Bernie Wexler. "Ken the faggot", as he thought of him, was seated where Jim usually sat.

At dessert, Natalie leaned forward and said sweetly, "Jim, you're not saying much at all."

Jim thought, ah-hah, I *am* supposed to have a reaction. I'm supposed to guess something. I'm supposed to see something. What am I missing?

161

He drove home thoughtfully and knew the answer by the time he reached his door. He called Natalie.

"I didn't know if I would hear from you again," she said.

"I need to talk to you," Jim said. They arranged to meet for lunch.

This time he was drug free. She examined him and saw that he was himself.

"What did you learn?" she asked.

He replied promptly, "You were trying to let me see how far I had slipped into the gutter, that I didn't belong in my special place any more. Natalie, you're wonderful."

She beamed, proud of him, and that was the end of his use of heavy drugs.

On the day of Jim's thirtieth birthday, Natalie said she and Bernie would be picking him up to take him for a Sunday brunch. He checked his face in the mirror. He was almost bald and his eyebrows were gone. He wanted to make sure he could put a sparkling expression in his eyes, and he saw with satisfaction that he could. He wanted to avoid, at all costs, sick, mournful eyes. He combed his hair half a dozen different ways, trying to make the most of what was left. He was sorry it was such a hot day that he couldn't wear a long-sleeved turtle-neck to cover the purple swellings on his neck.

He put on the nicest light-weight sweater he owned and went outside to wait. To his dismay, the wind disarranged his carefully combed hair. A couple strolling by looked at him idly and then, shocked expressions on their faces, looked away.

When Natalie and Bernie arrived with Nat's sons, there were hugs and kisses all around and he was reassured. He was in his family; he was safe.

Waiting for them at brunch in the Four Seasons Hotel in Yorkville were Bruce C., Bert N., and Brian B., all of them in a celebratory mood that dissipated Jim's nervousness at being on public view with his ghastly pallor and tell-tale gaunt body. The headwaiter announced that the Wexler car was ready. Jim expected they all would be going back to Natalie's place for the opening of gifts and was pleased to see a lavish limousine waiting in the hotel driveway.

"That's not for us," Natalie said, restraining him. "There's our limousine."

Behind the limousine were four pedicabs with a canopy of balloons floating over the seats. The lead pedicab, into which Jim was escorted, had a tape machine. Natalie said he must follow the instructions on the tape.

The first instruction was to go to Harbourfront, so the pedicabs set off in a row, bouncing down University Avenue, around Queen's Park, under the railway tracks, and out into the sunlight to stop by the sparkling bay.

The tape said, "Welcome to Harbourfront, Jim. We love you very much. Since you're such a good actor, you must now stand up in the pedicab and recite a scene from *Man of La Mancha*."

He knew what Nat was doing. She had been worried that he was hiding himself away in his apartment and was trying to push him into overcoming his fear of being seen in public.

Bravely, he stood up in the pedicab and declaimed lines from *La Mancha*, to the vast amusement of people thronging the sidewalk on their way to the ferry docks.

"I was so sick, and so scared, and it was wonderful," he recalls. "It was so wonderful."

The tape then instructed Jim to go to Nathan Phillips Square where he was to stand in the cab, chew bubble gum (which Natalie had supplied), and blow bubbles. He did this creditably, and the next stop was the Bellair Café in Yorkville. The pedicabs stopped at the curb, next to sidewalk tables packed with the lunch crowd. The instructions were, "Stand up and moo like a cow."

Here goes nothing, he thought, stood up, and mooed.

The eight jumped back into the pedicabs, rode the block to the Four Seasons Hotel, and alighted. They went to the main floor bar where the bartender had Jim's gifts stored on a silver platter behind the bar. There was a sealskin wallet from Bruce, a year's worth of free haircuts from Bert, a gift from Brian, and an antique gold seal ring engraved with a lion from Natalie and Bernie.

Rings are full of symbolism for Jim. When he threw Iris's wedding ring down a sewer, he saw it as a metaphor for the death of love. In the years since the break-up of his marriage, he has never bought himself rings, much as he loves them, because he believes that a ring represents love and must be exchanged between people who truly care for one another.

"I love it," he said, putting it on, too choked to say more.

Wonderful as the day had been, he was relieved when it was over and he was home again. He had been fighting waves of nausea much of the time, and the gaiety had a forced element that exhausted them all. Under the laughter and foolishness, Jim kept thinking that this was his last birthday, and he saw the same despair in the eyes of his friends.

That night he lay in bed, touching the ring, and tears ran out of the corners of his eyes, making the pillow wet. He wasn't sad. He felt he had known real love, and he was happy.

Chemotherapy resumed a week later, on July 3. Dr. Garvey decided that the brutal combination of chemotherapy and interferon seemed to be working.

Jim grinned. "That's just dandy," he told her. "Fire away. Whatever works, I say." And braced himself for the ordeal.

In August he was back in hospital again for further extensive tests of his throat, lymph glands, stomach, and bowel.

Dr. Garvey asked him to come to her office to hear the results. He prepared slowly. He was feeling much better, gaining strength every day. He didn't think he could bear it if she said he needed more chemotherapy.

She had astounding news. "You don't have a tumour anywhere," she announced triumphantly. "I've never seen anything like it in all the years we've been using chemotherapy. Everyone in the hospital is absolutely amazed."

He asked if that meant his cancer was cured, and she said no. Jim learned that cancer cells probably drift around in everyone's body, and that they certainly are never completely obliterated in someone who has once developed a tumour. The explanation he received was that if a person has 100 cancer cells and is hit with every kind of treatment the world possesses, 90 of the cells will be killed. If there are multiples, say 100,000 cells of cancer, the most effective treatment still will leave 10,000 cells. His tumours were gone, but not the risk that they might develop again.

"We'll watch and see," Dr. Garvey assured him. "Meanwhile, you just keep on getting well."

Jim went away elated. He felt confident that if he prayed enough to Jehovah, the cancer wouldn't return. In any case, Dr. Garvey was keeping a close watch. He was to return for a check-up every two weeks.

Natalie threw a cocktail party to celebrate her wedding anniversary. When she called to invite Jim, he protested. He was looking terrible, he said, "as you well know". She insisted that it didn't matter. She had phoned him first, in fact, and she wanted him to attend.

He dressed in the best clothes he had, but it was hard to walk into the room among Natalie and Bernie's elegant friends. Some people did start for a moment at the sight of his gaunt face, but they were polite and quickly recovered.

One guest asked Natalie if she could speak to her for a moment. In the powder room, she confided that she had shaken hands with Jim. Someone had just told her that Jim had AIDS.

She had been washing her hands frantically, but was she in any danger?

Natalie said there was no danger but that she understood how the woman felt. If she was uncomfortable about being at the party with Jim, maybe it would be better if she and her husband left. Which they did.

In September Jim paid a visit to Allan D., who was looking frail and desperately ill. Allan's young partner, Eric, was continuing to care for Allan, though Eric's face showed signs of the terrible strain.

Jim and Allan looked at one another with unspoken sympathy—Jim gaunt and almost bald from chemotherapy, Allan thin and mottled everywhere with Kaposi's.

Allan was stretched out on a couch in his living-room, a blanket over his legs. Jim lowered himself gently, his body hurting, and sat on the floor beside him. They didn't have much to say. There was a quietness and kindness between them; each was preoccupied with simply staying alive.

When it was time for Allan to take his medication, he asked Jim to hand him some pills on a table nearby.

"Look at me," he said with some bitterness. "I'm so weak I can't even stretch out my arm."

Jim leaned forward to hug him, but Allan waved him back. "No sense passing this thing around any more than we already have," he explained.

Whenever Eric touched him, he insisted that Eric wash his hands thoroughly afterwards.

Eric and Allan had been sexual partners after the illness was diagnosed, so Eric had gone for a blood test. To his relief, he was HIV negative.

"Dr. Stan Read calls it the luck of the draw," Jim shrugs.

The vagaries of transmission intrigue and baffle scientists. A Toronto seventeen-year-old had sex with a man only twice in his life and died of AIDS, yet active male prostitutes in New York continue to test negative. People who get AIDS, Jim concludes, are victims of the wrong circumstances at the wrong time with the wrong person. It is the same with the wide variation in how long people live after a diagnosis of AIDS.

Once, soon after Jim was diagnosed, he and Allan talked about which man had given AIDS to the other. Allan said wearily, "We don't know if I gave it to you, Jim, or you gave it to me when you came back from New York. We don't know. We'll never know. Does it matter?"

They decided it didn't. Thinking about it was fruitless and would only distract them from their real task, which was "getting out of this mess we're in", as Jim put it.

Jim says people with AIDS don't speculate much about the source of their infection, or about whether they unknowingly gave AIDS to someone else before being diagnosed.

"The guilt would be unbearable," Jim says. "For myself, I just figured whoever gave it to me, it wasn't going to help if I knew. And I can't let myself think about who I might have infected."

Jim was concerned about infecting friends, but he was taking his cue about that from Dr. Garvey. She was the expert in the disease, and he watched her carefully as she examined him, handling his body with ungloved hands and then washing thoroughly afterwards. His conclusion was that it was safe for people to be near him and that normal hygienic measures were adequate protection against infection.

Out of consideration for people less knowledgeable, he never was the first to offer to shake hands. A spontaneously affectionate person, he had a habit of hugging people he likes. Natalie cautioned him, "Jim, don't hug first. Wait and see if people are comfortable hugging you. Let them start it." After that he became watchful on encountering friends and waited until they made the first move. He had not kissed anyone since the diagnosis of AIDS. Maybe AIDS wasn't spread by kissing, but until he was sure he wasn't going to take any chance of infecting someone. Sex was out of the question. He hugged Bruce C., but that was all.

He became extremely careful about his own cuts, cleaning them with cotton that he promptly flushed down the toilet. The tissue he used to blow his nose went straight into the toilet, not into a waste basket where someone might touch the tissue when emptying the basket. When he slept at his father's house, he changed the bed linen himself the next morning and bundled it up with the towel he used after showering. Then he deposited the bundle in the laundry room in the middle of the floor.

"Eleanor," he would say, pointing to it, "this is my stuff *here*."

She would thank him off-handedly, but they both knew she would wash his things separately.

He started to worry about Shannon and Benjamin, the children of his younger sister, Karen. Because of a malformation in his glands, Benjamin had spent the first six months of his life in hospital having surgery on his tongue and throat. Afterwards he had open sores on his tongue. Jim was leery of being near the child, worrying that the boy's immune system was weak and unformed, making him especially vulnerable to contagion. Though the baby was drawn to him, Jim avoided touching the child. He knew that if Karen ever said to him, "Benjamin has AIDS," he would not want to live.

As Allan D. became sicker, he withdrew more into his thoughts and was unresponsive to callers. Jim didn't visit again, though he heard Allan was in hospital. Friends were surprised, expecting them to draw close because they had loved one another for a long time and were facing the same disease—each was almost the only person the other knew with AIDS—but the distance seemed to suit them both. Jim thinks their instincts were right: neither wanted to be a burden on the other. In fact Allan was much sicker than Jim was. The chemotherapy that had helped Jim had done little for Allan and his spots continued to increase.

Consistent with the vacillation that had always characterized the father-and-son relationship, Jim's father's mood had changed from testy and condemning to one of pure and selfless generosity. Karl read everything he could find about AIDS. Did Jim know about the treatment they were testing in Paris? Jim did. Did he want to go to Paris? No, he thought Dr. Garvey was doing fine. How about going to Germany? There was some talk of a new treatment there. No, but thanks, Dad.

Jim's room was filled with fresh flowers. Once, when Jim appeared to be close to death, his father hired private nurses at $100 a shift.

As Jim's strength returned, he was restless in his small bachelor apartment. He needed to be near the hospital, he felt, and closer to his friends. His father made a generous offer of $10,000 to furnish a new apartment downtown and another $2,000 to buy clothes, since nothing in Jim's closet fit him any more. The gift was a tonic. Jim loves shopping for clothes, and he has a nesting spirit that lends itself to time-consuming searches for the right drapery fabric and coffee-table.

He threw himself into both ventures with enthusiasm. He found a two-bedroom apartment on Sherbourne and made arrangements to move in when it became vacant. He wanted the furnishings to be elegant and simple, the mood serene. He took special pains shopping for the bedroom to ensure that it would have a comforting atmosphere. He assumed that there was a very good chance he would die in it. He wanted the last things he saw before he died to be lovely.

He returned to hanging out in gay bars, drinking with his cronies, going home alone. Paul D. usually seemed to be too busy elsewhere to join him. Natalie called a meeting of a handful of Jim's closest friends, including Paul. She explained that Jim was having a difficult time and maybe wouldn't make it. He had been close to dying at least once, she told them. To pull through the crisis he would need their support as never before.

She turned to Paul. "You're going to have to make up your mind, Paul," she said levelly. "If you're with him, be there. If you're not, it would be better if you dropped out entirely. Make up your mind."

Paul thought it over. "I'm out," he said finally.

One evening, a few weeks after the report that his cancer had disappeared, Jim was in Chaps, his favourite bar, in a reckless, frenzied mood. He felt himself becoming drunk but he didn't care. Then, out of nowhere, suddenly he was sober.

He drove home, perplexed by how odd he felt, his mind blank. He sat on his bed fully dressed and stared at a wall. He wasn't aware of the passing of time until it was dawn. The mood of unreality still with him, he went to Paul D.'s apartment to talk about it, but Paul refused to let him in.

With his car keys, Jim scratched on Paul's door, *Iris*.

He went to Bruce C.'s apartment. He could hear the shower running and had to knock several times before Bruce opened the door.

"Jim, you look terrible," Bruce said in alarm. "What's wrong?"

Jim started to cry. "I have AIDS and I'm going to die," he screamed.

Bruce drew him in and helped him into bed as Jim's pent-up grief burst out. He raved about Paul's rejection of him, about his sister's and brother's reluctance to let him near their children, about Allan D.'s dying, about the lost career in theatre that had almost been his, about friends who seemed uncomfortable to be with him, about his loneliness, about the God he had forsaken.

170

Bruce went to the telephone and notified his office that he wouldn't be able to work that day. Then he called Natalie and told her about Jim's breakdown. Her advice was, "Let him cry it out. It's time he did."

Jim sobbed and wailed until nearly two in the afternoon. When he was done, exhausted, he stumbled out of the room and found Bruce calmly reading a book. Bruce looked up and smiled. Jim, loving him for his kindness, went back into the bedroom and fell into a deep sleep. When he wakened the next day, he left a note of thanks for Bruce, returned home, showered, and went out for a bite to eat. Sitting over his coffee he thought, *now what*?

Now I have to make some decisions and see what can be done.

Back in his apartment, he looked up the telephone number of the Toronto head office of the Jehovah's Witnesses. He dialled and asked for the address of the Kingdom Hall nearest to Sherbourne. He reasoned that a congregation so close to the gay ghetto of Toronto, as the area south-east of Yonge and Bloor is called, would have more understanding of gays than he might encounter elsewhere. His decision in Cambridge to leave the Jehovah's Witnesses for ever no longer seemed wise. God was his only hope.

He went to St. Michael's for more tests. Dr. Garvey said there were bits and pieces of things developing that she didn't like. She wanted him to have more chemotherapy and interferon. He began the familiar gut-wrenching routine of two weeks of chemotherapy, two weeks of interferon. His hair, which had begun to grow back, began to fall out again.

Mornings when he felt well enough he dressed in his gym clothes and did exercises. Nurses coming to take his temperature and blood pressure found him doing push-ups.

"Are you sure you're sick?" they would ask, amused.

"No," he replied, puffing, "I'm here for a vacation. Isn't this the right place? The St. Mike's Hilton?"

171

One afternoon he obtained a pass so that he could inspect his new apartment and get the keys from the previous tenant. One of his favourite nurses, Barbara, seemed to be in a hurry. She explained she was getting off work because she had to meet some guy who was taking her apartment.

They went their separate ways. Half an hour later Jim knocked on the door of a twentieth-floor apartment in a Sherbourne Street building, and it was opened by Barbara.

His most troubling problem was a lack of energy. In the brief periods between treatments and tests, he was too weak to take any pleasure in the lovely summer that was slipping away. He was sleeping eighteen hours a day. With an effort, he would get up around lunchtime to feed himself, then fall back into bed. He always made himself eat some dinner, though his appetite was poor.

His father was annoyed. When he called at one o'clock one afternoon and realized he had wakened Jim, he snapped, "Come on, you can't be sleeping at this time of the day!"

Jim replied wearily, "Dad, I'm really ill. The disease is taking its toll. I think I should let my body do what it wants."

Karl apologized, contrite.

Jim loved the apartment and furnished it to please his senses and sustain him in his fight to live. He had chairs covered with pink silk, and there was a crystal chandelier over the dining-room table. He had indulged himself in the purchase of ornaments and lamps, having in mind that he would be alone for long periods in the apartment and it would help if he had beautiful objects around him. To offset the silence of his solitude, he invested in a VCR and good stereo equipment.

Jim believes that his father's financial support indeed did contribute greatly to his phenomenal recovery that summer from the invasive cancer. He watches other people with AIDS struggling with unemployment insurance forms, worrying about rent and eviction, and too short of money to buy warm clothes for their wasting bodies or treat themselves to a movie or a meal out. He is convinced that the anxiety brought about by a rapid descent into poverty is a contributing cause of death.

In his case his father gave him rent money and a generous allowance, removing from his shoulders any economic concern. The stress Jim had to endure that summer of 1984 with the cyclical return of his cancer was not exacerbated by financial deprivation. His father's gift to him was leisure to read or sleep or listen to music or go out to a restaurant as he pleased, so that fighting the disease was Jim's only problem.

Later, when Jim was part of the founding group of the PWA (People with AIDS) Foundation, his goal was for the foundation to reproduce, as best it could, the freedom from anxiety that he had known. Visiting friends with AIDS in hospital, he found that they were obsessed with fears of losing their apartments because they had stopped being able to meet the rent. Reflecting on his own good fortune in having a father who could afford to support him, Jim formed a theory that worry helps the HIV to kill.

Jim called the elder in the Jehovah's Witness congregation nearest him and was invited to attend the next prayer meeting. He didn't look well, he knew, and it would be difficult to explain his long absence from meetings. He hoped people wouldn't be too curious. That was water under the bridge, and he needed to return to the faith.

When he parked at the Kingdom Hall, he found it difficult to summon the nerve to get out of the car. He gripped his hands together, squeezed his eyes shut, and said a prayer for strength. Then he arranged his remaining hair to cover the bald spots and went inside. The peace of it swept over him. Listening to the discussion of the meaning of a certain part of Scripture, he felt he had come home. In a world gone crazy, here at last was an island of tranquillity and wisdom.

At the end of the reading someone approached him. Jim explained he was meeting a certain brother, the elder with whom he had spoken on the telephone. He was told the man was away. Jim gave his name and phone number and said he would be back the next week. He left in a mood of euphoria, bubbling with happiness, and said a prayer of thanks to Jehovah. He felt safe. Even if he died of AIDS, God would help him come back to life. He was safe again in the arms of his God.

He returned the next week and was interviewed by the elders, as protocol requires for a Jehovah's Witness entering a new congregation. To his surprise and consternation, they had been doing some research and they knew all about him. They knew that he had left his congregation, that he was divorced, and that he was homosexual.

"What are your intentions?" they asked. "Why are you here?"

"I have some serious things to reconsider," he explained. "My health is poor. I have AIDS."

He was surprised that they seemed indifferent to his admission that he had AIDS. They were more concerned with something else, his "moral standing". They wanted to know if he was still seeing gay people.

"Well, yes," Jim replied. "They are my friends."

They drew back from him. "You haven't left off all your contacts with homosexuals?" they asked.

Jim explained that the people closest to him for many years, apart from his family and the Wexlers, were gay. He wanted to rethink and rebuild himself as a Jehovah's Witness, but he also needed the support of his friends, especially at this difficult time in his life.

The elders looked at one another. "That's fine, Jim," one of them said. "We'll see you next week. We'll need another meeting about this."

174

It wasn't easy to return the third time. Jim was embarrassed and dismayed by the severe tone of the first meeting. He understood that the elders had a duty to safeguard the cleanliness of their congregation, but he had hoped for more compassion for his desperate state of health.

He listened to the prayer meeting with great pleasure, loving the familiarity of it. Afterwards he was again invited to join the elders in a small library room.

"We've reached a decision," he was told sternly. "This congregation will disfellowship you for living as a homosexual. You have maintained your evil friendships and therefore we can't believe that you are repentant."

"It's very hard to be repentant about something that one is," he told them in a broken voice. "It's like asking a black man to repent his colour and get rid of his skin."

The elders ignored the interruption. One of them said, "You'll be allowed to attend the prayer meetings on Sundays and on Tuesday nights, but no one will speak to you. We're going to announce from the platform that you've been disfellowshipped. You mustn't make it hard on the brothers and sisters who don't understand the circumstances. You should not talk to them."

Jim felt such a chill that he couldn't speak.

"The only thing you can do," an elder said, observing the young man's silent anguish, "is continue to come to meetings. If you persevere, and if you cut all ties with homosexuals and stop being a homosexual, we may be able to reinstate you after a period of time."

They read the proclamation. It made no mention of homosexuality, to his relief, but said Brother Jim Zanuk was "guilty of conduct unbecoming a Christian".

Jim was flabbergasted. Though he knew how harsh his faith could be towards those who were judged to be wrong-doers, he had expected kindness in his situation. His excommunication, in view of the fact that he was dying, seemed inhumane. He sat in his car, crying so hard that he couldn't drive; when his sobbing stopped, he prayed for help.

The solution that came to him was that he should accept the ruling. God must be trying to give him a message that being gay was intolerable. He saw a possible trade-off: if he gave up his gay friends, God would forgive him for being gay and he would be accepted into Jehovah's kingdom.

It was worth it.

His next check-up with Dr. Garvey was depressing. The cancer was back again. This time the tumour on his lymph gland would have to be removed surgically. A six-inch incision in his neck gave the doctor access to a tumour the size of a lime. After that the three-month sequence of chemotherapy and interferon commenced again.

The interferon needles were excruciatingly painful. Though Jim refused to complain, he sensed the sympathy the nurses felt for him. The skin of his arms had become callused by the needles, sixty injections a month for the interferon alone.

It was beginning to be difficult to psych himself up each morning for the eight o'clock interferon needles, knowing that it would hurt to the limit of his tolerance and bring him to his knees with vomiting by nightfall. When he rose at seven to shower and dress, he had to lecture himself determinedly to be nonchalant. He was hanging on—just—but it was becoming too much to bear.

He was finding comfort in talking to himself on tape. What was happening to him seemed so extraordinary that he decided he needed a running chronicle so that when he died his family and friends could hear how he had felt.

One night before another admission to St. Michael's for interferon, he taped this comment:

"It's 12:30 in the morning, a Tuesday, and I'm going in for interferon again. I don't like the needles and it makes me pretty sick, but it's interesting. The last Tuesday I had to go for interferon my temperature skyrocketed and they had to put me in emergency to get me settled. It's happening again tonight and I don't understand why. My temperature is about 39.2. I would like to think it's psychological, but it makes no sense. I'm a big boy, and I don't think I am overly anxious. I'm not going to emergency this time, I'll just wait it out and see what occurs.

"I don't think it's a foolish move. Everything is pretty well ready. Everyone knows what I want. I haven't put it on paper but I would like the funeral home on Mount Pleasant to look after the arrangements. The director there is Wayne Hamilton, a good friend. I would appreciate him doing the work, if he would, that's needed. I think everyone knows I want to be cremated. I would like my father to make the decision as to what occurs with the ashes. My first pick would be to be buried on the land where my grandfather died, but I don't think you can just be buried where you like. My second pick would be here in Toronto in Mount Pleasant Cemetery, which I've always loved. Away from the traffic, if you could, but it's not going to make much difference.

"I'm sorry about all the grim details. I'm tired of getting sick and getting better and getting sick and getting better. I think I've made my peace with Jehovah and I hope everything is finalized there between myself and my God."

Some hours later, just before dawn, he picked up the tape machine again:

"I have unfinished letters for my father and my mother and the others, directed to those persons who have known me through my life. I have more letters to write and more things to say, but generally everything is done. I'm going to crawl into bed. I'll drink some fluids. I don't know if a Tylenol will help, but I'm going to take one. See what happens, take my temperature, and if it gets outrageously high it might be time to call the emergency.

"Well, I love you all. You know that." His voice on the tape is calm. "I'm doing the best I can. Please, be strong and firm, hold your own. Good night."

A long silence, filled by the raspy tone of the tape.

Then, "I just have to add one more thing. In the back of my 1984 date book is a list of persons I've been closely acquainted with. If someone could call them, the names with the strokes through them, Natalie will know who else needs to be called.

"One other thing." A dry chuckle. "How many PS's can I get on this tape? Revelation 21, verses 3 and 4, says that God's kingdom is a 'new Jerusalem'. John talks about it. He said, 'and the tent of God will be with mankind and He will reside with them, and they will be His people and He will wipe out every tear from their eyes and death would be no more. Neither would mourning nor outcry, nor pain be any more….' It's because of my looking forward to that kingdom that I can have a little strength to make these plans and say the things I do. Please do your utmost to be there too so when I wake up I can see you."

Next on the same tape, a bright, brash tone: "It's Thursday night. I didn't die after all, whatayaknow. Here's the future. I'm standing doing dishes and thinking. Jehovah's design in natural things around us tells us something about him."

9

Jim started to telephone people close to him, beginning with
Bert, his hairdresser and friend for five years. He invited Bert to
come over and they had a companionable beer together. When
he felt ready for it, Jim told Bert that he had been shut out from
the Jehovah's Witnesses and could be restored to grace only if
he stopped seeing anyone who was gay.

"This is what God wants," Jim explained sorrowfully. "From
this time forward, Bert, I don't want to see you any more. I'd
prefer it if you didn't call me, because it will be hard enough
without that."

Next was a friend from the *Man of La Mancha* cast, who came
with his lover. The man was devastated.

"I can't believe this, Jim," he said. "You need your friends
now. You need people around you."

"*No*," Jim told him with more emphasis than he intended.
"God is trying to help me and I have to do this if I want to be
saved. I won't be able to see you any more."

The hardest parting was with Bruce C., who had seen him
through the day when his nerves fell apart, the man Jim has loved
most in his life. Bruce had just been diagnosed with AIDS. It
started with a foot that was sore and swollen. When it became
so tender that he couldn't ride his bicycle to work, he consulted

a doctor. Tests were done and the doctor told him it was cancer; he had AIDS.

Bruce's illness made the parting all the more painful, but Bruce was so understanding that it broke Jim's heart. "I know how you feel about your religion," he said, "and I understand why you're doing this. You've taught me a great deal about this God of the Bible and your hope for resurrection. I just want you to know I'll always be here for you. If you change your mind, even if it's five years from now, I'll be here for you."

That cut ties with the last person in the gay community who had been close to him. Jim had succeeded in saying goodbye to everyone. He was more alone than he had ever been in his life. His friends had been dismissed, and the congregation where he went to pray twice a week, when his health permitted, turned from him as if he didn't exist.

He had a fat letter in what he could scarcely recognize as Allan D.'s handwriting. Allan had sent some pictures of himself, a list of vitamins he ordered Jim to take to keep healthy, and a poem by Edna St. Vincent Millay:

Love is not all: it is not meat nor drink
Nor slumber nor a roof against the rain;
Nor yet a floating spar to men that sink
And rise and sink and rise and sink again;
Love can not fill the thickened lung with breath,
Nor clean the blood, nor set the fractured bone;
Yet many a man is making friends with death
Even as I speak, for lack of love alone.
It well may be that in a difficult hour,
Pinned down by pain and moaning for release,
Or nagged by want past resolution's power,

I might be driven to sell your love for peace,
Or trade the memory of this night for food.
It well may be. I do not think I would.

Jim had a panic attack that he wasn't doing enough to help himself live. His father agreed to stake him to a trip to New York so he could investigate what was happening there to help people with AIDS. It didn't take a genius to know that AIDS was going to kill a lot of people before it was stopped. If it was sexually transmitted, a good many of the gay community probably were carrying the virus without knowing it. Jim only knew eight people in Toronto, including himself, who had AIDS, but he didn't doubt that there would be hundreds, given the sexual behaviour of the early eighties.

He called the Gay Men's Health Center and was taken aback by the businesslike approach.

"I'd like some information...," he began.

"Are you sick?" he was asked briskly.

"Yes, I...."

"Do you have KS or PCP?"

"What?" Jim had never heard the abbreviations before.

The man patiently explained that KS meant Kaposi's sarcoma and PCP was pneumocystis carinii pneumonia.

"Oh," said Jim. "I have KS."

"Okay, here's the number to call. Ask for Arnie."

Arnie worked out of an office with a security system that obliged Jim to buzz and identify himself before the door unlocked.

Arnie said, "I've been around AIDS for a year now. Do you want a dream world, or do you want to hear it as it is?"

Jim opted for reality.

Arnie reeled off the life expectancy. Jim was shocked that he was approaching the limit, sixteen months. Arnie said no one was really certain about transmission yet, but it was found in body fluids so Jim should be careful. And there was no cure and no prevention.

Jim drove back to Toronto. He had discovered that they didn't know any more in New York, where there were hundreds of people dying of AIDS, than they did in Toronto, where few had died of it.

During the long drive back, he used his tape machine to record his thoughts about God and dying. He could not imagine how anyone could face death without believing in God. From the beginning of the human species, people had worshipped something—stones, stars, *something*. People had to believe that there was help somewhere for them when they were in trouble. His faith in Jehovah, he was certain, would get him through AIDS.

He often ran into people who were unaware that he wanted to isolate himself from the gay community. One of them, a mutual friend named Harvey, called to say that Allan D. was dying. Jim went to the hospital. As he came along the corridor he saw Harvey sitting in a chair just inside the room. Allan was out of sight around the corner, but Jim heard him pull off an oxygen mask and call out, "Who's there?"

"It's Jim."

"Go away, Jim," Allan said roughly. "It's not good here."

Jim hesitated.

Allan's voice softened. "I'm sorry, Jim. I'm not feeling well. Could you come back another day?"

"Okay, of course. Kisses and hugs, Allan."

He was somewhat relieved. He wasn't sure he wanted to see Allan at the point of death. He would rather remember him laughing and tanned, having fun.

They talked on the telephone a few times, once when Allan was hallucinating from morphine injections.

On the morning of October 30, 1984, Harvey phoned Jim to say that Allan D., aged thirty-six, had died peacefully in his sleep at 2:30 that morning. Allan was one of the first people in Toronto to die of AIDS, and his distraught parents called funeral homes in vain. None would agree to embalm the body. Finally they found one that would accept the body only on condition of immediate cremation in the body bag.

That same day Allan's parents took his ashes home for burial in London. They didn't take the time to notify any of Allan's friends. When Jim heard of the death, the service was over and Allan D. already was buried.

Jim is haunted by what Harvey told him of Allan's last two days. Allan was using the bedpan the day before he died, Harvey said, and he passed pieces of what looked like meat. On analysis it was found to be part of his stomach and bowel. The pain had been excruciating. The cause of death, in fact, was the haemorrhage from that disintegration.

Jim was committing monologues to tape on a regular basis. The machine performed the function of friend, much as his teddy bear had done when he was a lonely child. He reflected on Allan's death: "Allan used to swim and work out, trying to keep his stomach muscles flat. He loved the look of a well-conditioned body. But Allan is dead now, so what good is the time he spent trying to keep in shape? How much better it would have been for him to spend the time pursuing a better way of life. Once we're in the grave a beautiful hulky body is not going to help us. A God in heaven we've tried to serve, to learn about, to make a relationship with, this God can help us."

"It's November 5, 1984, one in the morning, and tomorrow morning at St. Michael's Hospital I have another appointment to see Dr. Garvey. I know she's going to recommend that we do chemotherapy. I don't want to go through it all again. Oh God,

I'm scared. I don't know what I'm going to do if she recommends that we start the chemotherapy again."

"Tuesday, November 27, 1984. Thursday I'm going to visit Dad. I've been pondering all morning my being disfellowshipped, why it occurred and how I can straighten out this problem. I think it will be time at the end of this month to approach the brothers with a letter and start bothering — or, rather, going after — them to reinstate me. My one problem may be that they may not feel that there's been sufficient time gone by, but I don't have much time to work with. So I'm going to have to do the best I can with what I've got.

"I've missed the last three meetings. Quite ill with fever, and I've started to get my interferon shots. They may not think that's a good sign, but I'm going to bring out in a letter that my meeting attendance isn't going to get any better. If anything, it's going to get worse and I'll need help to get tapes of the meetings. I'll do my best and see where I end up."

"Saturday, December 8, 1984. Not using the tape for a few days. Heading out in my car, thinking about the latest *Awake!* talking about world government...the training of persons on this earth from both sides, one side being Jehovah and His angelic government and the other side being Satan and his demon angels. Interesting to see how the two sides work...."

"Sunday, December 9, 1984. Wonderful visit with Dad and Eleanor, my sister Kathryn and Derek and Mary Ellen. I mentioned my progress with AIDS occasionally to keep it in the conversation. I hope my family won't think I'm trying to go after sympathy because that's not what I what. What I'm trying to do, just so they will know later, is not to try for emotional sympathy but to keep the subject alive in everyone's mind so there

184

isn't any pretending that the disease doesn't exist. So when I do die it won't be as much of a shock.

"Father asked me to move back to Brantford. Whomever I associate with will be most hurt. If I did that with Natalie or Mom or anybody, I think my death would be harder on them. I've chosen to stay in Toronto and keep pretty separate so they won't get hurt. I know I sound so noble that it's sickening. I don't mean for it to be like that. I'm just trying to do what I think is right."

"Wednesday, December 12, 1984. I had my chemotherapy this morning and now I'm sitting down to do some studying. At the moment I'm studying a chapter about Jesus Christ and I'm researching Proverbs 8...."

"December 19, 1984, four in the afternoon, almost a week away from the last chemotherapy. Feeling not too bad. I'm having trouble with my tonsils and my tongue is swelling. Looked at by Dr. Garvey. I had a chance to talk to nurses about blood transfusions and what Jehovah's Witnesses feel about them. I just touched on a few things briefly, although the different nurses, particularly Gloria, shut their minds immediately. They didn't want to hear anything about religion and what the Bible says. They said that old line that the Bible is open to interpretation. They weren't giving the subject a fair chance at all."

There is a pause in the tape, then background music and Jim's voice, drowsy and dreamy. "It's approaching midnight, my favourite time. I've closed the apartment, everything quiet, a cup of tea, put on nice music, the place is clean, the work is done. I can just sit and enjoy my surroundings. It's my favourite time, when everything is organized and in its place."

While he was visiting his father, a rumour swept the gay community that Jim had died and, like Allan D., had been buried secretly. Jim heard that people grieved, and he was moved.

"I didn't realize how much I am loved," he confided on the tape. "I didn't appreciate that some of the people whose lives I've touched in the past years as a gay man in Toronto, I didn't appreciate that some of these men I met and had a good time with, how much they care for me. It touches me very deeply to see how we all affect each other. There is nothing so important as how we conduct ourselves with other people....

"My health is deteriorating in many little ways." The voice on the tape is slurred. "My tongue is coated with some kind of white skin. It's extremely swollen besides, and my tonsils and throat are badly infected with something. I have some kind of a lump growing in my left ear and my pinkeye comes and goes and it's not pleasant. It becomes quite painful, the pinkeye does. My skin is going through some kind of trauma. It's extremely itchy and is covered with little red marks. I don't know if they're Kaposi's sarcoma or not. My face is breaking out, and the skin in my beard is breaking out. Lots of little things....

"I've been keeping my life before me constantly these past few days. I have a beautiful home. My father is a wonderful supplier, he's helping a good deal. But I don't think this is the way I want to die, a taker. Accepting help from my father and the love of my friends without having attempted to really give back.

"In my overall plan I had in mind that I would accomplish my best work in my thirties and forties. That doesn't seem like it's going to happen. I'd love to have everything organized and be all set. When I'm not, I give up. My best bet is to make a decision on goals and try to achieve them in what time there is available to me. I desperately want to help the gay community."

Later: "I want to serve Jehovah and I deeply want what He wants. I understand that being part of the gay world, going to discos and so on, would not be correct. I won't be able to change

186

the course of Armageddon, but perhaps I can use whatever abilities I have to relieve some of the pain and suffering. I know the truth, I know what's happening as we near the end of this system of things, the end of religious and governmental arrangements. The world is starting to cave in and things are speeding up, as Jehovah said. The best thing is to side with Jehovah and make it through the years of terrible darkness...."

A new tape. "It's Sunday, December 22, 1984, and Mom will come from Gravenhurst for the day. I have become a new uncle. Allan and Mary have a baby girl."

"Three a.m., December 26, 1984. Mom and Daniel and I are back from Allan's home. We visited the family and saw the baby. I am touched by Allan and Mary, so happy and proud. The miracle of making a new person. Michelle Johanna. Named for Mom. The most wonderful gift he could give Mom. It's been a wonderful day.

"Mom and Daniel are sleeping in the bedroom so I'm talking low. I have a chance to think. It seems with all the difficulties, 1984 has brought the family closer together. We appreciate each other. I think we see the real necessity of family life. I hope my brother and sisters raise their children in a secure atmosphere, learning about Him and His truth. I have trust in Jehovah and that will get me through, give dignity to my life however long or short it may be. I am doing the best I can in Jehovah's sight."

The visit of his mother was not without strain. She and his sister Karen were uncomfortable about seeing Jim since he had been disfellowshipped. They knew that to be correct as Jehovah's Witnesses they should not have any contact with him, but under the circumstances of Jim's quickly dissolving health they found it difficult to be obedient. Their decision was causing them to be censured in their Collingwood congregation, and they had to deal with disapproving elders, but they reasoned that Jim was working hard to be reinstated and therefore deserved their support.

"January 4, 1985. New Year's Day with Nat and Bernie. Saw a movie, went out to eat, back to another movie. I'm trying to chronicle my thoughts so I can be one of Jehovah's Witnesses and teach other persons coming behind me. I may not be able to do it in person very long because of my illness. I may soon pass away, but I hope anyone listening to these tapes can benefit from what I have seen and what I am experiencing. I am trying to redirect my life as best I can so I may have a hope for resurrection in the future. I continue to make mistakes but for the most part my conscience is as clear as it has ever been."

Jim spent hours in prayer, passionately repenting his sins and asking for forgiveness. He could make no sense of the fundamental contradiction that the God who had made him, and made him a gay person, disapproved of homosexuality. How could that be? His homosexuality was natural in him; it was not something he had sought or wanted. He had tried very hard to change it, to submerge it, but it was something he could not control. That being so, how could a God of love punish one of His creations for what that person is naturally?

He said on the tape: "I can't get that one together. It bothers me. The elders are trying to make me do something unnatural when they ask me to stop being homosexual. Will I have to lie about it for the rest of my life? If I am unable to stop all homosexual contact as they are trying to make me do, will I then be a liar to the congregation, and would that be better than telling the truth? Is it better to be a liar than to be gay?"

"Friday, January 18, 1985. I'm finding that as things hurt me, I'm just withdrawing. I hope I don't become bitter, though I can see that I am. I'm learning to turn life off. I'm learning not to be sensitive." His voice is broken and tearful. "I don't want anything to affect me any more, not a death, not a loss, not money. I don't want anything to get to me any more.

"Today a tragedy hit me. I was on a fast for a couple of days and I was doing pretty good, but I was very lonely. I was here by myself. Sometimes I think I'll go mad. It's very difficult to be here by myself. Sometimes I think it is worse than the prospect of death. I'd prefer to have died than to not be getting well. I'm struggling hard to stay alive, but without the proper things to be happy, why try? The major tragedy today is that I lost my ring. All my life I wanted somebody to give me a ring. Last year Nat and the family gave me a beautiful seal ring. Today I lost it. I just noticed it wasn't on my hand. I'm losing weight because of the disease and somewhere it slipped off.

"I got angry and drove in the car like a maniac, and then I shut it off. It was no longer important. I need to shut everything off.... I'm not glad I'm dying but I wish it could come quicker. Either not to be dying and be totally healthy or to die quickly.

"Oh, Cassius called. Roger F. died on Wednesday."

"Sunday, January 20, 1985. Midnight, my favourite time to sit and listen to beautiful music and evaluate. To do it comfortably my home has to be clean, spotless, with nothing to do. A lot has happened to me recently. I think I hit rock bottom emotionally. It's as much as I can take, as much of a front as I can manage for my friends and family. I've been alone a good deal and the loneliness just closes in on me. Sometimes I think that I will go crazy. A couple of days ago I was in my car driving and I couldn't stand to think of coming home because there is nothing to do here. I am so lonely and depressed. I really want everything to be finished, to stop. I don't know which way to turn.

"It's time for all of us to progress. Tomorrow morning I'm going to start preparing my voice again, doing what I do best. I'm a performer, I'm an actor. I'm good at it. If I'm able to get out of this mess with this AIDS business, I want to be a tuned actor and ready to work.

"Last week or so I haven't been happy with my stand on Jehovah God. I haven't been studying, and that's one way to sever relationships. I'm going to put my letter in for reinstatement with the congregation. It's time to progress. It's time to stop wasting time. It's time to tune myself as an actor, as a moral person in good standing with Jehovah God.

"The money from my father makes me a nothing. It makes my apartment, lovely as it is, not something I provide for myself, not something I was able to do....

"I don't know if I am going mad. I might be...."

A few minutes later he observed casually, "I am developing pneumocystis carinii pneumonia. I think I'm in my second day. If I knew for sure that the AIDS eventually would kill me, I would let the PCP accomplish that right now. It usually kills in eight days, so I figure I have about another six days to live. I'm so tired of watching my life disintegrate that perhaps it is a kindness to myself if I let myself die this week. I don't know that I shall do that, but I guess I'm mulling it over in my mind.... The hospital will have to be notified about the pneumonia. Tomorrow I start my speech lessons."

He had a gift from Bruce C., a tiny white kitten, with the explanation that Bruce didn't like to think of Jim's being so alone. Jim named the cat Alexander the Great. He'd been thinking about Alexander the Great of late, a young man who in his time conquered the known universe.

On January 30, 1985, Jim said on the tape: "Such a responsibility that goes with having a pet. Not such a necessity to run out of the apartment any more because now there is life here. I am progressing in building up my mental state."

He added, "The hospital thinks I may be developing PCP. I handed in my request for reinstatement to the congregation last Wednesday evening. The brothers didn't make any mention of it Sunday. I hope they're considering it."

When he couldn't stand his own company any more, he would drive to Gravenhurst to see his mother and his half-brother, Daniel, always dropping in on his sister Karen as well. He adored her children, Shannon and little Benjamin. He was particularly touched by the little boy, with his frail body and his small face still misshapen from the congenital defects that surgery slowly was remedying.

His letter asking to be reinstated was ignored. Jim decided he would have to try harder. He would have to stop seeing all worldly people, which meant the Wexlers. A devout Jehovah's Witness could not associate with such people.

Natalie had watched Jim's retreat from the gay community with dismay. She often talked to his discarded friends, assuring them that Jim had been through similar periods when he was frenzied and obsessed with his religion, and had always emerged. He would be out of touch for a while, she said, but soon he would need his friends. They had only to be patient. Meanwhile, she was the information pipeline and provided regular updates on the state of Jim's wavering health, particularly to Bruce, who called almost daily.

When Jim asked Natalie for a meeting on a Saturday afternoon in January 1985, she had no inkling what he intended. They went for a lazy drive in the country, as they often did. The mood between them was peaceful and relaxed, but Natalie, always sensitive to his moods, sensed that Jim was brooding. She put his silences down to depression from the disease.

Darkness was falling when they returned to the city, hungry for a steak at House of Chan.

191

"Nat," he said, when they had been served, "I'm in trouble. I need your help."

She gave him a sharp look, suddenly reading him correctly.

"I think I know what's coming, but I can't believe it," she said.

He drew a deep breath. "You've guessed it. I must stop seeing you. We must have no further contact."

Her face registered shock. "Oh, Jim," she wailed, "you've become a fanatic."

"I know what I must do," he told her. "This is what God is asking of me, and I must do it."

"You're cutting yourself off just when you need your friends most," she protested. "You're making a terrible mistake."

He would not be moved, even by her tears.

"Will you be okay?" she asked.

"We love each other very much, we'll always love each other, but we can't see one another ever again," he said with finality in his voice.

He went home and thought, "Now I have nobody. I can't talk to Jehovah's Witnesses because I'm dead as far as they are concerned, and I can't talk to my friends because I've told them all to go away, so what have I got here? I've got my close family members, who don't live in the city, and that's it."

In February he was in hospital. "High atop Toronto in the St. Michael's Regency," he said cheerfully to his tape machine. "We're going to start doing retesting this week to see if the cancer is totally gone or not. Hopefully, it is. The brothers haven't spoken to me yet about what they intend to do about my letter. I'm a little worried that the three brothers in the committee that disfellowshipped me have a poor impression...."

"February 6, 1985." Jim's voice is hoarse and slow. "It's been one incredible week. I've been in the hospital undergoing tests. We were hoping the cancer had gone, but it's spreading and they're finding more of it. It's continuing to grow despite the chemotherapy. I've had all sorts of thoughts this week, up and down. I thought a great deal about how life is." He is crying. "So much has happened. It's really difficult to put it into words." A chuckle. "What can I say, you really had to be there.... I'm so happy about my belief in the Jehovah God and the resurrection. It's a wonderful thing, and I hope that other persons who don't know of that hope yet will come into the truth and gain some strength....

"Tomorrow I have a major test. They're going to put a tube down my throat and into my lungs. I'm not too crazy about that, but I'll be asleep. It seems to me that most of the fellows who have had PCP had this done to them, so I'll just be another one of those guys...."

He begins to pray. "I am sorry for the mistakes of my body, which is dying. It was such a beautiful gift and now I'm going to die. It hurts me to see the poor body struggle.... God, please do not turn your face away from me.

"March 17, 1985." His voice is brisk. "A lot has happened since I last recorded my thoughts. I have been doing a lot of thinking about my position here in the time that I have left.... I have many anchors to hold me down in the hurricane, which many of the men in my situation do not."

In the deep winter months of that period, he often thought he was losing his mind. Whenever he was well enough, he went to movies alone, walked the streets alone, ate alone in restaurants. During his periods in hospital for surgery, tests, or chemotherapy, no one came to see him except his family. Nurses found it a curious contrast to Jim's first few times in hospital when his room was filled with people and flowers. He read a lot, prayed even more, and slept.

He went to congregational meetings nervously, bracing himself to endure the icy silent treatment that was his punishment. He always dressed carefully and made sure his hair was combed and his clothing spotless. Before getting out of the car, he bowed his head and prayed for forgiveness and for strength.

He always took a chair at the back of the room, took his Bible out of his briefcase, and reverently followed the proceedings. Just before the meeting ended, he would put away the chair and leave early, avoiding the embarrassment of being ignored.

Before every lonely meal, he bowed his head and prayed. God, in fact, became his constant companion.

He talked to Jehovah on his tape machine. Sleepless and wretched, he sat alone on the floor of his apartment in the darkness of midnight and poured his heart into a cassette so that after his death people would find an account of his faith:

"Churches have driven people to demon worship. It's cruel to teach people that when they die they aren't really dead, that they're somewhere else. Parents are left to wonder if their child is burning in hell or an angel in heaven."

On another occasion: "Jehovah's Witnesses have the only right answer. People are tossed around with no one to give them proper comfort, know for certainty that the Bible is the truth. Anyone with intelligence and a non-prejudicial heart would have to agree with that. What Jesus said in the Bible is so true. Churches are magnificent, but they have given people nothing to go on, nothing to help. White-washed graves, they are. If I don't make it all the way to Armageddon, to where Jehovah's system does come in, in the last year or so I've got of life there must be something I could do to help in the so-called gay community. Not in a sexual way, or get involved in socializing, but anyone who has seen the lifestyle—that's what's wrong. A thinking person could never condone the lifestyle and what it has done. Not just from the disease. There has never been happiness in the gay community. Bruce said to me he's always known the promiscuous gay lifestyle is wrong, that it doesn't work."

He continued to wrestle with a basic contradiction: his religious teaching said that all homosexuals are evil, but his own experience with his gay friends could not permit him to accept that they were evil people. "People are kind and sensitive, generally," he mused. "There is real beauty in these fellows and women. I'd like to help in some way. Healthy beautiful people of all ages are being destroyed....

"The Bible talked about it, prophesied it, but also said, keep your heads up, hold yourself erect, deliverance is near. That's the truth. Thousands and thousands of people will be killed. I don't believe medical science can help. It couldn't after the First World War in the flu epidemic. Organized religions have nothing in them that people can turn to. Only Jehovah's organization...."

Later: "Being disfellowshipped stopped me in my tracks. It made me think and study and really take a look. I'm sure the apostle Paul was very sorry when Jesus stopped him in his tracks by making him blind for a few days. He never would have changed when he got his sight back if he didn't think the truth. I'm in the same position. I'm glad I'm finally able to acknowledge what my life is really about, not to live a farcical life any more.

The voice on the tape is often weak, and the long rambling discourses about God are broken frequently by spells of convulsive coughing. At one point, however, when his tongue was covered with a white fungus infection, his voice is thick as he says, "I've come to the decision that I have to use my abilities to help other persons with AIDS. I didn't come to that resolve when I was diagnosed with AIDS. I just wanted to roll over and die. But not only you, Bruce, but also other people who need help. I'm going to try.

"I think the best way to go is to get involved with the AIDS Committee of Toronto that's just starting. I have to keep up my studies in Jehovah's Witnesses and my preaching activity, but more than anything I want to do what's right, particularly in Jehovah's eyes, because that's where the greatest blessings will come."

195

Jim thought about it carefully and decided that helping other people sick with AIDS was not consorting with the gay community, because he would take the opportunity to bring them the teachings of Jehovah. With that in mind he went to the cluttered space above a fast-food outlet that was the office of a new organization, the AIDS Committee of Toronto (ACT). Theresa Dobko, a sensible and compassionate ACT counsellor, told him that an AIDS support group made up entirely of people with AIDS was about to begin meeting every Tuesday.

She said a volunteer facilitator had come forward, Dr. John K., and he would help the men sort out the emotional problems associated with their disease.

On the next Tuesday Jim went nervously to see what it was like to be in a room full of people with AIDS. Would he fit in? Eight other men had gathered. To his dismay, Larry W. was there. Once he and Larry had had a brief sexual fling and they remained fond of one another. He hadn't heard that Larry had AIDS. There was someone who looked Filipino, Francis, whose face was puffy with sores. And Raleigh H., a middle-aged man with a look of importance. Someone named Norman, another named Mel, a waiter, Irv C., whom Jim knew slightly, and Michael T. and Lee W.

All of them appeared healthy. In fact, with his pallor, scrawny body, and almost-bald head, Jim looked by far the sickest in the room.

In late March he said on the tape, "I've become involved in a support system, a group of men who meet on Tuesday nights who all have AIDS or AIDS-related problems. We discuss death and the future and what we feel and what we think. Tonight, a Friday night, I have just finished an afternoon and evening in a drop-in centre where these men and their friends come by and informally discuss their feelings. Most of them are holding out quite well. One of them is such a gentle, easy-going, happy person, just getting into life. The disease is spreading across his face. His face is going through turmoil with the cancer, and now he has shingles...."

He wept a lot. After a while, to relieve the emptiness, he set his teddy bear in the living-room and talked to its kind face. He hadn't done that for years.

Later: "In the company of other men I find a comfort that I don't find with women. I married and tried to find that, but couldn't. I have done my best to understand these feelings.... The Bible condemns the carrying on of homosexual activity. I understand that. Rather than try further to sweep my emotions under the carpet, I will deal with that as I believe Jehovah expects. Is a promiscuous gay lifestyle correct? Of course not, but the feelings still exist and will exist always....

"I adore my father, and if he should listen to these tapes, Daddy I can't tell you how much your support has meant.... Thank you for being my father....

"Little Bruce continues to ignore the fact that he has AIDS, and I'm worried that somewhere along the line he's going to have a major breakdown. He's one of the kindest men I've ever met in my life and I hope that Jehovah will protect him and help him get through....

"My brother is remarkable in the way he's dealing with his new family. I'm proud of him and what he's doing. Allan, if you hear this, I'm real proud of you, big brother. Set a good example for Daniel.... If I should take a quick dive, I want you all to know I love you dearly and I'll see you in the resurrection....

"I was thinking aloud as I was sitting in the hot bathtub that I'm almost finished. I've got my apartment almost completed, which was my physical project to keep me happy and interested. I have done some paintings, which I love. I have made out my will. I have tried to show the men in my support group that with the proper mental attitude the body will make it a lot further. It may not make it live for ever, but it will go a lot further. I'm doing my best to teach everyone about Jehovah and to help them see the reasonableness of Jehovah's system. So if and when I die, almost everything is accomplished. I'm content. I'm happy…. I have loved…loved every minute of my life…. There's so much to accomplish and enjoy. I will continue in my teaching work and try to understand my love for Jehovah. I certainly hope that I'm resurrected…."

"April 5. Natalie doesn't see the need for Jehovah at the moment…. Perhaps she will, I hope she will. I've tried to teach her…. Next week I'll be going back to hospital for a retake. The cancer seems to be on the move. We'll deal with things as we deal with them."

"It's Monday morning, April 15, and I've been in hospital for three days…. The tests are slow in coming…. I'm feeling pretty good. If we should have to restart the chemotherapy, fine. Things are pretty well looked after…."

"Sunday night, April 21, 1985. I had a scope done of my stomach on Friday and there is no cancer in my stomach. They are very pleased with that. I have a scope tomorrow to take a look at the lower bowel system and then I have a few others coming up. So this week should determine exactly what's going to happen…."

An undated fragment, with Jim's voice slow and listless: "I had a rough week, actually. I'm tired of being alone, of having no romantic interest. I love my friends, they've been very kind. And my family. But no one really….I'm not at the centre of anyone's attention. No one really wants to know where I am all the time, and if I'm always happy, and if I need sex, and have I eaten well…."

Whenever Jim was out of hospital he would attend the Tuesday night support group, though the psychiatrist's way of running the group irritated him. John K.'s style was to prod each man to reveal his deepest pain. Tears were cathartic and people shouldn't bottle up their feelings. Jim disapproved. His firm belief in self-control was at odds with the views of the psychiatrist. He hated seeing men pushed to their limits. An edge of irritation was creeping into his relationship with the facilitator.

On the tape Jim complained: "The psychiatrist who sits in on these meetings, who I've always felt should not sit in but he does, has his own personality problems. He wants the fellows in the group to look to him for support. What that would do is undermine the fellows' ability to think for themselves, to reason that they have strength themselves."

Still, the group had its own synergy that worked for the participants. The beef sessions, in particular, did them all a lot of good. One man described the unfeeling way he was given the news of his diagnosis. When he called for the result of his blood test, his doctor gave him the news over the telephone. He said in an irritated tone, "You have AIDS," and curtly refused to answer questions, saying he was rushed for time.

Another had a worse experience. A technician told him the diagnosis, handed him his coat, and ordered him to leave.

Lee W., very embarrassed, talked about his humiliating incontinence. His bowel seemed to be dissolving, he said. Touched by the confession and the man's misery, the others offered what comfort they could. They all had experienced acute diarrhoea, they told Lee. It probably wouldn't last.

The room was an oasis of understanding. Each had been isolated by the diagnosis of AIDS. Poorly informed, not always understanding what their symptoms meant and what their treatment was supposed to accomplish, and in the dark about the means of transmission, they clung together and swapped what bits of information each could acquire. The group was a great place to air grievances against the medical establishment or uncaring families and friends. The group was a sympathetic audience to which they could voice their fears of the terrible fungus pneumonia they all dreaded, their hatred of the disfiguring purple blotches on their skin, their dilemma about celibacy. Was *any* sex safe for their partners?

They broke up reluctantly, often going down the street to the Golden Griddle Pancake House to continue the discussion over coffee. Lingering on the busy sidewalk, they exchanged phone numbers and arranged to meet for lunch.

The first AIDS support group expanded to a core of about ten regulars with the addition of Scott M., a blond youth who drove to Toronto every Tuesday night from Buffalo, and Bob F., a bisexual man with a wife and four teenage sons. They became a family, as people do in the face of shared disaster. Though a disparate group in many ways, the tragedy they had in common dissolved differences and they became very dear to one another. Raleigh pulled them together for splendid dinner parties in his huge home near Toronto's High Park.

A topic that obsessed them all was the international search for a cure for AIDS. They kept abreast of experimental treatments being tested in Paris, Mexico, and New York, griping that the Canadian government was showing no interest. They argued the merits of vitamin therapy and shared complaints about insensitive health professionals. Sometimes they talked of their own doom and how they feared death.

The look of their disintegrating bodies wrung their hearts. One said sadly, "We aren't going to die pretty."

Lee W.'s bowel did not improve. He had an open sore on the inside of his rectum that gradually ate through the wall of his bowel and gave him excruciating pain when he had an attack of diarrhoea. His doctors tried everything they could devise to heal the wound but it defied all attempts. Unhappily, his diarrhoea was almost continuous and his suffering great.

His will to live, however, was extraordinary, and he lasted month after month, coming faithfully to the group whenever he was not in hospital. He brought special protective pillows on which to sit.

Jim made a joke of it, "Lee, I always knew your butt would get you in trouble."

"Monday night, almost midnight, here I am alone again, playing my guitar and singing my love songs to myself.... I miss being in love. Worse than anything, I miss the ability to meet people and like people. Unless a cure is found for this disease I have, I can't come close to anyone romantically. I find that very hard to deal with.... When does it stop? When can I have some peace?.... You who have been listening to all these tapes, do you have an answer for me?"

Francis from the Philippines had a cancer on his face that was rapidly eating away the entire left side. The group wondered why his doctor didn't use chemotherapy but hesitated to undermine Francis's confidence in his treatment. Francis was devoted to Jim. Whenever Jim was in hospital, Francis would show up with beautiful flowers. Jim was horrified to watch the cancer spread until eventually Francis no longer could see out of his left eye. But he was cheerful about it. He told Jim that his doctor was trying radiation and thought it was working.

Francis told the group about his encounter with a cab driver who looked at his corroded face and said, "Buddy, were you in a fight?"

Francis replied, "I'm in a fight all right. I'm in a fight with cancer."

Jim and Larry W. went to lunch one day at Pickups, a little café and deli on Jarvis Street. Jim arrived first and took a table by the window. When Larry got there he asked to move to the back. He was losing his sight, he said, and the light hurt his eyes. They laughed a lot that day about "getting out of this mess, AIDS".

Jim went to visit a friend, John W., a physician with AIDS whose lungs were filling with the fungus growth of the PCP. Jim found a big expensive get-well card with a good joke and John read it appreciatively. Then he kissed it and handed the card back to Jim.

"I won't last much longer," he explained. "Give someone else a laugh."

Jim didn't know what to say. He squeezed John's big toe through the blanket, gave it an affectionate wiggle, and left. John died two weeks later. People said his lungs filled up so slowly that he was gasping for breath for two hours before he died. His friends held him down because he was thrashing around the bed as he slowly suffocated. Jim didn't feel like going to the funeral.

Jim was finding himself increasingly at odds with the psychiatrist who was acting as facilitator in the support group. To have the men crying and blowing up at one another was all very fine for John, Jim thought, but it was leaving them all ragged and exhausted at the end of the evening. He wanted to see a positive emphasis so that the men would leave the group feeling stronger instead of shattered.

The disapproval each felt of the other grew into active dislike. One evening John took Jim aside as the meeting was breaking up. He ordered him to drop out of the group.

"You're a disruptive influence," he told Jim. "You've been staging a power struggle and I won't stand for it. It's bad for the group."

The group disagreed.

"If anyone is going to go," they assured Jim, "it will be John."

The group met that week in Jim's apartment over muffins and coffee and agreed to ask ACT for a new facilitator. They admired the half-finished painting Jim had on a easel and Jim invited each of them to paint something on the canvas.

Later, when all the men were dead, Jim gave the painting to ACT.

Also undated on the tape: "Today, earlier today, I went down to the operating room for an examination of the opening in my penis. The pain was excruciating and the staff was hard on me. I can't remember ever having been in as much pain in my entire life. When it was over I found that one of the St. Mike's doctors had just died after catching a hepatitis-B infection from a patient he was operating on. So when I went down and had to be worked on, and of course there was a bit of blood and I have this diagnosis of AIDS, I was treated pretty rough. I couldn't understand why, and then I learned what had happened."

The support group agonized over Bob F.'s situation. He was the bisexual who lived with his wife and four sons. His family was unaware of his double life as a gay man. He hadn't found a way of telling them that he had AIDS. His explanation to his wife was that he had cancer. He told the group he didn't know which to tell her first, that he was bisexual or that he was dying. And what would his sons think of him?

The group advised him to be honest—he needed his family's support. They discussed with him exactly how he would break the news. When Bob reported back, he said that his family had accepted it very well.

Soon after, Bob stopped coming to the group's meetings. The men worried as the absence stretched into weeks. They decided that Jim, the most diplomatic among them, should call to see if Bob was all right.

A boy answered the phone. Jim identified himself as a friend. He wasn't sure how much the boy knew but he gave his name and asked to speak to Bob. The boy answered that his father had died. How had Jim known him?

Jim wasn't sure how much the boy knew so he answered evasively, "I used to see him Tuesday nights." The boy's tone warmed. His father had appreciated the support group very much, he said. The family would want Jim to relay its gratitude.

Norman was growing sick. He announced one Monday night that he had heard of a miracle cure in Montreal and was leaving to try it. He promised to keep everyone informed but no one heard from him. Then Jim had a phone call in the middle of the night. Norm had died in Montreal.

"Good afternoon. It is the evening of May 9 and I have just checked into room 602.... We're going to do a biopsy tomorrow and we'll see what happens. So far the tests are coming back negative, but I have more spots growing on my shoulders and back, which means the cancer is growing again...."

"Well, you're going to find this interesting. It is July 3, 1985. I am once again in St. Michael's Hospital. The biopsy took several weeks to heal and it is indeed cancer. They've started chemotherapy again [heavy coughing].... It was my birthday on June 24 and I went out and danced and I relaxed and I spent the entire week getting plastered, quite plastered. And I didn't care about my health. And I did it again the next weekend. I'm just tired now as we go into the second year of all this. I now realize that there may be no end in sight, other than death, and I think I'm tired of waiting now. I think the emotional strain is starting to get beyond me.... After my second binge I got quite ill. My temperature skyrocketed and I have shingles breaking out on me. They started a few weeks ago, so I'm watching my skin rot. I may have pneumocystis carinii pneumonia again. I don't know how long a person can take, watching himself slowly disintegrate, before enough is enough. Those two binges I had, those two weekends, I actually hoped that they might kill me....

"I'm going to talk to one of the psychologists at St. Mike's and find out what other patients do when they come to the end of their rope. I'm just tired of this....

"In the last few weeks two people in the support group have died, so we're down to six, though we have added a bunch of new people. Larry doesn't look very well and some of the other guys are quite ill. We're all quite ill....

"I'm just tired of the mental strain. Usually when I come into hospital I make sure that I have everything in order and everything's packed, and I come in with guitar and books and games and papers and whatnot to keep my mind occupied. But this time I just walked in with a duffel bag. I'm so tired of that, the futility. This time I was brought in in a wheelchair and pushed around. I didn't care which room I got. I just was sick and lay in bed. That was good in a way. It let me relinquish some of the control I always maintain in my life. I usually try to keep totally in control of any situation I'm in....

"Last night I was so sick I was delirious and I was hoping I would die. I was hoping it was all over, I could stop the nonsense and just relax, just drift away, *but* wouldn't you know, these tough Ukrainians, I just bounced right back. This morning my temperature broke and I came back to earth."

10

The new facilitator in the AIDS support group was an extraordinary woman, Linda Boyd, an American who had been counselling people with AIDS and their families on a volunteer basis for the AIDS Committee of Toronto. Her background included counselling in an intensive care unit of a hospital in Atlanta, Georgia. She had come to Canada during the tumultuous years of the Vietnam War and got employment as a counsellor for people with problems of sexual dysfunction and sexual identity. After that she worked with severely disabled adolescents in the Bloorview Children's Hospital.

Linda Boyd was thirty-six when she came to the group, a big woman who dressed in an amazing wardrobe of vivid colours with eye make-up and long glossy fingernails to match. She wore rings on every finger and smashing earrings. Her hair usually was ash-blonde, but on a whim she would dye it bright pink or add a streak of sapphire blue. Smart and funny and kind and perceptive, she was just what the PWAs needed.

She began each session by asking the men to join hands, close their eyes, and say briefly how they were feeling.

"I'm very tired tonight," one man said.

"I'm depressed and worried," said the next.

"I'm very tired *and* depressed and worried," said the third with an inflection that invited laughter.

The mood of the group eased with the arrival of Linda Boyd and a co-facilitator, a quiet, friendly man, Roddie McFadzean, with a calm, reassuring presence. Jim had known Roddie before, but Linda was someone new to him. He loved her style, and then he loved her. He says that she was the best friend that people with AIDS ever had.

"She gave us emotional support and wasn't afraid to be our friend out of fear that we would die on her," Jim explains. "That begins to happen. After a little while, I'll tell yah, you get a little scared of who you make friends with."

The tape: "It's the first day of August 1985, and boy, do I need to talk. Made it this far and I didn't expect I would. I'm at St. Michael's Hospital, back with some kind of gastro problem. I'm connected with IV now. I'm baffled, I'm confused. I'm a fighter and I'll go down fighting, but I'm losing hope. I'm frustrated, I'm tired of all this, I'm tired of this hospital business, I'm tired of being sick, I'm tired of the elders teaching me how to love God and how to hate my fellow man. I'm sick of the way people treat each other. I have planned suicide several times, but I don't think that's the answer. I have an obligation to my friends to fight to my last breath.

"It makes no sense to me to keep poisoning me and hurting me and stabbing me and sticking me with needles. Putting me in hospital, making me eat rotten food, watching myself deteriorate, watching my hair fall out, my skin rot, and disease crop up all over my body....

"Perhaps it would have been better to let me die last year.... When death comes it will be like an old friend...."

Jim's voice is brighter on the next tape: "It's August. First of all, I've thought it over. Better to try than die. How do you like that one? I talked to my father and Natalie. Both agree there is not much hope here. If we're going to stop this disease before I get too ill it's time to go to Paris. I'm preparing names and contact points. I hope I can be a forerunner for my friends here. Larry's in the intensive care unit. He's extremely ill and on the verge of death. He's on a respirator...."

Jim talked to Dr. Garvey about the proposed expedition to Paris. His father was willing to finance it, he told her. What did she think?

She replied thoughtfully. "If you want to try some other treatment in Paris, or wherever, that's fine with me, Jim," she said. "I'll make your test results available so there will be no trouble about having the work done again. But, Jim, we're all connected on this one. This is a serious disease and within days of any of us finding something that works, anywhere on the planet, we all know about it. I'm worried about the emotional cost to you if you go looking for something, and it doesn't help."

Jim decided against it, though everyone who could afford it at that time was rushing to Paris. He knew one man, Steve B., son of a politician in the Atlantic provinces, who had moved to Paris for the treatments. They did him no good and the loneliness, he reported, was unbearable.

The next death in the group was a newcomer they called "Little Norman". Then Francis died, half his face eaten with cancer.

Larry's health worsened. Jim went to visit him in a hospital palliative care unit. Larry's lover, Peter, intercepted Jim. He said Larry wanted to see no one except his sisters and Peter. A few days later, Linda Boyd called to say that Larry had died.

On the tape Jim said: "Well, it's Monday, August 12, and later today I'll be going to Larry's funeral. I went to Chuck's on Saturday, and now Larry's. I'm glad that it's over for him. I wish it was over for me. Just not to have to worry about the needles and things.... I hope that Jehovah forgives me for the mistakes

I've made. It's been pretty rough so far. I'm pretty tired. Good night, Larry. Sleep tight...."

The day of Larry's funeral was cool for August. The remnants of the support group attended together, thin, pale men in heavy sweaters. The burial was in Mount Pleasant Cemetery. Larry's parents, plainly dressed people, stood clinging to each other as the coffin was lowered into the ground. Jim was seized by grief for Larry and for himself. Would he be in a coffin next? Would that be his parents weeping by a hole in the ground?

The third series of chemotherapy was begun. Dr. Garvey said there was more cancer. It wasn't too serious, she assured Jim, but he would need more chemotherapy and interferon.

He submitted with a sick heart. His arms were so callused from the interferon needles that it took considerable strength for the nurse to puncture through the thickened skin. The pain was becoming unbearable.

On the fourth day of the interferon, as the nurse was laying out the customary six syringes, he was embarrassed to find tears in his eyes.

"Rosie, I'm sorry," he said. "I'm really sorry, but I can't go through this any more. I can't."

She seemed relieved. She reported to Dr. Garvey, "Jim can't take any more."

Dr. Garvey considered. "Well," she decided, "that's not too serious. The interferon has done all the good it can, and I think it has helped a lot. We'll have to see how he goes with chemotherapy alone."

Jim's voice on the tape is slurred. He is drunk. "Well, well, well, it's August 22. You still listening to these fucking tapes? You've got a lot more resilience than I've got. Tonight was very interesting. I tried to kill myself. Smashed up the car. Ran it into a pole. Well, I'm still here as you can tell. The car has a few dints in it, but it still runs. I did 180 KPM all the way home from Huntsville to Toronto. I was hoping one of the tires would blow, the car would flip, grow into a huge fireball and throw me and I'd be dead. Well, it didn't happen....

"I stopped this goddamn therapy, which is all poison and no treatment. I was sick of it. I'm tired of it. It's no therapy at all. It would have been kinder to let me die of the cancer when I was full of it last year.... I don't know what to tell you except that the depressions get longer and more scary. I've become more bold about trying to kill myself....

"I'm the black sheep. How nice it would be to be straight, to grow up nice and straight like my brother and have a wife and children. But I wasn't born that way, and I'm tired of being persecuted because I was born. I'm tired of being pushed and taunted and given shots in the newspapers and media because my sexuality is different from someone else's. How easy it would have been to be straight. To take a wife, a woman. Everyone would be happy because the boy has taken a bitch to fuck instead of a man to fuck. It is a sickie world...."

One night in late summer 1985 he decided he could not stand another meal eaten alone. He cooked for two and set his dining-room table with two places—linen placemats, sterling silver, crystal glasses, his fine china plates. He lit the candles and, when the meal was ready to serve, he placed his childhood teddy bear in one chair and sat in the other. He ate slowly, making light conversation in a cheerful voice to the silent bear.

Halfway through the meal he began to cry. *I am going crazy*, he thought to himself. I am a grown man, a dying man, eating alone and talking to a teddy bear. What have I done that is so wrong that I deserve this? I'm not going to die of AIDS, I'm going to die of loneliness. He had never hurt anyone, he had tried to do his best all his life, and he was ending up a madman talking to a teddy bear.

He felt strange. Nothing in the room looked familiar. He went to his balcony and stood looking at the ground, twenty floors below. Without any plan, his despair so deep his thoughts were formless, he climbed on the railing and stood there, one hand braced on the wall beside him.

I am going to jump, he thought. *I can't take any more*. His muscles tensed and he prepared to push off.

It was midnight and the street was quiet. He looked up at the night sky. "God, is this what you want me to do? Do you, the God of love, want me to jump off this balcony?"

He climbed down to think about it and stood shaking. If Jehovah was a God of love, surely he didn't want Jim St. James to go stark raving mad, talking to a teddy bear, cut off from almost all human contact while he faced a fatal disease.

"Something's wrong," he thought. "I've made a mistake somewhere. I've missed something. There is something desperately wrong, either with the Jehovah's Witnesses or with me."

What began to emerge in Jim's mind was the thought that the elders didn't know him, they didn't love him, they wouldn't care if he jumped or not. People like that might not be speaking for God after all. They were bigots. They had totally rearranged his life and he had listened to them because of his blind faith in their wisdom, but they were—after all—only people. He had been about to kill himself because of the prejudice of ordinary people.

He spent the rest of the night curled up in a peacock rattan chair on his balcony with a blanket wrapped around him. He prayed for help from Jehovah, and he cried and prayed some more and talked aloud, until he saw the dawn break.

"I'm gay," he said aloud. "There is nothing anyone can do to change that. They can chop off my head, but my heart will still be that of a gay man. I had no choice in this. It can't be God's way that I'm evil because of something I can't help. Somewhere men have screwed up."

211

It came to him in one piece that he would never return to the Jehovah's Witnesses. He would be grateful always for the moral upbringing he had known in the Kingdom Halls, and the fellowship, and for the wisdom of the Bible, but the religion was without heart.

Over the next few days he searched the Scriptures for answers. He found something in Romans that talks about the laws in the Bible being impossible to follow; there were too many of them. He found tax evasion mentioned in Romans, and adultery, and pre-marital sex—in fact, all the weaknesses to which humans are prone. The conclusion was that no one could keep all the rules. The point was to try, to the best of each person's ability, and God would forgive.

A few nights later his mind was clear. He lay in bed looking at the stars out his window and addressed God: "I may die of this disease, but I think I know how I'm going to live what time I have left. If the congregation doesn't want me, that doesn't matter any more. I've done the best I can do. I have to leave it to you, God. You'll have to figure it out. I'll live out my life as a gay man and live it the most responsible way I can. If that's not good enough, I have nothing else to give. You'll have to decide whether to bring me to life after Armageddon. It's now in your hands."

He considers that he has an agreement with Jehovah and it has been his comfort ever since. He does his best to be a good person, as a gay man, and he leaves the rest to the deity.

He called Natalie the next day. She burst into tears and shouted, "Get over here right away! I need a hug!" They talked for hours while he poured out the story of his new-found serenity. She gave him her total attention and encouragement. She said, grinning through tears, that she had been waiting for him to come to his senses, she knew it would happen eventually.

He went about repairing his friendships very slowly. The first person he called was Bert, his long-time hairdresser and buddy.

"It's Jim, Bert," he said. "I was wondering if you have time for a coffee."

Bert said, "Whaaaat? Do you mean it? That's great!"

Bert's warm reaction was repeated with every call he made. No one was huffy with him about being dropped so abruptly, and no one treated his decision to return with anything but a spirit of welcome. He called Bruce C., who said "Come over at once."

Bruce was living with a man named Carlos in an apartment near Dufferin Street. He sounded fine on the telephone, but Jim already knew that Bruce was too ill to work. His entire leg was swollen with cancer and he was in great pain.

He found Bruce hobbling around the apartment by hanging on to the furniture. They hugged and Bruce wept when Jim told him about the night on the balcony.

Bruce and Carlos were making preparations to move to Vancouver to be near Bruce's family. The parting was poignant, but the two men promised to stay in touch. In the weeks that followed, Jim made no effort to call or write. He wanted to pretend that there was no urgency, that Bruce was fine.

Jim was also deeply ashamed. During the first months after Bruce had been diagnosed with AIDS, Jim had locked himself away in what he had come to describe derisively as "the time when I was drowning in the glory of God". He knew from his own experience that the first months of AIDS can be spirit-breaking. Bruce had been there for him when he had his attack of hysterical weeping, but he had made himself unavailable for Bruce.

When Bruce was in hospital having treatments on his leg, Jim had been in his apartment raving to Jehovah, but when he, Jim, was in hospital for chemotherapy, Bruce came every day.

Twice during the chemotherapy treatments Jim's fever had lifted him into delirium and the doctors had notified Natalie that they thought he might die. Natalie had called Jim's father and brother, and Bruce, who had raced to the bedside. Jim has no

213

memory of one occasion and only a hazy recollection of the other. He recalls that he was ready to give up. He was sweating with weakness and shattered with a sense of hopelessness.

"I can't stand any more," Jim gasped. "I can't hang on."

"You must," Bruce said, holding his hand tightly.

Too light-headed to be rational, Jim looked around wildly. "Why should I?" he cried, "Look at this messy room. No one comes to clean."

Bruce went to the nursing station in a fine rage and commanded cleaners. Someone came to clear away the litter, as Bruce stood by beaming with pride that he had been helpful. Loving him for his kindness, Jim began to feel better.

He holds it against himself that he had not helped Bruce in the same way during the first part of his ordeal. It is something Jim can't forgive the Jehovah's Witnesses or himself.

Scott M., only twenty-two, stopped coming to the meetings of the AIDS support group. He was a Jehovah's Witness in Buffalo but had been "smart enough", as Jim put it, to stay in the closet. When he was diagnosed with AIDS he didn't want to reveal his homosexuality by contacting the AIDS group in Buffalo so he joined the one in Toronto. His mother bought him a little car so he could make the long trip every week. Once Jim drove to Buffalo to visit him there. Scotty complained about "the spots". He was covered with a hundred Kaposi's spots on his torso and limbs.

Jim felt his stomach tighten. He couldn't get away from Scotty fast enough. Scott's spots looked just like Allan D.'s. What flashed in Jim's mind was the story of Allan's stomach coming out his rectum. Was this to be Scotty's fate?

The last time the support group saw him, Scotty's face was covered in spots, which he found humiliating. That time his mother drove him because he was growing too fatigued to make the trip alone. The group loved her.

They never saw or heard from Scotty again. They assumed that he was dead.

One night when the support group had drifted to the pancake house for coffee, Jim was drawn to a newcomer, Michael T., a big, bearded, intelligent man with long dark hair. When their eyes met, there were signals of kindling interest.

The awareness of one another continued over the next few weeks. They began spending nights together, but neither was ready to risk having sex. They tried it one night but Jim was so worried about giving Mike his infections or getting Mike's that he lost his erection. Instead, they preferred to cuddle. Jim discovered that Mike gave wonderful massages and was willing to continue for hours to lulling music, with candles to light the room. The attraction for both was the physical contact; they were starved for physical touch.

The relationship lasted for a few months and gave them both comfort. Then Mike drifted away from Jim and the group. His was a curious situation. The group heard that there was a possibility that Mike's cancer wasn't related to AIDS after all. His doctors had jumped to that conclusion because he was gay, but the diagnosis was not certain. No one in the group ever saw Mike again; they heard he moved in with a woman who had cancer.

New people joined the support group in such numbers that it was growing, despite all the deaths. There was Randy, once a good friend of Jim's, and Dennis B., who came up from Key West where he once had run for mayor. Everybody liked Dennis. He had become prosperous through investments in Florida real estate but his lover, Carl, lived in Toronto. When Dennis was diagnosed with AIDS he came to Toronto so that Carl could care for him.

Jim met Dennis in St. Michael's Hospital. Dennis had just arrived from Key West and was in a wheelchair. Carl introduced them and the two men liked each other on sight. Jim found

215

Dennis an intelligent, composed person with whom he could share his hopes for making a contribution that would be helpful to people with AIDS and the gay community in general.

Dennis deteriorated quickly. An accomplished, successful man accustomed to command, he was appalled at the swift and disabling spread of his disease. One night he lost control of his bowel and made a mess in his bed. Carl helped clean him, but the shame of it was shattering to the pride of the sick man.

After that his bowel system fell apart and he was obliged to wear diapers. That humiliation was more than he could bear. Jim talked to him about making a fight and tried to instil in Dennis his own zeal for thinking positively. Dennis responded to the younger man's spirit and together they would vow that Dennis was going to recover bowel control. They kept on in that optimistic vein even when the tumour in Dennis's brain resulted in paralysis that made it impossible for him to leave his wheelchair.

For a few weeks it looked as though the cheerful approach was working. The cancer in Dennis's stomach seemed to be in remission. The group was delighted for him. Then Dennis discovered that he was going blind. Jim watched Carl tenderly caring for Dennis and hoped, for both their sakes, that the end would be quick.

Get it over with, Jim thought. To have the disease and die is bad enough, but to go like this, little by little, is unbearably degrading.

The tape again, with Jim's voice slow and dragging: "Well, it's October 16, 1985. My health seems to be hanging in there although the last weeks I've had a problem with my throat. I've got candida albicans at the back of my throat, which makes me cough a bit....

"Two weeks ago something happened which is causing me a great deal of trouble. I met someone and I brought him back to my apartment. He saw the marks on my arms and decided I had AIDS. He lit into me. Since then I've seen this young person around and he gets more vicious. Kurt says I shouldn't be going out in public. I was in Chaps four days ago and I met a young man and we sat and talked a while. I went to the washroom and this hurtful person went up to the man I was talking to to make sure he knew that I have AIDS....

"We just buried another guy. That brings us up to about eleven...."

"It's November 7, very late at night, and I'm happy. My friends and my family have gotten me through a very rough time of adjusting. Although I still have my ups and downs I think that helping other people, giving them strength, has given me the strength that I needed to get through this....

"I'm not sure that the cancer will return in January as Dr. Garvey expects. Probably it will, but we will cross that bridge when we get to it...."

That December of 1985 Raleigh threw a Christmas party for the support group. No one expected that Lee W. would come. He had lost a great deal of weight and the pain of his rotting rectum had become intolerable. To everyone's surprise, Lee turned up with his lover, Brian. Lee, emaciated to the bone, was bundled up in layers of sweaters. Everyone helped Brian carry him in and arrange him on a sofa in a cocoon of blankets.

Lee responded to the party mood. His face brightened and he joined in the conversation and carol singing, and the gentle ribbing. In a while he was sitting up—talking, laughing, drinking wine—as merry as anyone there. In fact, at two in the morning he was the last to leave. Lee lived another two or three months.

"Mind over matter," was Jim's explanation.

Jim chose his Christmas gift for Dennis with care. He selected a blue crystal heart because it sparkled and he thought that

217

Dennis might be able to see it, and certainly he could feel the shape. Dennis unwrapped it and held it in his hands tearfully.

"Can you see it?" Jim asked.

Dennis said triumphantly, "I can. I can just make it out. It's blue!"

Carl hung it on the Christmas tree the couple had in their apartment. He reported to Jim that it was Dennis's favourite ornament and he was proud of himself that he could see it.

Jim went to visit. It was obvious that Dennis would not live much longer. He sat in his wheelchair facing the tree. Jim sat on the floor beside the wheelchair, leaning against Dennis's leg so Dennis could touch him, and they talked gently, with many silences, all afternoon.

Jim thought about Bruce every day but heard no word and couldn't bring himself to call. In truth, he didn't want to know how Bruce was doing, fearing the worst. One afternoon close to Christmas 1985 Jim came home to find a message from Bruce on his answering machine. In a weak voice, Bruce said, "I just wanted to call and tell you I love you. Everything's okay between us. I understand perfectly what happened. Here's my number. Please call me if you get a moment."

Jim called at once and they had a joyful conversation. The point of the call, it emerged, was that Bruce wanted Jim to stop feeling guilty. Knowing his former mate so well, he realized that Jim was suffering because his withdrawal had coincided with Bruce's diagnosis.

There were no recrimminations and he wouldn't hear Jim's stumbling attempt to apologize and explain.

"I want you to know that I've always loved you, Jim," Bruce said. "I understand, better than anyone else you know, what you were going through when you couldn't see me. You shouldn't blame yourself for that. I understand and it was all right with me then, and it is now."

Bruce was being cared for by his family. Carlos had AIDS too and had returned to Toronto to be with his own family. Bruce said he was fine, not too badly off. They exchanged expressions of their love for one another.

They promised to stay in touch. "Hugs and kisses," Jim said at the end of the conversation, as he always did.

"Love you," Bruce replied, as he always did.

Two weeks later, on December 15, 1985, Bruce C. died. Jim seems to have blocked the memory of how he learned of that death. He hasn't the slightest recollection of receiving the news.

Jim liked to visit Dennis B. He would sit on the floor, his head against Dennis's knee, and they would talk optimistically about their disease and their hope for a cure. They imagined how in a few years they would laugh to remember how frightened of dying they had been. Dennis had a son he adored, and Jim listened to the familiar grief of a gay father separated from his family. They talked of Dennis's mother, whom he loved dearly, and Jim spoke of his affection for his own parents.

Dennis was the next to die. Linda Boyd called to tell Jim. She was becoming the continuity in all their lives, the one person who was at every bedside, the one who made the phone calls.

Dennis had loved roses, and there were roses by the hundreds in St. James chapel where the funeral service took place. Someone sang "The Rose". Jim cried, thinking of Dennis, missing him deeply, missing Larry, feeling his own death heavy on his heart.

Afterwards friends went back to the apartment Dennis had shared with Carl. There were drinks and desultory talk. Jim left early.

Carl, Dennis's lover, grieved for a year and then became a volunteer facilitator in a support group for families and partners of PWAs.

Lee W. was next. Then Bill McC. died. He had joined the group only a short time before. The PWAs were beginning to

219

see that the disease was erratic. Some died within months of the diagnosis and others, like Jim and Raleigh, were still alive almost two years later. Raleigh, a chubby, jolly, middle-aged man, prosperous in real estate, had lived in a steady relationship with his lover for seventeen years. When he was found to have cancer, doctors didn't suspect AIDS at first because Raleigh didn't fit the young-swinger profile of the average gay man with AIDS.

Jim and Raleigh noted similarities in their disease. Both started with Kaposi's, both had a rough time at the beginning, and both seemed to be almost in good health—a few additional lesions here and there every few months, but otherwise stable and holding.

Irv C. was one who went quickly. He became shockingly thin soon after his diagnosis. Irv had a magnificent apartment on St. Charles Street where he lived with his lover, Mark. Irv was a hulky 190-pound man, and he and Mark were waiters at a chic Toronto restaurant. When the management discovered that Irv had AIDS, they fired him. He protested and was offered a large sum of money as severance pay if he would keep quiet about the reason for the firing. Irv agreed. Two weeks later Mark also was fired.

The restaurant where the two men had worked was owned by a group that had investments in a number of other fine Toronto restaurants. In the weeks following the firing of Irv and Mark, the restaurant group fired all staff whom they suspected of being gay.

In Irv, AIDS manifested itself by disintegration of his bowel. In six weeks, constant diarrhoea stripped the flesh from his body. Jim went to visit him in hospital and walked in as nurses were helping Mark clean Irv. He was dumbfounded. He had never seen anything like Irv except for photographs taken in death camps. The man, screaming incomprehensibly in pain, was reduced to no more than seventy pounds. Irv's skin was stretched over his bones so that every rib was prominent. Jim could see plainly the outline of Irv's heart beating inside his chest.

Jim looked at the living cadaver and whispered to a nurse, "How can he be alive? He can't possibly be alive."

She said grimly, "He's got a pretty strong will."

Irv died a few days later. Jim shudders to think of him. His cancer, like Irv's, tends to recur in his bowel. Will his death be like that? Jim's stomach once was covered in cancer. Will it come back there and will he, like Allan D., die with pieces of his stomach coming out his anus? Those two deaths haunt him.

Jim spoke of Irv on the tape machine. "I can't even remember Irv's funeral," he mourned. "There's been so many you start to confuse them. Who sang, what was said, who conducted it. A couple of friends, Barry and Steve, also lived in the Bay-Charles Towers where Irv lived. Steve was also diagnosed with AIDS. I adored Steve. He was a tall, blond accountant and had his own firm. He went to Paris for HPA 23 and was very happy with the treatment. I knew he would be a close friend and ally. I went to his apartment, a lovely summer day, was it eighty-five or eighty-six? Maybe the spring of eighty-six.

"He had a lovely apartment. We talked about our fathers and how alike they were. I got a phone call when Steve died. It seemed so quick. I had been hoping he would be a good friend, and then he was dead.

"I went to his funeral. People were crying and they talked about how young he was and how brave he had been. It seemed so *quick*. I got in my car after Steve died and I cried."

Jim's voice is almost a wail. "Luc was in his forties, a freelance announcer with the French network. He got sicker and sicker. They used to bundle him up. He'd sit on his couch in his home and he'd put on a little toque. I tried to encourage him to get out of the apartment and come to the support group but he never did that. I saw him sometimes in the bars. He was losing his hair from chemotherapy.

"He became so thin, so skinny. His friends rallied around and tried to make him feel comfortable but he became so skinny. Then he died."

A deep breath. "Mal was twenty-two when he died. His friends were on one side of his bed and his family on the other, arguing because the family didn't want any mention of AIDS at the service and the friends said that wasn't what Mal wanted. Mal couldn't talk because his throat was full of scabs and thrush and all that. And while they were arguing about the service, Mal died. Isn't that an amazing story?"

Not long after, Jim was in St. Michael's with a high fever. He counted his admissions to date: seventeen. The worst of it was the nights when he wasn't sick. He had trouble sleeping and the time dragged heavily. To amuse himself, he liked to go into the corridor hooked up to his IV and use the wheeled tripod on which the solution bottle was suspended like a skate board. Other sleepless patients roared with laughter to see him zip by.

He was on his IV skate board the night his fever began to subside. He heard the sound of a man crying. The room was dark except for the light from a television set suspended on a long arm next to the bed and Jim could see a young man in the bed. He appeared to be trying to make a telephone call and he was crying.

Jim asked if he could help. The man explained through tears that he had cancer in his spine and he was paralysed. The doctors told him that he wouldn't recover the use of his legs, and that maybe the cancer would move the other way to his brain and paralyse his arms.

Jim sat down beside him and talked of Jehovah. "I'm in pretty bad trouble myself," Jim said, "but even if I should die I have the hope that I'll come back to life and live on earth again in a heavenly kingdom."

Jim's message, or his voice, or the kindness of his presence soothed the man. His tears dried and he shook Jim's hand gratefully.

11

Numb with shock and grief, Jim and his friends went to one funeral after another. Jim reflected once that when his father had been his age, the only funerals he had attended were those of his parents. For Jim, at only thirty-one, funerals of contemporaries were becoming common, everyday occurrences.

He had started to make a list of the dead: Allan D., John, Bruce C., Bob F., Norman, Little Norman, Francis, Larry W., Dennis B., Lee W., Bill McC., Irv C....twelve young men. Kind, gentle people who got a fatal disease from making love.

For a while only one funeral home in Toronto—Humphreys— would bury a person with AIDS. Those of the gay community who attended the AIDS funerals became experts at finding their way around that funeral home. They knew where to find the coffee maker and where the extra sugar was stored. Most of them had only one suit appropriate for funerals, so even the wardrobes became familiar.

When Rosar-Morrison, a funeral home on Sherbourne Street, made itself the second one in the city willing to bury people who had died of AIDS, the gang rapidly learned to find the coffee machine there too.

"He's in the big room," people would inform arrivals. Or "He's in the green room." Everyone knew the rooms.

Jim had resumed having sexual relationships, usually with someone he met in the support group who also had AIDS. Even so, both men would be anxious to avoid getting whatever opportunistic infection the other had. They had sex outside the body by means of mutual masturbation. If someone tried to kiss Jim on the lips, he always turned his head. Occasionally he had sex inside someone's body, wearing a condom, but he always withdrew before orgasm for fear the condom might break.

What he enjoyed most was the long cuddle after. Jim loves to be touched.

The gay community was avid for information about how AIDS was transmitted. For them, the information was a matter of life or death. All of them noted that health professionals familiar with the disease were very casual. Most wore gloves to touch the lesions but some, like Bernadette Garvey, touched with bare hands and simply washed thoroughly afterwards.

News from the research centres increasingly discounted the scare stories about AIDS being spread by saliva or tears. Once when Dr. Stan Read withdrew some blood from Jim, he stood swirling it in an open vial and it splashed out, running down his arm.

"Stan," Jim cried. "You've got my blood on you!"

"Jim, we know a lot about this disease now," the doctor told him. "Transmission by blood only happens in certain situations and this isn't one of them."

In the support group one night a man confessed to the worry that when he died his friends would find his apartment wasn't clean. Dirty dishes in the sink, maybe. It was crazy, but that really bothered him. It turned out that the same concern had been on the minds of almost everyone in the room.

"I worry that my bills won't be paid," someone else said gloomily.

Heads nodded about that too. No one wanted to die and leave a mess.

By the end of 1985 everyone in the first AIDS support group had died, except for Jim and Raleigh, who was preparing to move back to Florida. Newly diagnosed men replaced those who were gone, and the group was growing in size. It seemed that every day in Toronto, someone was being diagnosed with AIDS. The media were full of alarm, but the Canadian governments—municipal, provincial, and federal—were slow to respond, even though it was becoming obvious that health services were approaching a state of crisis. In such centres as Toronto, Vancouver, and Montreal, the increase in the number of PWAs was rapid and shocking.

Jim had an entirely new list of telephone numbers and addresses. One of the newcomers to the support group he liked best was Russell A., forty-two, a repairman working on the printing presses at the *Toronto Star*. Russ was a big, handsome, solid, intelligent man who gravitated to Jim and became his most loyal friend. They found they had the same sense of the ridiculous, and when the group broke up on Monday evenings they would linger over coffee somewhere and chuckle about something that had happened in the group that both found absurd.

Russ developed a sense of Jim's depth under the buoyant exterior. It was always Russell who knew when something in the group had been hurtful or had plunged Jim into sadness. He'd sling an arm around Jim's shoulders and say, "Come on over for lunch and we'll talk about it."

Russ had been an alcoholic, one of those derelicts who stumble into parks and sleep on the grass. Through determined efforts over a period of years he had finally succeeded in staying dry. He had established himself as a respected person in the gay community and lived in a comfortable apartment filled with paintings he collected. Even the discovery that he had AIDS didn't shake his determination to stay away from alcohol. Kaposi's lesions and all, he faithfully attended Alcoholics Anonymous meetings.

Russ rarely complained about his fate, but once, just before he died on his forty-third birthday, he said to Jim, "This isn't fair. I pulled myself up by my bootstraps. This isn't fair."

Ross A. was another newcomer to the support group. The AIDS organization in Edmonton, where he was the first person to be diagnosed with AIDS, is named for him. Ross was a bright, bubbly, funny man. What Jim remembers most about Ross is his fear. Behind the joking was a scared man, and he died quickly.

Jim can't remember Larry A. very well, except for Larry's horror about death. The group often talked about death, which was so much on everyone's mind, but Larry's terror had a dimension that was different from the others'. He died only a month after joining the support group.

Randy F. was next to die. Randy endeared himself when Jim was in hospital by giving him a card showing a teddy bear climbing up some steps and inscribed WE WILL MAKE IT. When Randy joined the group he was looking for support to face the double ordeal of informing his parents that he was gay and then telling them that he had AIDS. Randy's lover, Tony, came with him to the group, and the men discussed how Randy could make the disclosures.

It was painful but familiar ground for many PWAs. Some of the men in the group couldn't do it. For a man to tell his parents that he was dying of AIDS would mean that the parents would conclude that their son was gay. Men therefore were telling their parents that they had cancer or pneumonia. Parents shut their eyes and believed it.

Others used the disease as an opportunity to be honest at last with their parents about being gay. In some cases there was acceptance that healed the years of evasions and pretence; in many, there was rejection of the dying man.

In either case, every man in the room had an opinion on how Randy should conduct himself, and he listened to a din of advice.

Linda Boyd observed of these early PWA support groups that Jim St. James was always the strongest person when problems had to be resolved. The others, she noted, came to depend on him for leadership, and in this case Jim's views that Randy should trust his parents to love him carried the most weight. He went to Vancouver to tell his parents and sent Jim letters of profuse gratitude.

"You were right," he wrote. "I talked to my father just the way you told me to do it, and it wasn't as bad as I worried it would be. Jim, you keep up your strength. We all need you."

Randy returned to Toronto and died there. A year later, Randy's lover, Tony, discovered that he too had AIDS.

As Christmas approached Jim was feeling useless. His third session of chemotherapy was behind him, and his hair was beginning to be thick again. Though his strength had not returned enough for him to go to a job every day, he was well enough to work out in a gym from time to time. He painted, mostly abstracts, and even sold a few. He spent a long while on a painting for his living-room, a huge white canvas that incorporated a rough piece of cloth drawn across the surface.

That still left a lot of time for him to be restless and dissatisfied. He wasn't doing enough, he felt, to assist people with AIDS who were fighting both the disease and public sentiment against them. The papers were filled with negative publicity about AIDS and the gay community, a lot of it suggesting that homosexuals deserved what was happening to them, and there was talk of quarantine and compulsory testing.

One article made a particular impact on Jim. It quoted a doctor who declared that the disease was spreading because the gay community was irresponsible about sex, and that AIDS would eventually kill thousands upon thousands of heterosexuals as well.

Jim talked with Ed Jackson at the AIDS Committee of Toronto to ask if there was something he could do to help offset the bad press. He offered to help out as a public speaker, or whatever ACT needed in that line. He told Ed that he had been an actor "before AIDS" and that he thought he could perform all right as a sort of spokesperson. Would that be useful?

ACT very much did need someone with AIDS who was willing to go public. The disease as yet had no human face. At a press conference that autumn to highlight the funding crisis that ACT was in, a reporter had asked to speak to someone with AIDS. Ed had known there was a PWA in the room, but he also knew that the man's parents didn't know he was gay.

He had answered, "There's no one available right now."

Ed told Jim that there had been a problem finding someone with AIDS who was confident in appearing in public. If Jim was willing to do it, maybe he could help turn around public attitudes. That had strong appeal for Jim and he agreed. A few days later ACT received a phone call from Ellie Tesher, a writer at the *Toronto Star*. She asked if ACT knew of anyone with AIDS who was willing to be interviewed. Ed promised to have someone call her and notified Jim.

Jim hesitated. The offer to represent people with AIDS had been made spontaneously for a mixture of reasons. It came out of his restlessness and a sense that his brief life had not been useful, and also from the pain of feeling helpless to fight back against AIDS. Interestingly, there was much in his impulse that sprang from his training as a Jehovah's Witness. He would be a witness, in a sense, for his people. By presenting himself as an openly gay man who was a respectable person, he could meet his commitment to Jehovah to make his life worthwhile. Now that he was faced with following through on his offer, however, he wasn't sure he could do it. Very few men in Toronto had acknowledged in public that they were gay. Those who did, like George Hislop, who headed a gay organization and had run for political office, and Peter Maloney, a lawyer who also had run for political office, had suffered for it.

He mulled it over for a few days. There was the worry about how his family would take it; on the other hand, he might be able to do a lot of good. An article about him in the *Star* might counteract the negative picture gays were getting. Jim thought of Jobikins, the nurse who had said that meeting him had changed her mind about homosexuals. Maybe he could have the same effect on some of the *Star*'s vast readership. He made up his mind. It was time to stand up and be counted. He called Ellie Tesher and said he would see her.

The reporter, an experienced, elegant woman, was exceedingly careful. Using a tape recorder, she interviewed him several times in his apartment and over lunch, showing no nervousness at being in his company. It was a different story when it was time for the photography. The first photographer assigned to the story refused to do it. A second photographer, Dick Loek, agreed. Dick Loek is a charming, skilled man who shook Jim's hand without hesitation.

Jim looked almost as healthy after a year and a half with AIDS as he had before the disease. Half the forty-five pounds he lost during the three sessions of chemotherapy had been gained back, and his neatly trimmed thick dark beard concealed the hard boniness of his face. Some of the pictures were taken in his apartment on Sherbourne; in others he was shown strolling the streets, just another man in the crowd, though taller and handsomer than most.

On the night of Friday, December 13, 1985, Ellie called him to say the article would be appearing in the next day's paper. Jim thanked her and felt the edge of panic. What had he done?

He phoned Natalie and Bernie to tell them to watch tomorrow's paper.

"Are you all right with this?" Nat asked him.

"I'm fine," he assured her, but in truth he was badly frightened.

He spoke about it to his tape machine: "I'm really scared, but this is what I have left to give. I hope my family will be supportive. I'm going to fight. I'm going to get out there and do what's right...."

In part his concern was for his own safety. He feared that people in his apartment building might attack him in the belief that he was putting them at risk of infection. Others in the neighbourhood might find his address and see his apartment number in the lobby. He remembered what had happened in New York. The reason the Gay Men's Health Center had such heavy security at the door was because once an assailant had walked in and thrown acid in the face of the receptionist. Motorists driving by the offices used by New York PWAs not infrequently threw stones at the windows. There was a good possibility some crazy might try to hurt Jim.

Early the next morning Jim went to the apartment superintendent with a story that he was "having marital problems". He asked the super to remove his name from the list of tenants on the buzzer system in the lobby.

"I'll do it first thing Monday," the super promised.

"No!" Jim cried. "It has to come off today."

The super was irked. "I'll try to do it later on," he said, "but right now I'm busy."

Jim got a screwdriver and removed the glass plate over the buzzer system himself. He replaced his name with a blank.

He bought a *Toronto Star* as soon as the papers were delivered to the corner newspaper box. The article was easy to find. It took an entire page. He read it quickly, read it again more slowly, read it a third time very very slowly. A bit sensational, he thought, but all right. It was accurate and it was sympathetic. Now AIDS had a human face.

Under a page-wide picture of Jim strolling in a crowd of people on a busy street was the headline: "*In the shadow of death, I cried all day*."

The article began:

His scrapbook opens to a photo of a bright-eyed, rosy-cheeked baby: James Stephen Zanuk, born June 24, 1954. He flips pages to his high school diploma.... It will end—cut off in mid-story and mid-life—tragically soon for the ambitious young man. Zanuk, 31, is a victim of AIDS....

The AIDS threat never leaves. A scar on his neck marks where a huge cancer lump appeared and had to be removed. There are 20 dark purple Kaposi's sarcoma cancer spots on his arms, legs and back. He has suffered severe depression, been in hospital with raging fevers, with wheezing lungs, and for treatment of candida, a white fungus that covered his tongue, made it swell, and caused his voice to fail.

Dr. Stan Read, an infectious-diseases specialist with an international reputation, was quoted. "Jim must have a better than usual immune system to have done so well this long.... We know of no exceptions to eventual fatality from AIDS. Only a few people in the States are still alive three years out. Only one man in California has lived close to four years."

Jim winced and regretted his frankness when he read: "He still has sex, he says, with a lover who also has AIDS. The two men practise what is known as 'safe sex,' with no exchange of semen or saliva, now advocated by the homosexual community to avoid the spread of AIDS."

The article noted that Jim was about to endure his fourth round of chemotherapy treatment. His quote on that was, "I don't know how long I can keep doing this and keep my mind healthy."

Ellie Tesher concluded: "Jim spoke to the *Star* in the hope of helping others who have AIDS, and of dispelling cruel prejudice."

Jim thought, "Holy smokes. I don't know if this took guts or insanity."

On the same page was an article from San Francisco by the *Star*'s Lynda Hurst. It began, "The AIDS epidemic is killing homosexuals in this city at an average monthly rate of 40...."

Jim waited nervously by the phone. The first call was from a woman he hadn't heard from since high school in London.

"Are you the Jim Zanuk who used to be in the drama class?" she asked. When he acknowledged he was, she burst into tears. "I just want to tell you how sorry I am about your illness," she sobbed.

Jim hung up, relieved. He had been braced for hate calls. Then his mother called. Expecting a tirade, he was astonished by her calmness. She said she had read the article. "You've made it difficult for me and for Karen," she said with mild reproach in her tone. It had been hard enough for them to defy the elders when Jim wasn't seeing any of his homosexual friends, but she had a real dilemma now that Jim was flaunting his homosexuality in public and even admitting that he had a male lover.

"Why did you do it?" she asked sadly.

He explained that he wanted the public to understand that people with AIDS were human beings and that they were worthy of compassion and help.

"Why you?" she said. "Why not let someone else do it?"

Because, he answered, he had been so fortunate. He had a family who had stuck by him, and loyal friends, and financial support. Many people with AIDS didn't have those advantages. He owed something back to his community.

"I felt I had a responsibility to do what I could to help others," he said, choosing his words carefully. Everything hung on making her appreciate that he had acted in good faith, that he had been trying to be a good person and to help others.

There was a pause. His mother said, "Karen and I will have to think about what we'll do. You understand our problem, don't you?"

Jim said numbly that he did.

"I'll call you," his mother said gently, "when we decide."

Friends phoned to congratulate him on his courage. He had set an example, they said, and people would get a very different impression of gays and people with AIDS. They liked the picture of him in the crowd. It said a lot: people with AIDS weren't demons with fangs. They looked like human beings, with just the same humanity as anyone else. Natalie called to express her admiration.

Jim was grateful for all the support, but he could scarcely breathe. There was a very good chance, he realized, that he would never see his mother and sister again.

The promised call from his mother came the following week. Johanna had consulted the elders of the congregation. Their verdict was that she must sever all connection with her son. He was officially dead.

"From now on I can have no further contact with you," she said quietly.

"I know that, Mother," he said. His concern was for her. She couldn't go against the elders, and it would only hurt her more if he protested that his heart was broken.

"You've tried so hard," he told her. "You did your best to raise all four of us and you've done a good job of it. I love you very much and I want you to know I understand the position you're in. It's a choice between your son and God, and you can't live without God. There's no need for you to have any regrets about this. Don't worry about me. I'll be all right. Hugs and kisses."

Jim's mother has neither seen nor spoken to him since that day in December 1985. He came out as a gay man with AIDS in order to help his community, and maybe he did help, but Jim often regrets it. He's not at all sure any more that he made the right decision.

"It cost me my mother and my sister," he reflects. "I think the price was too high."

Messages have passed between mother and son by way of Jim's brother, Allan. He tells Allan, "When you see Mom tell her that I'm well and everything is fine." She tells Allan, "Tell Jim we love him and we're praying for him."

Jim misses her dreadfully. He is rarely able to speak of her without weeping but he never criticizes his mother for her decision. Instead he feels for her anguish. He knows she could not tolerate joining him in his exile from the Jehovah's Witnesses. Her faith is her life.

Once in an argument Jim's sister Kathryn lost her temper with her mother and said, "Look what you're doing to Jim. You're turning your back on your own son when he's dying." When Kathryn told him about it he was appalled.

"Don't do that to her," he told Kathryn. "You'll kill her. She's had two bad marriages and she's not a young woman, but she's trying to raise a young son. She was forty-three when she had Daniel. Think how difficult that was. All she's got is a God who she believes can fix everything for her after Armageddon if she follows what the elders tell her she must do. We can't take that hope from her."

He added, "If she did defy her faith, when I die what will she have left? Nothing."

Jim hoped that his father wouldn't see the story, since Karl Zanuk rarely reads the Toronto papers, but Kathryn phoned with bad news. Karl had read it and was in a rage. Worse still, a relative had called Karl to berate him for having a son who shamed the family name.

"Jim, don't go near him," Kathryn warned. "Don't even phone. He's ready to kill you."

His sister Karen called next. She and her husband, Vince, had agreed to say goodbye to Jim in person. She invited him to come to Gravenhurst for farewells. Jim went shopping for gifts for the children, Shannon and Benjamin. Knowing this would be the last time he would see them, he wanted them to have something lasting to remember him by. He selected a sturdy bright wagon for the boy and a charming clown doll for Shannon.

Karen and Jim sat at the kitchen table, the children swarming all over their uncle as they always did. Eventually Karen sent them out to play and said to Jim with tears in her eyes, "You know we can't see you any more. I understand why you did it but I have my own family to think about. I believe in Jehovah God and the teachings of Jehovah's Witnesses, so this will have to finish it for us. We love you dearly and we'll be rooting for your recovery, but we can't see you any more."

Jim kept his composure. He couldn't see any point in making her feel worse. He told her he appreciated that she had made a conscientious decision and he respected her for it. "Don't be upset," he said. "Somewhere it will work out."

His brother, Allan, often shows him pictures of Karen's family. Jim is astounded at how Shannon and Benjamin have grown. He would hardly know them any more. He treasures the crayoned notes they have written to thank him for presents. "I LIKE YOU," Shannon wrote blissfully after he started her on a collection of pigs.

Jim waited a few more days for his father to calm down and then drove to the farm without announcing himself. Entering the house as always by the rear door, he found Eleanor alone in the kitchen. Her expression was full of alarm.

"I'd like to talk to Dad," he said.

"He's in his office in the basement," she told him. "I'll call him."

She went to the top of the stairs.

"Karl," she called. "We have company."

"Aren't you going to tell him who it is?" Jim whispered.

"If I do, he won't come up," she whispered back.

Jim noted that his hands were trembling. When his father saw him, he burst into tears, sat down heavily at the table, and sobbed like a child.

"Pop, let's talk."

"How could you do this?" his father wept. "How could you shame our family so?"

"I haven't…," Jim started to say, but his father interrupted him with an explosion of wrath greater than Jim had ever seen.

Jim took a storm of abuse humbly and without defending himself. Karl called his son a disgusting pervert. He said he was sorry that Jim hadn't yet died of AIDS. It would have been better if he were dead. As the rage went on, Jim saw that what had hurt his father most was the stripping away of his privacy. For him it was unbearable that everyone would know that he, Karl Zanuk, had a son who was a homosexual.

Jim thinks that his father remains baffled by homosexuality, despite the efforts Jim has made to discuss it. He can't shake the notion that Jim is simply being perverse in remaining homosexual and that maybe psychiatry would cure him. Jim suspects that sometimes his father even blames himself for it and wonders if there was something wrong that he did as a parent, or if maybe the Zanuks have an errant gene.

Jim waited for his father's fury to subside, as it always did eventually. He tried to explain why he had done it. "I'm watching my friends die," Jim said desperately. "I'm watching them rot. I had to do something. This was my way to make life easier for people with AIDS. Someone had to do it." Couldn't his father appreciate that it was time someone had the guts to show that people with AIDS were human beings like anyone else?

237

His father shouted that he couldn't appreciate any such non-sense. Jim was grandstanding again. He shouted his views of that and finally, exhausted, slumped into silence.

When he spoke again his voice was quiet and flat.

"The story's out and there is nothing we can do about it," he said, looking hard at Jim, "but you are never to use our family name in public again. If I ever see you call yourself Jim .... in a newspaper or anywhere else, I'll disown you."

Jim was braced to hear how he would be punished. He expected that his allowance would be cut off. His father usually did that when he was angry. Probably he would take back the car as well. He was relieved when his father pronounced the sentence. Jim could keep the car but his allowance would be cut in half.

Jim went back to Toronto feeling depressed. He wouldn't be able to appear in public again, but the need for someone with AIDS to speak out was still there. At the next meeting of the support group he called for volunteers to replace him. No one could. Russell A.'s mother didn't know that he had AIDS. A couple of men were living at home and thought their parents would kick them out. The rest said they didn't have Jim's stage experience and they wouldn't be comfortable speaking in public.

They told Jim that he had to continue. Why not? The worst had already happened. He already had lost his mother and sister, and his father had cut him off. He had nothing more to lose.

"Yes I do," he said quietly. "I could lose my father."

He talked to Kathryn. She had the suggestion that he use his stage name, James St. James. She pointed out that many people who knew Jim from the period when he was pursuing his ambitions as an actor didn't even know another name. Theatre people always thought of him as Jim St. James. He had won an award with that name; he already had a public presence as James St. James. She reminded Jim that their father hadn't objected to Jim's going public but only to his use of the family name.

Jim was too nervous of his father's temper to discuss it with him, but he tested the water. As James St. James he gave an interview to a reporter for a St. Catharines paper. He waited for the earth to shatter. When he didn't hear from his father, he accepted a request from a Toronto TV news show to comment on a development in AIDS treatment. Still a silence from Brantford. He could not be certain his father even knew about it. When they met, neither mentioned it.

Then his father announced that he and Eleanor were going to Florida for four months to escape the winter.

Their absence came at a good time. Jim was in great demand, the first man in Toronto to go public with AIDS. Because he was also articulate and attractive, he was getting dozens of requests to make speeches and give interviews. Whenever there was a new announcement about AIDS, reporters called Jim St. James for a comment.

Jim became one of four speakers on whom the AIDS Committee of Toronto could depend for meetings all over the province. Jim was "putting a human face on AIDS", as more than one reporter described it. His sessions usually ended with question periods that lasted an hour or more. In St. Catharines one night someone wanted to know why he was making public appearances. He replied: "There was such an overwhelming need I could not bury my head. Somebody had to come out to alleviate the fears. It makes me feel I'm doing something to help. I'm not a scientist. I'm not a psychologist. But I can help by telling my story."

When his father returned Jim was established as a media figure. He waited nervously for a reaction, but there was nothing. By spring Jim couldn't bear the suspense.

"I've done a few little interviews," he told his father tentatively. "I don't know if you're aware of them. I call myself Jim St. James now."

"Yeah, I know," he said. "Allan told me. I can handle that, so long as I never see you use my name."

Zanuk is not Jim's real name. Out of concern for his father, the family name has been changed in this book, along with other identifying details.

His father never speaks to Jim about anything Jim has done in public. When Jim appeared on CBC television's prestigious *The Journal*, he hoped that his father would take some pride in it. Instead there was only silence. Whenever Jim tries to tell his father about a speech he has made, or a commercial he did for the Canadian Public Health Association, the older man curtly changes the subject.

Jim thinks that perhaps the problem is his father's difficulty, most of his life, in communicating his love for his son to Jim. Jim has never heard his father say that he's proud of him, though Karl Zanuk occasionally has praised Jim to Natalie Wexler. Sometimes he tells Natalie Wexler that he loves Jim. Natalie tells Jim, who is always deeply pleased to hear it.

"I'm Dad's Achilles heel," he explains. "It's very hard for him to have a son like me."

Jim met the financial problem caused by his reduced circumstances by taking in a roommate, Glen P., to share his Sherbourne Street apartment and help pay the rent. Glen had just broken up with his partner, Gord W., and was looking for somewhere to stay.

The relationship worked out well for them both. They turned out to be perfectly compatible and Jim was pleased to have someone in the apartment to make it seem less lonely. He wondered that Glen didn't appear concerned to move in with a man with AIDS. Glen said it never crossed his mind to worry about it.

A year after the *Toronto Star* article, Jim's sister Karen and her husband, Vince, and the children visited Jim's father, who didn't warn them that Jim was dropping in. Jim, who had also been in the dark about his father's attempt at a reconciliation, was surprised and overjoyed to see them again. Though Vince left the room without speaking, Karen greeted him calmly. The children stared at him. Jim wondered what explanation Karen had given for his sudden absence from their lives. Then Shannon crawled into Jim's lap and put her arms around his neck, hugging him without speaking. Benjamin clung to his knee.

It was too painful. Jim unclasped Shannon's arms and gently set her on her feet, hugged Benjamin, and left.

Jim's fourth bout of chemotherapy, which was directed at cancer in his stomach, started January 2, 1986. Jim was feeling fed up. He was tired of having AIDS, tired of treatments, tired of the suspense.

"Why am I still alive?" he asked Dr. Garvey. "It's beginning to be embarrassing. I'm the only one of the original support group left alive. I'm almost the only one of the second support group still alive. There's a third wave of PWAs just starting. Am I going to bury all of them too? And if so, why me?"

She said the chemotherapy happened to work well for him. It didn't always work, but his response to the treatment was truly amazing. As well there was Jim's positive attitude. "That helps a lot, Jim," she said, "but also you have an unusual constitution. You're a very healthy man, except for AIDS. You have the advantage of being raised on a farm with lots of good, nutritious food, and you come from sturdy stock."

There was another factor, not yet understood by anyone. All over North America the only people still alive two years after a diagnosis of AIDS were gay men of previous good stamina whose disease started with Kaposi's and who did not get pneumonia.

Though Jim had had the pneumonia, he was in the slim category of the fortunate.

Jim reflected he was drawing on a lot of resources, pulling from all the corners—including whatever interest Jehovah was taking in him. None the less it was exhausting. He caught himself sometimes wishing it would end, one way or another: Let me be truly well or truly dead.

On the tape he said: "It's very hard to remember nineteen eighty-five. When I try, things are like a cloud. I can remember bits and pieces but I don't know when they happened in relation to each other. The time between eighty-four when I was diagnosed and eighty-six seemed like I was walking in an unreal life. My love of life seemed challenged. It was hard to know how I was going to deal with this. When I asked Natalie and my friends not to talk to me any more, I wonder if I was bargaining with God. If I gave Him my most precious things—and my friends are my most precious things—if I gave my treasures to him, would that make me better? I wonder if I was bargaining. I hope not...."

"I guess nineteen eighty-five could be summed up for me as waiting for the other shoe to fall. I remember at one of the group meetings, one of the first ones, looking across the room at Norman, he's dead now, who was talking about seeing a psychiatrist. I leaned over and said, 'No one else can help you now but us. It's us who are closest to you. We're the best help you can get because we understand'....

"I want to talk about the nurses on 6A South in St. Michael's Hospital. If it wasn't for them I never would have made it this far. They have been my family, my strength, my truly understanding people. They used to put me in 601, the biggest room on the floor. They called it the king's suite. Sometimes when I knew Dr. Garvey would be checking me in I would call 6A South and say, 'Any chance of getting 601?'...

"The head nurse is an efficient, together woman. The thing I like best about her is her big heart, her kindness. Several times

Garvey would be checking me in I would call 6A South and say, 'Any chance of getting 601?'…

"The head nurse is an efficient, together woman. The thing I like best about her is her big heart, her kindness. Several times she would come in and I might be crying softly to myself and she would take the time to sit with me….

"The best time in my hospital stay would be when Dr. Garvey stopped to talk to me. It probably was that relief from stress, which Dr. Garvey's presence did for me, that has prolonged my life…. She's been careful not to overdo drugs with me, not to overdo therapies. Very careful not to guinea-pig me. Probably the most fortunate thing that ever happened to me was falling into the hands of Dr. Garvey…."

Soon after the fourth round of chemotherapy treatments began, his hair started falling out again, beginning as it always did on the sides of his head. In a flash of irritation, he got out his razor and shaved his head except for a Mohawk plume down the middle. His anger continued to build. He started to wear torn jeans and construction boots. He had an ear pierced and wore a gold hoop in it. When he returned to hospital for the final session of chemotherapy needles he was in a belligerent mood, far removed from the charming and urbane man that 6A had always known.

Dr. Garvey ignored the change in Jim's appearance and manner, but the nurses eyed him uneasily.

"Interesting earring, Jim," one ventured.

"That is what I am," he snapped. "I'm gay."

Linda Cohen, a social worker in St. Michael's Hospital who worked with the AIDS patients, came to see him.

"How's it going?" she asked.

"How should it be going?" he replied testily. "I'm dying and they're going to give me more chemo."

"Come and see me after your treatment," she suggested.

"I'm perfectly fine," he assured her. "I'm just fed up."

He was ornery and impossible with the nurses.

243

She said, "When I first saw you in the hospital you were beautifully dressed and you were a considerate, fine man. What's happening? I think we should talk about how you're feeling."

He was grumpy with her. What did it matter? he asked. He had lost his mother, lost his sister. He wasn't allowed to use his own name any more. His father had cut his support entirely, and he had been obliged to apply for welfare on the grounds of his disability. His friends were dead or dying. He had tried to help other people but all that happened was that he was worse off for it.

He later called it his *why bother* stage. Linda Cohen worked with him patiently, once a week. It was many sessions before he was able to discuss the separation from his mother. She prevailed upon him to keep hoping that something would happen, it would improve. He said she didn't know anything about Jehovah's Witnesses; it wouldn't change.

"Okay, you've got problems with your father and you've got problems with your mother," Linda said. "Who else?"

"Well," Jim said, considering, "there's my health. But I am going to continue to speak out. It's time we all stopped hiding in the closet. Someone has to be out there telling people what's happening, that we're seeing death after death after death. If you hide in the closet, you die in the closet."

"It sounds to me as if 1985 was a waste of time," she said. "Why?"

"I wasn't feeling well enough to do anything," he explained.

"Not according to Dr. Garvey. She said you had several periods between chemotherapy treatments when you could have been doing something. Why not go back to acting?"

"There's no point to it," he told her. "I'm going to die."

"We're all going to die," she retorted. "Does that mean that we should all quit and lie about?"

A few weeks later she hit him with it. "Jim, I think you're afraid to go back to acting. You're afraid that maybe you're a lousy actor. Your last show was in 1983. Maybe it's easier to be a dying swan with one good show than to get out there and test yourself."

"That's not true," he protested hotly.

"Then prove it. You may have limited time, but so what? Use it."

He walked a lot during those weeks, thinking. On a sunny, breezy, pretty day in spring, he saw a mother pushing an empty stroller, followed by a golden-haired toddler who was stooping, enchanted, to look at a butterfly. It was a perfect scene except that the child was without arms. Her hands were connected directly to her shoulders.

The thought he had was that he had been a vain and selfish fool. "You're moaning and groaning about what you don't have," he lectured himself. "What kind of a life has this child? How can you say, *why me*? Look at her and think about the life ahead of her. Why her?"

He heard that the Scarborough Music Theatre was doing a production of A.R. Gurney's *The Dining Room*. He knew the script and loved it, especially the role of Actor One. The role has seven parts, ranging from a child of three through to a grandfather in his eighties who has a speech in which he outlines how he wants to be buried.

Jim got rid of the earring and shaved off the stupid Mohawk crest of hair. That left him completely bald, so he selected his clothes carefully to offset that disadvantage. He dressed for the auditions in a black shirt and a white jacket and white trousers and picked up his briefcase. He checked himself in the mirror: distinctly odd, but not unattractive.

He took a place among others lounging in the theatre waiting their turn to be tested. People stared at his bald head but not with distaste. They seemed to take his look as something avant-garde, very Telly Savalas. His attitude, carefully struck, was nonchalance. He was going to prove that Linda Cohen was wrong: he was a good actor, and he was through fooling around.

The director was Lin Joyce and the producer was Herschel Rosen, who had produced *Man of La Mancha*. When everyone had finished auditioning, Lin invited a handful to return the next day for another audition. Jim was one of those invited to come back. When the second audition was done, he waited with the rest for the decision.

Lin Joyce announced she was giving the part of Actor One to James St. James.

He was astounded. He blurted out, "What about my bald head?"

"This is the theatre," she replied sunnily. "We can give you hair."

Herschel Rosen took Lin aside with a worried look. He told her that Jim had AIDS. Maybe his health wasn't going to be reliable enough for the six-night performance run. Maybe there were other problems. Jim was fairly well known. Maybe audiences would stay away. Lin wasn't disconcerted in the least. She said that Jim was the best actor for the part and the AIDS thing didn't matter. In fact, he wasn't the first actor with AIDS she'd directed.

After the first read-through with the rest of the cast, two men and three women, Jim spoke with Lin Joyce.

"I feel funny about working with them when they don't know I have AIDS," he said.

She asked, "Can anyone get AIDS from working with you?"

He said no, it wasn't possible.

"Well then," she said, "I don't think it's anyone's business. If it can't be transmitted by casual contact, why bother telling them? None of the women is going to inform everyone that she had a hysterectomy, none of the men is going to to discuss his medical history. Forget about it."

Still Jim was uncomfortable. He waited until rehearsals began. He had become close to one of the actors, Daphne Duncanson, with whom he had several scenes. He decided to tell her and allow her to inform the others.

He asked her to have a coffee with him and began tentatively, "My health isn't that good."

"We all know that you have AIDS," she told him. "A couple of us went to the AIDS Committee of Toronto, and we got information that reassured us that we're not in any risk. We're all comfortable with it now and I hope you are too."

Cathy Dunphy of the *Toronto Star* later interviewed Daphne. The actress confessed that she had been concerned because there is a scene in the play where she kisses Jim. "So I went out and did some research," she explained. Jim told her they would not kiss on the mouth. "Jim is such a great guy, such a great actor," Daphne told the *Star*, "that sometimes I get carried away working with him and want to give him a big kiss on the mouth. But he always turns his head away. I forget; he's always aware of it, always in control."

Jim relaxed and began to enjoy himself, as he always does when working in theatre. His depression lifted and he basked in the affection others in the cast showered on him. He was touched by notes and cards from them that he found in his dressing-room: "Keep up the good work, Jim." "We're rooting for you."

Because of his habit of being supportive and encouraging to people around him and because he was the most experienced actor in the group, he became something of a father figure. He gave counselling when others brought him their love-life problems. When nerves snapped in an argument between the producer and the director, Jim was the mediator. It was vastly satisfying. He had braced himself for the possibility that he would be a pariah, but instead he was an important, valued member of the group.

Late in June 1986 the cast was nervously approaching opening night. One afternoon they were working on the children's birthday party scene in which they all played the roles of six-year-olds, each of them wearing a cone-shaped hat with an elastic under the chin. Jim's role called for him to turn off the chandelier when the candle-lit cake was carried on stage. On the cue, he hit the prop switch and turned his attention to the cake.

To his surprise, it was a real one with real candles blazing. The cast sang, "Happy birthday to yoou, happy birthday to yooou, happy birthday dear Jiiiim...." and he saw that the cake was for him. His thirty-second birthday was two days away.

Jim gets very emotional when he recalls that moment. "That said a lot to me," Jim says. "It said I was still a human, I was still part of the human race."

Opening night was July 17, 1986, and the Wexlers sent Jim a huge bouquet of flowers. Lin Joyce, wishing her cast well, gave Jim a big hug. The play was a great success and audiences gave the cast tumultuous ovations at the curtain calls. Jim loved every minute of it, though his role was difficult. The part he could almost not bear to do, night after night, was the final scene when Actor One, made up as an old man, sits in the dining-room in the dimness of twilight and describes for his son the funeral he wants.

Under the circumstances, the emotions of that scene were difficult for Jim and for the rest of the cast. A pall settled backstage while he did the lines. The hardest time of all for him was when his father and Eleanor came to see the show. Jim felt a double meaning in every word of the funeral scene because he has tried several times to discuss his own funeral with his father, but Karl Zanuk won't listen.

Jim's return to the stage drew much media attention. He told all reporters that it was "magnificent" to be back working.

With the show over, Jim's depression returned. He groaned to himself that he could have predicted that it would. Every show he's ever done, he hates the final curtain that means the party is over. The kindness shown him by the company made it especially poignant and he felt absolutely sunk as he joined them for the wrap party.

Natalie had made preparations to ease the blow, arranging for the two of them at her expense to spend a few days in an elegant country inn near Toronto. Despite the luxurious surroundings, Jim was in a flat, detached mood. Natalie tried to get a rise from him by being her animated self, but he didn't respond. She tried a joke card: "I love you. PLEASE QUIT SMOKING ." Jim laughed. He had started to smoke, and he found it calmed his nerves. The woman from the *Star*, Ellie Tesher, had been appalled to see him light up.

"You shouldn't be smoking!" she exclaimed.

"Why," Jim asked with a grin. "Will it give me cancer?"

12

Driving back to Toronto with Natalie, Jim maintained the polite fiction that he was feeling fine, only a bit tired. Though she was suspicious, she was obliged to accept his story. In truth, as she suspected, he was feeling forlorn.

He wandered about his empty apartment trying to find something to distract him. His roommate, Glen, was away. Glen was trying a reconciliation with his former partner, Gord, and was staying with him. Television didn't work, so Jim put on some music. That proved irritating. He turned off the tape and picked up a magazine, only to throw it down.

His mood was strange. He couldn't analyse what was happening to him. He was engulfed by a sense of the pointlessness of his existence. He had promised Jehovah to live as good a life as he could, and he made a mental check-list of the tasks he had assigned himself when he made his deal. For one, he had proved to himself and to others that he really could act. That had been gratifying, but he didn't need to do it again. By surviving as long as he had with AIDS, he had demonstrated his theories about the importance of not giving up. Even if the person couldn't beat AIDS, as he always said in the support group sessions, it was enough of a triumph to put up a fight. Well, he'd put up a fight all right.

What else? By going public, he had led the way for other people with AIDS to talk about the illness. To improve the image of gay people, he had behaved always as a courteous and thoughtful person. His behaviour had been exemplary, and he had shown ability as a natural leader in every situation in which he found himself. In the support group, he was the strong one. His positive attitude had helped many—he had thank-you notes to prove it. He went to every funeral. What more could he do?

He could think of nothing.

He undressed and pulled on some old jeans. Barefoot and bare-chested, he paced the apartment, stopping from time to time before a tall mirror. The body looked great, he decided, except for some purple cancer lesions here and there. He had to admit it was a great body. It had come back after four bouts of chemotherapy. Doctors found that remarkable.

He decided to go out and have a few drinks with the boys. He called his drinking buddies, Rafe S. and David B., put on a shirt and shoes, and went bar-hopping. He got slightly drunk on spritzers, but it didn't change the strange way he was feeling. He thought of himself as Bette Davis in the film *Dark Victory* where she knows she's going to die and she's being brave about it, not telling anyone. That thought was chased by a moment's wry amusement at how theatrical he was becoming.

The analysis of his life continued in his head. Maybe his life had given other people hope, he thought. He had lived two years and four months with AIDS. A Canadian record, Stan Read told him.

Sadness began to fill him to the brim. Was there anything more he could do? No, not a thing. So what was next for him?

He went back to his apartment and opened two bottles of champagne. He took off his shirt again so he could admire how healthy he looked and went out on his balcony to sip the wine and look at the sleeping city spread below. He prayed to Jehovah to help his friends. He explained to God that he had been doing his best to help others, and he hoped God was satisfied with him.

He drank both bottles of champagne. Extremely drunk, he lingered on the balcony, mourning that he had never known love. All his life he had been searching for a relationship that would last for ever, but he had never found the person. The marriage with Iris had failed. He had hurt the two men he cared most about, Allan and Bruce. Now both were dead.

He didn't feel like going to bed. He stayed on the balcony, head back, looking at the empty sky. Around five in the morning the drunkenness suddenly evaporated. When he stood up he was perfectly steady.

He had an urge to walk so he drove to Toronto's east end beaches. The sky was still dark as he walked the length of the boardwalk, still barefoot and shirtless. The waves lapping the shore made a contented sound. He felt light-headed but perfectly sober.

As dawn began to break, he sat on a park bench and watched the squawking gulls wheeling and the passing of early morning joggers. His thoughts had fixed on one idea: that there was nothing more that he had to do. He could put down the burden. He had tried to make something of his life and while it hadn't always worked out, he had always done his best. He could take pride in that, but it was done.

His mood soft and calm, he drove back to his apartment. He parked his car exactly in his assigned space in the garage, taking time to get it perfectly straight between the two lines. He locked the doors and stood admiring the sparkling clean finish. He checked his apartment to make sure it was spotless. He scoured the bathtub and sinks, put out fresh towels, and made the bed with clean sheets. He opened the cupboard doors and made certain the glasses and mugs were in straight rows. As he puffed up the pillows on the sofa, he realized that he was preparing to kill himself.

He looked in the mirror and felt sympathy for the person he saw. That person in the reflection had a sad life. He was sick with a terrible disease and he had never found his love.

Jim laid out the clothes he wanted to be wearing in his coffin. On the coffee table, where no one could miss them, he put the farewell letters he had written to friends and family and the tape he wanted played at his funeral.

He showered, shaved, and put on cologne. He slipped into a clean jogging suit that he wears as pyjamas. He opened his medicine cabinet and took out an almost full bottle of Halcyon sleeping pills. They wouldn't be enough to kill him, he decided. They would need help to stop his lungs and heart. He found some Tylenol 3s, a codeine prescription given him for pain. That would do it.

He looked into the eyes in the bathroom mirror. He thought, *I'm so alone.*

He said aloud to the man in the mirror, "I'm sorry to do this to you. You've really struggled, but it's time to stop."

He dumped the pills in his hand and washed them down with water. Now there was no turning back. He felt great peace and relief. A picture came into his mind of a pond, very still and beautiful under a motionless sky.

He thought, pleased, It's over. You did it. Now you can relax.

He put the pill bottles away neatly, turned off the bathroom lights, and climbed into bed with his teddy bear.

A thought struck him. It was possible that he wouldn't be discovered for several days and his body would have started to decompose. That would be unpleasant for the person who found him. He got up and put a message on his telephone answering machine: "Hello. It's Jim and I'm sorry that I'm not available. Please leave your message. I have loved you all. Goodbye."

For the first time he began to wonder how his death would affect others. The people in the AIDS support group looked up to him. Maybe his death would make them discouraged.

He found paper and a pen and laboriously wrote a note urging PWAs to keep on fighting. He didn't want to set off a rash of suicides. It was becoming difficult to write but he persevered. He addressed individuals in turn, urging them not to give up. "None of you should give up…."

He put his funeral music on the machine and crawled dizzily into bed.

The next thing he saw was a white ceiling. He looked around and there was a swarthy man sitting beside him, reading a book. A green shade had been pulled down over a window. He tried to move. He was naked and his hands and legs were fastened.

He shook his head. His vision was double and wouldn't clear.

"Untie me," he told the man.

"I can't," the man responded.

Jim was terrified. What was happening? He started to thrash and scream. Linda Boyd appeared beside him, speaking in a soothing voice. Behind her was Rafe, his drinking buddy. A nurse appeared and then a doctor. It seemed outrageous to Jim that all these people were in the room but no one was making a move to untie him. He cursed them all at the top of his lungs.

"Rafe," he yelled. "Call the newspapers! They have me tied down here."

Dr. Garvey arrived. "My goodness, you have strong lungs," she observed mildly.

Jim immediately calmed.

"They have me tied down," he complained to her.

She said, "Just leave it for a little while, Jim. Relax. We're looking after you."

"What is happening? Why am I tied down?"

He got no answer.

The room cleared, except for the stoical guard. Someone brought Jim a coffee, which he sipped through a bent straw. He discovered he was attached to a catheter. His mouth felt funny. After a moment he apologized to the swarthy man for his rudeness.

A woman who said she was a psychiatrist came to test his reflexes. "Can you follow my finger?"

He could, but with difficulty. He was still having trouble focusing.

"Do you know where you are?"

"Dr. Garvey was just here, so it must be St. Mike's Hospital."

"Right," she grinned.

"What happened to me?" he asked. Suddenly he knew. "My God," he groaned. "I tried to kill myself."

Late that afternoon a nurse removed Jim's catheter and unfastened the restraints on his arms and legs. He went to the bathroom, followed closely by the swarthy man, and saw that his mouth was filled with what looked like black tar. He brushed his teeth and tried to make himself presentable. A nurse gave him his jogging suit and he got back into bed to think.

Dr. André C. came in.

"André," Jim asked. "What happened?"

The doctor reconstructed the sequence of events for him. It was now Friday afternoon. Jim had taken the pills, as near as the hospital could estimate, around seven on Thursday morning. Glen had called Jim about two hours later, a very unusual thing for Jim's roommate to have done. Glen rarely called Jim during his periodic attempts at reconciliation with Gord, and he never before had called early in the morning because he knew that Jim likes to sleep in.

Glen was alarmed by the message on the telephone answering machine. Jim's voice sounded strange and the "I have loved you all" had a ring of farewell. Glen called Linda Boyd, who dialled Jim's number and listened to the tape. She didn't like it either.

They decided something was wrong. Glen volunteered to go to the apartment and let himself in with the key to check if Jim was all right. If Jim was in trouble, he would phone Linda at once and she could let Natalie know.

Glen had a ominous sense as soon as he entered the apartment. The place was too still. He looked in the bedroom and saw Jim lying on his back, his eyes half open and glazed with coma. When the friend called Linda, she immediately summoned an ambulance.

A team was waiting in St. Michael's emergency with a pump. To absorb the drugs, they filled his stomach with charcoal. Jim regained consciousness while they worked on him and raved a stream of insults, directed mostly at a hapless young doctor doing a residency in psychiatry. Someone called Jim's father to say that Jim wasn't expected to live. Karl and Eleanor rushed to St. Mike's and waited with Natalie all Thursday afternoon and into the evening while doctors struggled to keep Jim's heart going.

By Thursday night, the crisis was over.

Jim was restricted to his room. The swarthy man was replaced by another man. Jim realized that they were guards. He protested and was told that they were there to make him feel more calm and safe. He could accept that, he really didn't want to be alone. Everything sharp had been removed from the room— razor blades, scissors.

For four days and nights he was under close surveillance, even when he used the toilet or shower. Then Jim was left to himself, though restricted from leaving the room. Jim allowed himself to think about the suicide attempt and wonder why he'd done it. Sitting before a window one dreary, overcast day, he tried to puzzle it out. He was a man who had everything—he lived like a prince. He had just finished playing the lead very successfully in a play. His apartment was beautiful. He had fine clothes, thanks to Natalie, who took him shopping occasionally, and to his father, who would lend him his Visa card. He had plenty to eat. He had friends. He had a good reputation in the community. He was healthy—very healthy, considering.

He had everything. What was missing so much that he had wanted to be dead?

He couldn't blame it on AIDS. He had been very lucky with his AIDS. Allan D. had died with pieces of his stomach in a bedpan; Francis with half his face gone. Others were covered with Kaposi's tumours. John W. had drowned in his own phlegm. Those men had gone through hell, Jim reflected. His life was a piece of cake in comparison.

He didn't want to see or speak to anyone but his family and Natalie. He needed privacy to think. His door had a NO VISITORS sign, and his phone calls were intercepted. For several days, Natalie refused to visit. She explained to Jim's father that she was so angry that she didn't trust herself to see Jim. When she and Bernie turned up, she smouldered silently and let Bernie do the talking.

The visit was brief. "Bernie," Natalie said, standing up. "We'll have to leave before I slug him."

Jim was drawing some conclusions. One was that he was a person who would always need to have a project. The suicide was caused in good part by his feeling of purposelessness. The closing of *The Dining Room* had left a void; he had nothing to fill his days. How foolish he had been. He was young and smart and fit. Surely he could find something worthwhile to occupy himself.

The difficulty was the uncertainty of the disease. A normal job was out of the question. He was always popping in and out of hospital, and for long periods weakness would overcome him. All people with AIDS were in the same situation. Because they were young, they were accustomed to being active and productive. The disease put them in limbo, too ill to continue working but well enough, sometimes, to want to be busy at something. But what?

He didn't have an answer, but he resolved to find one. The other major problem, his loneliness, would be more difficult. He was finding it increasingly difficult to tolerate waking up alone in his bed, spending his days alone, eating alone, going to bed alone. He couldn't look for the deep attachment he longed to have because of his AIDS. If he did find someone to love, someone who would love him, that person would have to be prepared to watch Jim die. Who would want that?

He had thought before of teaming up with someone else with AIDS. They both would know the score, that one or both of them would die young. He reflected that he hadn't looked enough. So many people were getting AIDS. Surely he could find one person among them with whom he could live lovingly.

He left hospital with two resolutions: that he would make a project for himself to keep occupied and that he would find companionship and maybe love among people with AIDS. He was pleased with himself for clarifying his goals. His energy and confidence returned. He felt alive and ready to go forward.

He resumed attending the PWA support group, which had been badly rattled by his suicide attempt. Linda Boyd explained to a friend, "They felt that if the strongest person in the group, the one who was their spokesman, could want to kill himself, why did they bother to keep going?"

Steve G., a comptroller, was a handsome blond youth with astonishing blue eyes. Jim called them "surfer-boy eyes" and always thought that Steve looked like a California beach boy. For a time, as long as his health would permit, Steve volunteered to help a group of people who were planning to establish an AIDS hospice in Toronto, called Casey House, but he had to drop out when he started to become blind.

Steve and Jim became playmates. Their theory was "if people are going to drop around us, let them drop—we're going to go disco." Both loved to laugh and to hang out in bars. They went straight from the tragedy-drenched group discussions to Chaps for a beer.

When Steve's sight started to go, Jim led him to the bars. Strangers sometimes stopped them to say to Steve, "Pardon me, but you have the most beautiful blue eyes I've ever seen." Steve, unable to see who was speaking, nevertheless would thank them merrily.

Steve lived with his father, an alcoholic. One night his father ordered a pizza, put it in the oven to warm it, and then forgot it was there. The box caught fire and Steve smelled the smoke in his upstairs bedroom. He fell down the stairs in his haste to reach the fire and groped blindly at the stove for the source, burning his hand severely. He filled a pot with water and threw it in the direction of the heat, managing to put out the blaze.

When Jim dropped in a few days later Steve told him about it, making a joke of it, but Jim could tell that Steve had been badly frightened and was shaken still.

Jim had encountered a massage therapist not long before who told him that massage is very helpful to the blind, because of the touching.

"Strip down," Jim told Steve. "When you've seen one man, you've seen them all. Take off your clothes. I'm going to give you a good rubdown."

While Jim rubbed Steve's body, they talked about Steve's death. "I know it's going to happen," Steve said calmly. "I just want it to happen soon. I've thought of taking pills. I don't want to be useless like this any longer."

Jim silently held him in his arms. Neither cried.

When Steve lay dying in hospital, Linda Boyd persuaded him to start putting his life story on tape. Steve embraced the project eagerly and had almost completed the autobiography when his illness overtook him.

That example proved useful. Jim often advises PWAs to get their life story down. It's a way of surviving.

John H. was Steve's friend. John raised a storm with the Canadian National Institute for the Blind because some official there was reluctant at first to assign someone to help Steve. John, a flamboyant dresser, was one of those PWAs who got "the lean disease", wasting away because of bowel destruction. He accepted that with debonair grace, never losing his poise in Jim's presence, and devoted himself to attending to Steve until he died.

His spirit broke, however, when he noticed one day that he was losing his eyesight. He went into a black depression. Jim believes that John committed suicide. He didn't have the look of a man who was ready to die of AIDS. Jim knows the look well, and John didn't have it.

Carl H., a tall, handsome, easy-going man, worked in gay bars. Jim knew him only slightly but was a friend of Carl's lover, Steve. When Steve introduced Jim to Carl as someone who also had AIDS, Carl shook his hand with a warm grin.

"I've got it too," he said. "I'll just have to work with it, see if I can beat it."

He kept his affable nature and composure to his death. His attitude was that other people were worse off than he was. He'd had a good life, he'd do his best to get through AIDS, but it was all right if he didn't make it. In the group he was never bitter and never morose. Jim watched him with admiration and respect, and took a lesson. Carl was not letting AIDS change him. That was Jim's idea about AIDS too.

Carl died quickly, only a few months later.

Ron McL., a balding man with an athletic body, was a bus dispatcher. Jim and Ron had had a sexual fling eight or so years earlier and Jim still found him a sexy, alluring man. He suggested they have an affair again, but Ron, who lived on the outskirts, couldn't arrange to stay in town.

Other PWAs in the group, those not attached to lovers, were coupling with one another. Two PWAs could relax together. While each took precautions against the other's virus, neither wanting to get someone else's bug, there was at least the relief from the need to start the relationship with a lecture about safe sex and endure inspection of one's lesions and purple blotches. PWAs understood better than anyone that there could not be sex with penetration—but that that still left many pleasures.

Ron came to the group for about two months and promised Jim he would spend the night with him in the next week or so. That was the last Jim saw of him. Ron missed three or four group meetings and then one night Linda Boyd told the group that Ron McL. was dead.

Jim is curious about deaths that happen that fast in people who apparently are still healthy. He always wonders if there was a little help. Paul L.'s death is the one that makes him most suspicious. Though Paul's AIDS had been diagnosed six months before, Paul looked absolutely fit, like a man in the pink of condition, and seemed out of place among the support group's coughing, haggard men.

One morning, only three days after a healthy-looking Paul had been at a support group meeting, they read in the paper that he had died of cancer.

"Cancer doesn't kill anyone that fast," the men agreed, "and neither does AIDS."

Rumours floated around that people with AIDS were contacting Britain's Hemlock Society to get information about painless ways of committing suicide. Jim understood why. For most it was the fear of suffering. They all had listened to the screams of dying men; no one wanted to die in agony. Others could see themselves becoming a burden on family and friends. Some wanted to die before the disease made them ugly.

261

Terry G., whose AIDS had resulted in spinal meningitis, confided to Jim that he was stockpiling sleeping pills. Jim told Terry, "Don't try to kill yourself when you're depressed. That's the wrong time to do it. Believe me, I know."

Terry's death soon after looked suspiciously sudden.

Brooding about all the deaths with a friend, Jim said, "It's like someone taking away my history. These are the people who knew me in my twenties. I'm only thirty-two and I should have all these friends, but they're gone. It's so abnormal, so unnatural."

Bill McC., a sweet, quiet man with shaggy sand-coloured hair, lived on a farm near King City with his lover, Ernie, an affectionate, vulnerable man possessed of a wicked wit. An established couple for many years, they took up farming in order to enjoy privacy and have time together. Bill and Ernie had a pack of dogs and other animals, cultivated a kitchen garden, and loved to cook together. In the gay community, they were regarded as an ideal couple.

When Bill's parents learned that their son was dying, they attempted to secure title to the farm and were able to afford to retain a battery of lawyers to help them. They put pressure on Bill, who had Kaposi's and pneumonia, to change his will, and they reviled Ernie with the usual insults that some people heap on gay men.

The group furiously threw its depleted energy into encouraging the men to hold firm, and word was that Bill had refused to change the will. Linda Boyd called around one day to say that Bill had died and his parents were taking Ernie to court. To everyone's satisfaction, Ernie won the case.

Mario M., a small man with a reputation for his prowess in bed, was only in the group a short time before he became too sick to attend. His contribution, however, was memorable. His passion was that people with AIDS should keep in touch. He arrived at the group one evening with a chart shaped like a tree, bearing names and telephone numbers and connecting lines.

"We'll call one another," he explained enthusiastically. "We'll each have a copy of this chart and we'll talk to one another whenever we feel blue or we have a problem."

Jim appeared to be the only one in the room who was dismayed. He thought of his own long list of names of people he knew who had died. There were nineteen. He didn't think Mario's plan would be much of a morale booster, but Mario was bubbling with enthusiasm and heads were nodding.

Jim tried to stop it.

"I love your idea, Mario," he said. "It's important that we get together to help one another, and I see what you're getting at. But maybe we shouldn't go quite so far as this telephone tree you're suggesting."

"Why not?" Mario asked belligerently.

"Well, I'm the veteran here," Jim said slowly. "I hate to say this, but I've had some experience with lists. I can tell you that in a few weeks or months from now, there are going to be a lot of holes in that chart. It can get pretty depressing."

Jim was overruled, and Mario distributed copies of the chart. Very soon there were four names crossed out. And then, two more. One of them was Mario.

Jim can't remember Mario very well. On the tape where he was recording his thoughts he said, "How can I forget the people I've spent time with, the people who have passed away? There have been so many and so many funerals. It's overwhelming. People wonder. They ask, Why haven't you gone crazy? I wonder myself why I haven't gone around the bend. I knew those people. They were young, they were just starting off in life. Like me, just starting a career. I've watched them all die. It's not great being the longest-living AIDS patient, I'll tell you. Sometimes I envy Larry and Dennis and Brucie and Allan. They haven't gone on year after year watching a new crowd of diagnosed patients come in and then seeing them die, one by one, struggling for a chance at hope."

The group, for reasons of privacy, had moved out of the busy, congested ACT office and was meeting instead in the reception room of a psychiatrist's suite of offices, which were unused on Monday evenings. One evening Jim walked in and found Lawrence P. sitting there.

"Oh no," he groaned. "Not you, Lawrence."

Jim knew Lawrence as a member of the gang that Bruce C. had hung out with.

Lawrence gave Jim a twisted smile. "Yep," he said. "Me too."

Lawrence, a small, squarely built man, was a gifted school teacher who inspired affection and respect in his colleagues and students. Like Steve G., he was part of the steering committee to found Casey House hospice and capably served on sub-committees.

Lawrence loved to talk about his family, and some of the stories were painful. As his health worsened, he moved in with a sister, but he could see that his presence was having a disastrous effect on the sister's marriage. Torn between her husband and her dying brother, she chose the latter. Jim heard later that her husband had left her. Then Lawrence died.

When Jim was in St. Michael's Hospital with one of his fevers the head nurse asked him to visit a young man two doors away whose AIDS was affecting his brain. Brain damage from AIDS was unusual at that time. Oddly, dementia was to become a common calamity among people dying of AIDS, but few doctors knew then that a species of the AIDS virus could attack brain cells directly. St. Michael's doctors wanted a brain-tissue sample in order to confirm that the man's problems stemmed from AIDS.

"He's petrified," the nurse told Jim. "Maybe you could talk to him, calm him down. His name is Sam R."

Jim had been planning to visit other patients in the hospital and was dressed in slacks and a shirt. He knocked on Sam's door and was invited in.

"I'm Jim St. James," Jim said, "and I understand you're having a rough time."

"Yes," Sam replied grudgingly. "I have AIDS and they want to open my skull. I don't know if I should let them."

Jim made some general comments of reassurance about the skill of the St. Mike's surgeons. "A lot of people have faced this disease," he continued. "I've seen a lot of cases and I have seen that fighters come through. You have to get your confidence going...."

Sam was not impressed. "I really appreciate you coming to see me," he snapped, "but you don't know what it's like. You don't have AIDS. Look at you, you're the picture of health."

Jim replied, "I have AIDS too. I've had it for almost two years."

"Whaaaaat!" Sam cried. "You look wonderful. It's not possible."

"Sure it is," Jim grinned. "And you can do it too."

Jim gave him his standard pep talk about "keep going, keep trying, keep on truckin' until there's no more strength to go on", and Sam listened, enchanted.

For as long as Sam lived, it was his goal to be as healthy as Jim St. James. He and his lover, Gary, marvelled at Jim's appearance and one or the other would bring up Jim's name whenever they felt discouraged.

Jim went with Russell A. to Sam's funeral to be a support to Gary. Gary was one of the regulars at funerals for people who died of AIDS. The gang of regulars was almost a travelling club.

Sam's funeral was very tearful. Gary was very busy when it ended, shaking hands with Sam's huge Lebanese family, and he didn't spot Jim until the funeral cortège was about to leave. He got out of the limousine and gripped Jim in a hug.

Struggling for control, he said, "Jim, we wouldn't have gotten this far but for you. You made Sam a fighter."

Jim remembers Tom R., tall and awkward, as the one they couldn't stop from talking. He used the group as a sounding board to absorb his pain, and they decently put aside their own needs and listened as he rambled on about his life and his fears. They figured him for a lonely man. He was living with his parents in a small town near Guelph, and he had yet to tell his family that he had AIDS.

Meetings that Tom attended left the others feeling ragged, but the complaining was good-natured and gentle. He died soon after Sam.

From time to time Jim took someone home with him to stay the night or for a few days, someone with AIDS. He found, to his great embarrassment, that he could not sustain an erection. For a man who once had been something of a sexual athlete, it was crushing to his ego.

He encountered Dr. Stan Read at a party and on an impulse told him about it.

"What medication are you on?" Stan asked.

Jim told him. The list included something new that he was taking for the fungus-like candida albicans infection in his throat. Stan told him that thrush medication was famous for killing libido.

"Jim, you couldn't get it up if you tried," he grinned.

Nathan S. was a thin, intellectual Mennonite whose family had been understanding and supportive when he told them he was gay. They prayed about what they saw as an unfortunate situation, but they were not fanatics and the thought of rejecting their son apparently never crossed their minds. "Pretty together people," Jim observes enviously.

Nathan's reaction to the diagnosis that he had AIDS was one that Jim frequently observed. He changed his habits completely in a desperate effort to mend his health. Where once he had enjoyed a hamburger and french fries, he now turned to steamed broccoli and wheat germ.

"It's a bad mistake," Jim thinks. "I've seen how it turns out when people go on a health kick based on something like an extreme macrobiotic diet. I'm convinced it's a bad mistake." Jim believes that the special diets are fine for a well person, but that a sick person needs the nutrition of a balanced diet. "The macrobiotic diet is too little, too late," he says. The stricken body, in the fight of its life, hasn't time to adjust to a drastic change of routine.

However, Jim never discourages anyone who firmly believes that such a diet or alteration of habits will make him well. As Nathan described to the group his discipline in adhering to the severe regimen he had prescribed for himself, Jim listened without comment. "Add the vitamins," he would have said if asked. "Get more rest. Eat healthier food. Buy spring water to avoid whatever is in tap water these days. But don't give your body such a shock."

Nathan died very quickly, which Jim attributed in good part to poor nutrition.

Jim had a call one day from Bill H., a man of twenty-two whom he knew only slightly. Word was that Bill was broke and close to dying. Jim checked his wallet to make sure he had some cash and went to see him. Bill was lying on a couch, weeping. He hadn't eaten and the rent was due, but his main concern was for his cat. He hadn't been able to afford cat food and the animal was hungry.

"Take the cat to the Humane Society for me, will you, Jim?" he asked. "Have him put to sleep. Do it for me, and do it fast. I don't want any goodbye."

Jim scooped up the cat and paid twenty-seven dollars to the Humane Society to have the cat put down.

The next time he saw him, Bill was in hospital. The youth was unkempt and depressed. He poured out the story of his grandmother's funeral, which was very much on his mind. He had gone to the funeral with his father and he was struck by his grandmother's beautiful oak casket. He told his father that when he died he wanted a casket like that.

His father turned on him. "I'm not putting a pervert in a casket like that. You buy your own coffin, because I'm not getting you one."

Jim held Bill in his arms and promised the emaciated man that he would be buried in a fine casket. When Bill died, Jim borrowed the money and bought a fine oak casket. Bill's father didn't attend the funeral.

13

Jim slowly evolved an idea for a organization made up entirely
of people with AIDS with the single purpose of enabling them
to help one another. The idea met a need in him that he had
expressed many times, to do something useful with his life.
Ever since the beginning of his illness, he had been yearning
to make a contribution that would help the gay community and
people with AIDS. He wanted to create something in which he
could take pride, something that perhaps would make his father
proud of him. That hope had sustained him through many black
depressions.

Early in 1986 it began to be clear that persons with AIDS faced
two grave problems in addition to their disease. One was poverty.
With a generosity he could no longer afford, Jim was handing
out money—ten, twenty, even fifty dollars—to help PWAs in
financial straits. Some, he knew, were not eating properly. Too
sick to work, they were living on welfare incomes that barely
covered their rent. The other problem was social isolation. The
AIDS support groups met only once a week, but people with AIDS
craved company more frequently. Those who were too sick to
work and too well to be in hospital had empty time on their
hands. They needed a central place where they could drop in for

coffee and be with people who could share what they were going through.

As well, the "veterans", people like Jim who had been in the AIDS support group for longer than a year, were tired of going over the same ground with newcomers—discussing what the treatment drugs might do to them, or what the pneumonia was like, listening to the man whose eyesight was going speak hopefully about the treatment he was taking, which everyone in the group knew had never worked to prevent blindness for anyone.

Jim was weary of going through it, week after week, and longed to be able to meet with other PWAs on a social basis, without the depressing repetition of pathology. Using his own survival as an illustration, Jim believed that PWAs would live longer if they didn't have the burden of financial stress and if they could be together to gain strength from one another. Poverty was enough to make a healthy person sick; for someone who was already extremely ill, poverty could hasten death.

He went for advice to Dennis Holbrooke at the Ryerson Poly-technical Institute. Dennis, author of a paper on PWA support groups in San Francisco, agreed strongly that people with AIDS needed a mechanism to draw them together for comfort.

"No one wants to be alone," Dennis told Jim. "When people first get the diagnosis, they feel very alone. They need to be with others who have the disease and can give them some idea of what to expect. There's strength in numbers."

Jim could see that raising money for AIDS projects was a problem for other groups. The AIDS Committee of Toronto was always in crisis for lack of funds. The committee trying to put together a hospice for AIDS was in similar trouble. He reasoned that an organization of people with AIDS wouldn't have the same problems. The public was certain to be touched by the poignancy of such an organization.

Certainly there was acute and urgent need for financial support for people with AIDS. ACT had just instigated a program to provide modest financial help for PWAs, but ACT itself was poor. Jim knew at first hand PWAs who were homeless and frequently hungry.

He decided he would pull some PWAs together and get a group rolling, but first he needed to know how such projects worked in other cities. He drove to New York City to see what was happening there and was greatly impressed. He found a drop-in centre and soup kitchen for people with AIDS, run by people with AIDS, and thronged with gaunt, hollow-eyed men talking and eating quietly together. In New York, PWAs also ran their own information and distress centre.

. Back in Toronto he made calls to some sixteen PWAs he knew from the support group. Seven expressed interest—Russell A., Franz H., Ray Barnard, Chris N., Danny B., Daniel D., and Leo J. He invited them to his apartment on August 28, 1986, and served orange juice and cookies while telling them his enthusiastic plans.

"I don't think this is how IBM started," he grinned, "but I'll bet we can do it."

He said they all needed to get together without the clinical discussions that happened in the PWA support group. "There are other things to talk about besides AIDS."

Everyone thought it was a great idea to have a clubhouse where PWA s could get emergency help and have some laughs. Maybe they could show funny movies, the way Norman Cousins described in his book *Anatomy of an Illness*.

What should they call themselves? Someone remembered that Vancouver had such a group, the Vancouver Persons with AIDS Coalition. Why not be the Toronto Persons with AIDS Coalition? They would need posters to tell other PWAs that they existed and a letterhead on which to write appeals for donations. That meant getting an identifying logo. One of them knew a graphic artist who might help. Could anyone type? Chris N., who arrived in such a weak state that he could scarcely walk, said he wasn't sure he had the strength, but he would try.

"I'm not *really* that ill," he said weakly.

The others looked at one another uncertainly, but Jim thought it would do Chris good to have a project.

A printing house ran off a hundred posters announcing that the Toronto PWA Coalition was open for business and giving a phone number to call for information. The group had no money to rent an office, so it was agreed that on a temporary basis, until they got some funds, the phone would be in Ray Barnard's apartment. Each of them would take turns answering it.

As the small group scurried around tending to tasks Jim assigned, Chris seemed to revive. He went with Jim to put posters on telephone poles and hoardings in the area of Wellesley and Church streets and churned out letters asking corporations to donate funds.

Jim talked to Lorraine Manley, fund raiser for the AIDS Committee of Toronto, and to Jim Shea and Rebecca Bragg of the Casey House hospice committee to make certain that his group wasn't stepping on anyone's toes. From them he learned how to apply to the Gay Community Appeal, which collects money in the gay community to disperse to worthy gay and lesbian causes. Jim studied the ACT application asking the Gay Community Appeal for $11,500 and discussed with the other PWAs what would be an appropriate amount for the coalition. It was agreed to ask the Gay Community Appeal for $12,000, the amount estimated for the rent of a clubhouse for a year.

In the expectation that their request would be met—who could deny dying men?—they started to hunt for space. A few weeks later they received a pleasant letter from the Gay Community Appeal and a cheque for $500 "for PWA initiatives".

"What's that supposed to mean, initiatives?" one PWA asked furiously.

Jim replied, "I'll tell you what our initiatives are—we're burying everybody."

The search for a headquarters was abandoned.

To their consternation, other responses to applications were also poor. A few individuals gave twenty dollars or so, but the corporations from whom Jim had hoped to get thousands of dollars weren't interested. Some articles appeared in the press, resulting in a flurry of interest that died in a day or two. Few people called the Persons with AIDS Coalition telephone, and many who did call wouldn't give their names. Jim's impression was that the PWA Coalition was an embarrassment that both the gay and straight communities wished had not surfaced.

The tiny PWA Coalition threw a Hallowe'en party for themselves. A new member, Jacques D., had a brilliant idea for a costume. Jacques' AIDS had manifested itself in repulsive open sores, some of them two inches wide, that had spread all over his body and face. The costume he chose was a Second World War soldier's uniform worn with the tunic open. The sores on his face and chest looked like wounds of battle.

Other PWAs were joining, but the group still wasn't getting anywhere. Corporations were asking for a tax-deductible receipt, and Jim learned that the organization would have to be more formal. The coalition would have to register with the Ontario government as a non-profit organization; then it would have to get incorporated; and then it could apply for tax-deductible status with the federal income-tax department.

Jim was horrified: all that red tape and bureaucracy just so a handful of dying people could help one another?

A friendly lawyer offered to help. First they would need a statement of their objectives. That was a breeze. They wanted to provide the public with firsthand information about living with AIDS; they wanted a drop-in centre; and they needed a supply of money to be used at the discretion of the group to help PWAs in financial emergencies.

The lawyer said they would also need by-laws. None of them had any idea what a by-law looked like. Jim and Russell A. looked at the by-laws used by the AIDS Committee of Toronto and concluded that by-laws weren't so difficult after all. The group sat down and whacked out a satisfactory list of simple rules that stated the qualification for membership in the PWA Coalition (a diagnosis of AIDS) and how officers would be elected.

They went back to the friendly lawyer. What next? He said that he couldn't apply for letters patent or incorporation until the group had officers. How many? Three, at least.

The next meeting was in Jacques' apartment. Jacques served tea and coffee and proudly showed off his newest acquisition, a glass-topped coffee table. The guests commented derisively on Jacques' exquisite taste in art—the walls were adorned with posters of male nudes.

"If we're going to get incorporated, we need a president, a secretary, and a treasurer," Jim explained. "Who wants to do what?"

Russell A. volunteered to be treasurer. Chris N. said that because he could type he would be secretary. In the pause that followed, Leo J., stretched out on the couch, said lazily, "Jim, you'd better be president since you're doing all the work."

"I don't know about that," Jim responded. "I hate paper work. I simply can't be bothered with it. And I don't know much about business...."

"Come oooon, Jim," Russ protested.

"Okay," he conceded, pleased. "Whatever you guys think."

They left the incorporation and tax status matters to the lawyer. He explained that he was a busy man, and he warned of red tape and long delays. It could take months. Meanwhile the group should try to keep track of income and expenses. An accountant volunteered to help, and Jim accepted gratefully.

The group was gathering support. James Beckwith, a member of the Toronto Board of Health, spoke highly of the organization. "St. James and the PWA Coalition focus on a high quality, long life for people with AIDS," he said. People admired the spunkiness of the coalition's motto: "We stand and fight."

Jim was in demand as a speaker. He explained to audiences all over Toronto, "It's the stress that helps activate the AIDS virus. So paying the mortgage, socializing, buying the drugs, looking at mental therapies and alternative medicines are all important. If persons with AIDS need financial help with that, then we'll give it. We'll do anything we can to keep them calm and relaxed, and we'll go for anything that will keep them alive."

Of himself he said simply, "My work has brought me back to life."

On the stroke of midnight on Christmas Eve, 1986, Jim stood in front of the Ontario Legislature at Queen's Park and sang "Silent Night" in memory of "those who have lost". In a gesture borrowed from Martin Luther, he left a proclamation on the main doors: "Wouldn't now be a good time to help the people? Do whatever is necessary to end AIDS."

Chris grew thinner and weaker. He insisted he was well enough to type, but sometimes it would take him an afternoon to finish one letter. One day he called Jim to say he would have to be inactive for a while because he was going into hospital. Linda Boyd told the next support group meeting that Chris was very sick.

She didn't have to elaborate. "Very sick" is the AIDS euphemism for death's door. Everyone realized that Chris, only twenty-four years old, was dying. Jim couldn't bring himself to visit. He told himself that he was too busy today, he'd probably go to see Chris tomorrow, but he never did. He didn't want to watch Chris die.

Linda said that Chris asked about Jim and wondered why he didn't come. Then she relayed a message that Chris understood why Jim didn't visit, and that it was all right.

"Tell Jim to keep going," he said to Linda. "And tell him that working in the PWA Coalition helped me a lot. It felt good to be useful."

Chris's main concern during the last two weeks of his life was for his two dogs. He lived alone, and the dogs were dear to him. Because he knew no one who would care for them, he asked Jim to arrange to have them put to sleep. When Chris died, Linda took the dogs to the Humane Society.

The rest of the PWA Coalition founding group attended Chris's funeral with shattered expressions on their faces. One down. *Who would be next?*

Ray Barnard stepped into Chris's position as secretary of the group.

Jim and his father had a frightful row. Karl Zanuk accused his son of laziness. If he was well enough to run around starting an organization for people with AIDS, he was well enough to work for a living, he said. He was cutting Jim off immediately. Jim would not get a cent from him ever again.

Natalie and Bernie Wexler acted as conciliators, as they always did after the rows between father and son. They explained that Jim's health was always uncertain. In fact Jim had a number of troubling symptoms. For one, he seemed to have a perpetual cold, and Dr. Garvey was arranging for him to have surgery to clear his sinuses. In addition the thrush infection in his throat kept recurring and Kaposi's had settled in his left leg, which had erupted with a dozen purple boils.

This time his father was adamant. Jim was cut off.

Jim had some savings and husbanded his money as carefully as he could, but eventually he was broke. He was forced to do what many PWAs do and apply for welfare as a disabled person. The

276

Family Benefits program pays a single person only about $500 a month, but it made Jim eligible for free prescription drugs—an important consideration—and a rent subsidy. He started looking for a cheaper apartment.

That summer of 1987 Jim discovered a wonderful place to relax, a quarry outside Guelph where gay men swam and sunbathed in the nude. He went with his drinking buddies, David and Rafe, and sometimes with PWAs from his support group.

One afternoon David and Rafe gave Jim a bag of Magic Mushrooms. He knew they were hallucinogenic, but he hadn't done illegal drugs for a long time and he was curious to try them. He took the entire bag at a party that evening and went home stoned, wondering what the Magic Mushrooms would do to him.

Just inside his door, he was flooded with a memory of Bruce C. so piercing that he began to sob. His weeping grew out of control and became hysteria. Frightened, he called his friend Terry and got an answering machine. Terry didn't get the message until the crisis had passed. When he discovered what had happened, he tore into David and Rafe for giving a sick man hallucinogens.

Despite the lack of tax status or formal organization, the new PWA Coalition was gaining acceptance. Dennis Holbrooke, Jim's psychologist friend at Ryerson, sold tickets to a Sunday afternoon cocktail party that raised six thousand dollars. Owners of some of the gay bars, Trax and the Barn, took up a collection from staff and customers and turned over the proceeds, a few hundred dollars for each occasion. Two men gave a party at Ryerson with catered food, the draw being a speech by Jim St. James, and that realized a few thousand more.

After the phone and printing bills were paid, most of the money received by the coalition was distributed in amounts of fifty dollars and seventy-five dollars, on a casual basis, to PWAs who asked for help. Jim estimated that the coalition had been

277

able to assist close to forty people; in some cases, money was provided to help pay for funerals.

Jim was notified that his application for a subsidized apartment had been accepted by the Metro Toronto Housing Authority. A one-bedroom apartment was available on the seventeenth floor of a high rise near Bloor and Sherbourne. Normally the space rented for more than $500 a month, but with the subsidy it would cost Jim only $97. In February 1987 Jim moved from his spacious apartment on Sherbourne Street to the new place. It was much smaller than the apartment he had occupied for two and a half years, but he enjoyed making it cosy and beautiful.

One Sunday morning Jim was wakened by a knock on his door. A dishevelled stranger stood there, carrying a small gym bag. He said he had AIDS and could he come in? Jim sleepily made him some coffee and pushed a bowl of potato chips at him. The man ate one or two, then a handful, then wolfed down the rest.

His money had run out, he told Jim sheepishly. He had been diagnosed with AIDS the week before, and his lover had kicked him out with only the clothes he wore and a few things he had hastily shoved into the gym bag. For three nights he had slept in a steam bath for eight dollars a night, but then he couldn't afford even that, so he had been sleeping for the past two nights in a park. He hadn't eaten since breakfast two days earlier. He didn't know anyone he could turn to.

Jim called Russell, waking him up. "I need a cheque right away," he said. "We've got an emergency here."

Russ said, "Sure, how much?"

Jim calculated, knowing the reserve was low. "Well, two hundred and fifty right away and probably more later."

Russ yawned. "Who do I make it out to?"

Jim held the phone away from his ear. "What's your name?" he asked the stranger.

The man looked away. "I don't want to tell you."

"Get back to you later," Jim told Russ.

Jim took the money out of his own account, using a bank machine.

Jim consulted the friendly lawyer. The coalition was often running into people with AIDS who were so ashamed of their poverty that they didn't want to tell their names. He needed to keep cash on hand for such situations, he explained. Would it be all right if he and other directors drew out cash to distribute as they found the need? The lawyer said it would be fine. The volunteer accountant advised Jim that a cheque made out to "cash" was a sloppy way of doing business. He recommended that the directors make out the cheques to themselves.

Innocently, they did so, signing cheques made out to themselves. Jim kept the coalition cash separate from his own money and doled it out to help PWAs meet rent payments or buy a meal. When Jim worried about the appearance of things, one of the group grinned, "Don't worry about it. By the time they come to do the audit at the end of the year, we'll all be dead."

The details involved in running an organization, even a small one, were overwhelming. Fund raising was proving an exhausting job they all hated and for which no one was suited. The compassion that Jim believed would result in large donations either wasn't there or they didn't know how to tap it. Sometimes it was a problem to pay the phone bill, and there never was enough money to rent a drop-in space of their own.

Their problems with fund raising were hurting their credibility. As the numbers of people diagnosed with AIDS continued to rise, the coalition's inability to respond to the growing demand for financial help was giving rise to criticism. The morale of the founding group suffered. Increasingly people found excuses for not doing their shift at the telephone, or else simply failed to show up at all. Jim got angry complaints from PWAs who called the number day after day looking for help and got no answer.

Using Ray Barnard's apartment as a headquarters had not proved the best of ideas. Ray was a casual housekeeper and the place was untidy. Files were often misplaced and letters lost. The group needed a proper office, someone to answer the phone dependably, and someone to hustle money and speed up the organizational process, which continued to drag. Meetings were turning into wrangles about the missed shifts on the telephone and the lack of funds. Increasingly it became obvious that one of them would have to take responsibility for the organization on a full-time basis.

Russ had an idea.

"Jim, it looks as though you're going on salary."

The PWAs met in Russell's apartment, and Jim left the room while they discussed Russ's plan. When they called Jim back, they had made a unanimous decision. He would be paid the same salary, twenty thousand a year, that ACT paid secretaries.

"I'll make a deal," Jim said. "Whatever money I can raise will be used to help PWA s who apply for assistance and to pay the bills for telephone, postage, legal fees, and that sort of thing. If anything is left after that, I'll draw a salary."

The group thought that was a good plan. "That way, Jim, " one man observed genially, "you'll *have* to be a good fund raiser."

Jim was ebullient. "My goal for the first year," he promised, "will be $200,000."

They asked advice from the friendly lawyer. Could Jim be paid a salary and still remain president of the organization? The lawyer said that would be perfectly proper. Jim couldn't take money for being an officer, but it was acceptable for him to be paid as a fund raiser. Jim later wished that he had asked for another opinion.

As for the incorporation papers and application for the tax-exemption number, the friendly lawyer said he was doing his best, but everything takes time.

Meanwhile Jim hustled around the gay community to organize house parties and special events in bars. Money was loosening up for ACT and the Casey House hospice, and some of it flowed to the PWA Coalition as well, despite the handicap of a lack of tax-exempt status.

On May 3, 1987, the AIDS Committee of Toronto organized a memorial service in Trinity/St. Paul's United Church for people who had died of AIDS. Attendance was sparse, but the service was very moving. Steve Manning, a former priest who is executive director of ACT, spoke simply about grief and loss. A few people stood to talk of friends. One of those who spoke was the valiant Linda Boyd, and then there was the naming of the dead during which people with heads bowed said the names of those they were remembering.

At the end, everyone filed silently to the front of the church to light slim white candles, each symbolizing a prayer, and plant them in a bowl of sand. As the church slowly and sadly emptied, the forest of candles was a beautiful sight, like a white chrysanthemum on fire.

The coalition obtained free office space on a temporary basis in a handsome Victorian mansion purchased by the Casey House hospice committee. The building needed renovations and furnishings but work was not expected to begin until after the summer. The hospice provided desks and chairs, worn but serviceable, and Jim bought a coffee machine and moved the telephone from Ray's apartment. With a stack of styrofoam cups, the PWAs had their drop-in centre at last.

As phone answering improved, some twenty new PWAs joined. At first PWAs were uneasy about visiting because they saw Casey House as the place where they would die. The feelings of horror eventually dissipated and the office became a popular gathering place. The only complaint was about the coffee. It wasn't *healthy*, they said. Why wasn't there hot chocolate?

Gram C., a graphic artist with AIDS, designed a PWA Coalition logo that pleased them all. He drew a muscular archer in silhouetted profile drawing a bow: a warrior fighting back. They were advised to change their name to facilitate incorporation and they chose to be called the Toronto Persons with AIDS Foundation.

PWAs strolled into the new office and found Jim merrily sitting at a desk. He dispensed money and listened to the shop talk of people with AIDS—who was "getting sicker", who was trying a new treatment, who had just been diagnosed, the new turn the disease was taking. A new strain of the HIV virus was emerging, one that went straight for brain cells and formed a fungus-like tumour between skull and brain that resulted in dementia. People were dying crazy. Also, there was an increase in the number of PWAs who lost their sight. *What next*? they asked one another.

Most PWAs were in need of money. Some had been waiters living in apartments renting for $600 or more a month. After the diagnosis they would be in hospital for weeks or a month at a time, during which their incomes ceased. To hold their apartments, they would have to apply for assistance. If they obtained welfare, payments were $655 a month. The men needed help to survive while waiting to die.

Most days Jim simply cleaned out his wallet and handed over whatever he had.

Jim and Ray Barnard were all over the city, attending benefits and fund-raising receptions in order to receive a cheque for the foundation and thank the sponsors. Often people would split the proceeds three ways, ACT, Casey House, and the PWA Foundation. That was fine with all three.

By May of 1987 Jim's health began to deteriorate. To his chagrin, his clothes hung loosely on him. Even in hot weather, he wore big, loose, long-sleeved sweatshirts to conceal his scrawny torso. His left leg, always a problem, erupted in fresh cancer tumours and required radiation treatments, first in one place then in another.

During the fifth such treatment he made his expression bright and interested, the only way he can ask such a question, and inquired, "Doctor, will I lose my leg?"

"No, Jim," the doctor smiled. "We can keep you going for a long time with this radiation. If that stops working, we'll find something else."

His old foe, fatigue, returned. Though the foundation office in the hospice was only two blocks from his apartment, Jim found the walk tiring and limped with the pain of his ravaged leg. He always found his telephone answering machine jammed with messages. One day he counted twenty-two, most of them impatient voices wanting an immediate response.

A good many calls were from the media. Jim was the most accessible person with AIDS in Toronto: the others were either dead or keeping their condition quiet. At every development in the unfolding AIDS crisis, Jim would be called for a comment. The Canadian Public Health Institute discovered that he was a fine public speaker and began sending him across the country to talk about AIDS.

On August 9, 1987, there was a second memorial service for people who had died of AIDS, this one at the Church of the Redeemer. One hundred people came, among them some white-haired members of the congregation. A weeping man played the piano, accompanying a man playing the flute. He announced with dignity that one of the pieces was his own composition. He was playing it at the service for his friend who had died, and would never play the piece again.

Russell A. invested heavily in meditation exercises from a man who drove in to see him once a week from a small Ontario town.

There was always someone contacting the gay community with a sure-fire cure for AIDS, and meditation was that year's hottest craze. Another was a mixture of ant poison and butter, which a man insisted would work wonders. Someone else was trying tea made from mashed wood, and there was a woman who urged everyone to try high-energy yogurt. Jim never ridiculed anyone's treatment, however bizarre. When Russell pointed out that he had nothing to lose by trying meditation, Jim was skeptical but told Russell that it certainly was worth a try. For someone with AIDS, someone the world-wide medical establishment couldn't help, anything was worth trying.

Jim watched Russ emerge from three-hour meditation sessions totally exhausted. He was uneasy, not because Russ looked so worn out and was spending so much money, but because he didn't think that Russell really believed in the power of meditation. If Russ didn't believe it would work, Jim reasoned, meditation couldn't help him.

When the purple boils of Kaposi's sarcoma started to cover Russell's face, Jim knew that his friend and colleague was dying. Russ was ashamed of his ruined appearance and wore long-sleeved shirts to cover his raddled arms. Jim thought he looked seventy years old, with his purple eye sockets. Sometimes Russell's mind wandered and he talked disjointedly. His memory was no longer reliable.

Jim wept at the sight. Russell was his anchor. How could he manage without him?

Jim was going out of control himself. Sometimes his temper exploded and he would kick furniture or pound the walls and scream. Often he was testy with friends.

His scalding fever returned and he checked himself into St. Michael's Hospital.

Linda Cohen, the hospital social worker who had encouraged him to return to acting, sat beside his bed and looked him straight in the eye.

"Jim, enough is enough. You have done everything you can. It's time to quit helping everyone else and take care of yourself. Read my lips." She mouthed *No*.

Jim looked away.

"Jim, say N-O, *no*."

He murmured "no" under his breath.

"Louder," she commanded.

"*No*," he shouted with a grin. "All right, I've got it. *No*."

Linda rose to leave. "It is the end, you know, Jim," she said softly. "You'll have to quit the foundation or you'll die."

Jim told the foundation that he would be stepping down as president at the end of August, around the date of the first anniversary. They would have to find a replacement.

Around the same time the foundation was given notice that it would have to move out of Casey House. The hospice was about to start a massive demolition needed to make the medical floor accessible to stretchers.

No other space was volunteered so the files were returned to Ray Barnard's home. Jim asked the volunteer accountant for ledgers and other records and was informed, with embarrassment, that nothing had been done. Five months of accounts and receipts and cheque stubs were returned to Jim untouched.

Natalie gave him the name of an accounting firm, which Jim hired to begin sorting out the mess. The Ontario government, which was preparing to make a grant to the foundation, asked to examine the books and found them incomplete and confusing. Of the $38,500 that the foundation had taken in from various fund-raising events and donations, many of the dispersements were not documented. No one had collected receipts from PWAs who had been helped with cash gifts.

The date of the first annual meeting of the Toronto PWA Foundation was set for August 26, 1987. A sandy-haired, businesslike man came to see Jim. He introduced himself as Rodney Polich, thirty-six years old, said he had AIDS, and gave Jim a three-page résumé.

"I hear you're stepping down as president," he said, "and I'd like to offer myself as your replacement."

Rodney presented some ideas he had for the foundation. He thought there should be a nation-wide network of PWA organizations and that the Toronto organization could be a catalyst in bringing that about. Jim liked him and liked his ideas. He pulled in Russ and Ray and they agreed with his assessment, so Rodney was asked to stand for election as the next president and preside at the annual meeting.

What Jim has since described as "that awful week" began on the morning of August 23 when Doug P., known as " Digger", died. Digger was one of the disco crowd who hung out in a place called Stages. They had a reputation in the gay community for drug use and wild weekends. At about eleven on a Friday or Saturday night they would take their drugs—MDA, acid, hash. The effect of the drugs peaked at about two in the morning and so did the music. Towards dawn, with men coming down with the aid of tranquillizers, the music also mellowed out.

By about seven, with the sky light, the disco crowd would be too jittery to sleep and would move on to what was called the "morning party". Gathering in someone's house, they would pull the drapes, light candles, take soft drugs, and play soft music. During Jim's brief fling as a drug user, he went to seven disco-gang weekends. After he stopped the drugs, he was wistful for the friendships.

When the AIDS epidemic began, everyone expected that the disco crowd would fall like flies because of the abuse they inflicted on their bodies. To everyone's surprise, the crowd seemed to be immune. It wasn't until 1986 that two of them, Digger and Andy A., were diagnosed. The news that AIDS had finally invaded the disco crowd came as a shock. They clung together, feeling exposed and vulnerable.

Digger joined the PWA Foundation because Jim was there. He put up a valiant fight for many months, though he lost a great deal of weight and his body was horribly wasted. Then, abruptly, he seemed to give up and died in a few weeks.

The afternoon of the day Digger died, Jim visited one of his closest friends, Terry D., another foundation member and a friend from the days when young gay men were healthy and beautiful and loved to party. Terry was a wild man, a painter from New Brunswick with a fiery talent. A spiky-haired adherent of the leather-and-chains set, he was always broke and lived in shabby circumstances.

Jim thought that Terry, bright and quick and tormented, was a genius. Though Terry was a comical man capable of warm and loyal friendship, he lived in a state of suppressed fury, which escaped in his art. Whenever Jim saw Terry hanging out in the whips-and-leather bars, he was struck by the hunch that the man was trying to punish himself for being gay.

For a while Jim and Terry had a sexual fling. Afterwards there was a sweetness in their relationship. Whenever Jim was depressed, he went to visit Terry to be cheered up. They would part with hugs, and when Jim reached home he would find that Terry had slipped a note in his coat pocket: "Love you, kid."

Terry could always sense when Jim was discouraged and needed to be silly. Whenever Jim was feeling down after chemotherapy, hating the way he looked, Terry would call to meet at a burger bar and make Jim laugh.

When Terry first noticed the tell-tale purple marks on his arms, he decided maybe it wasn't AIDS, maybe it was too much drug use. He quit drugs completely and waited for the blotches to go away. When they didn't, he consulted a doctor and was told he had AIDS. Jim was the first person he called.

"You've got to make a fight of it," Jim counselled him. "Be strong. Look at me, it's been more than three years."

Terry resolutely stayed off drugs and started attending a self-help group for addicts.

The first time Terry was in hospital he covered every inch of the walls of his room with lurid paintings. Jim stood transfixed by the garish array and was touched to notice that one of the pieces taped to the wall was a picture of him. Every level surface of the room was covered in teddy bears of all sizes. Terry had dressed one of the bears in leather and given him a whip.

Terry had pneumonia and was also suffering from a brain infection, but he climbed out of bed to greet Jim with a hug. He had a rule about that. One should always hug friends.

Someone Jim didn't know came in and looked around the room admiringly.

"When you die, Terry," he asked, "can I have the teddy bears?"

Terry went back and forth to hospital every few weeks. The tumour growing against his brain often left him disoriented. He clung to Jim in terror that he was losing his mind.

"Don't worry," Jim assured him with a grin. "No one will notice the difference."

Terry was amused. They could always cheer one another.

When Jim heard that Terry was in hospital again and near death, he went to see him bearing gifts of a balloon cluster, some big crayons, and a drawing pad. His friend was stretched out on the bed, dark glasses covering his eyes and a cloth on his head.

"Ssssh," he whispered to Jim. "Everything is extra big. No noise. Please be calm."

The room was full of quiet, sad people, seven or eight in the small space.

Jim said in a genial tone, "All right, Terry, but I think you should be a good host. This looks like a party. Get up and serve the drinks."

Terry smiled fondly and said, "Shut the fuck up."

Terry was taking treatments, administered in an IV drip over a period of five hours, which made him violently ill. He told his doctors it wasn't worth it. The treatments weren't working anyway.

He ordered his doctor, "Stop the treatment and let me die."

Terry looked exhausted and he appeared to be in great pain. Jim gently squeezed Terry's foot through the sheet and Terry winced. "Jim, don't touch me," he whispered. "I'm too sensitive everywhere."

Jim didn't linger. He thought there were already too many people in the room for a sick man. He kissed Terry gently on the cheek and said he'd be back the next day.

As Jim got in his car, he thought, "That's the last I'll see of Terry."

Linda Boyd phoned the next morning. Terry was dead.

Jim went to tell Ray Barnard. They sat together for a long time without speaking, without needing to speak. Jim felt that his heart was breaking. The intensity of his pain over Terry's death caught him unawares. He hadn't realized he cared so much for the man. It was almost as much grief as he had felt for Allan D. and Bruce C. How could he go on?

Jim and Ray went together to the foundation meeting a day later. Some thirty people had gathered and as Jim walked in someone pulled him aside.

"I have bad news," he said.

"I already know," Jim told him. "Terry's dead."

"It's not Terry," the man said. "It's Dan B. Danny died this afternoon."

Dan B., a small immaculate man, had been a friend of Jim's since high school in London. As teenagers, they each had wondered if the other was gay but it had been impossible to ask. When they met again ten years later in a gay bar in Toronto, they laughed about it until the tears ran.

Danny had stopped his chemotherapy treatments half way through.

"I've watched what happens with others," he told his doctors. "It's treatment, treatment, treatment, pain, pain, pain—death. I think I'll skip the pain and do it nicer."

He signed some forms to absolve his doctors of all blame and went home. For a few weeks he saw his friends as usual, did some shopping, dropped into the bars, and made his preparations. As he got sicker, he lived on pain-killers but wouldn't go to hospital. He called Jim.

"I'm doing the best I can," he said. "Thanks for your help and good luck to you and everyone else."

Dan didn't waver in his refusal of treatment. He died quickly.

The August 26 foundation meeting was stormy. New people turned out, objecting to the structure of the foundation. They were furious to learn that Rodney Polich had been chosen as the new president and they protested that PWA s who were not members of the foundation couldn't vote. Most of all, they complained that the meeting was closed.

Rodney distributed copies of the by-laws, but this only increased the complaints. The by-laws were hotly debated and no consensus emerged. Rodney decided that the meeting was getting nowhere. He suggested another meeting on September 23 that would be open to all interested PWAs.

Rodney wasn't well but insisted to Jim that he would be able to carry on. Jim was not so sure. Rodney's AIDS had turned into spinal meningitis, which was crawling up his spine towards his brain. Three times a week he went to a hospital out-patient clinic for an IV drip containing a new drug, amphotarazine. Jim had little expectation that the drug would help Rodney because so far it hadn't worked on anyone.

Raymond C., another foundation member, died a few days later. Andy A., a big handsome former bartender at the Barn and one of the Stages crowd, died on September 10. A member of the foundation, he was a long-time friend of Jim's.

Jim attended a benefit party for Andy at the Barn when Andy became too sick to work. Andy's friends put on a comical this-is-your-life-Andy skit and raised about $500. Andy, about to have surgery to have his spleen removed, attended festively attired in pyjamas and dressing gown. The last memory Jim has of Andy is of him in hospital, moving slowly down a corridor pushing a walker.

Jim noted the pattern of his life: Wake up feeling pretty good, think about the day while making coffee, looks all right...*ring ring*.... "Hello, Jim here.... Hi, Linda, how are things?... Okay, I'll make it easy on you. Who's dead now?... No, I hadn't heard.... Okay, wait till I get a pen. All right, when is the funeral?... Are you okay?... Thanks for calling. Hugs and kisses."

The tragedies created a mood of tenderness in Toronto's gay community that grew more pronounced in the autumn of 1987. Everyone has lost someone. A few, like Jim, know forty or fifty people of their own age who have died. George Hislop, attending a funeral service that winter, observed bleakly that every day that week, for seven days, someone he knew had died.

As in a garrison under siege from a merciless enemy, gay people tended one another. Nobility emerged as people turned their minds to living each day as if it were their last. Stories of extraordinary kindness abounded, and expressions of affection were less restrained. A gentleness settled on the community; its suffering brought with it dignity and strength.

Jim has never met a gay man who doesn't believe that he is sero-positive for the human immunodeficiency virus. Gay men live in the shadow of a guillotine, wondering if a bruise or a sniffle or a sore shoulder or a headache is the beginning of full-blown AIDS.

One man who couldn't bear the suspense went to be tested and was found to be HIV-negative. The shock of it, after being braced for bad news, was so great he went into a depression. Two weeks later he insisted that the test be repeated, but it was negative again. Four months after that, he came down with PCP, the pneumonia peculiar to AIDS. He told Jim bravely that in many ways the reality of his diagnosis of AIDS was easier for him to bear than the years of uncertainty.

Jim finds it inspiring that so many people in the gay community's crisis are behaving nobly: uncomplaining in pain, unselfish in helping the sick, courageous in dying. People are making it through, he notes: lovers faithfully attend the diapered dying, volunteer buddies push wheelchairs, respects are paid at funerals.

Jim notes that most deaths from AIDS are peaceful. People close to death from AIDS know the signs in themselves because they have seen so many die. Usually they approach their final days strangely calm and composed.

Doing It!, a Toronto magazine for the gay and lesbian community, took note of the PWA coalition that spring, describing Jim as "Canada's longest surviving PWA, whose remission baffles many in the medical community, who is perhaps the most vigorous leading force behind the development and growth of the PWA Coalition".

Jim was quoted in the article as saying, "As of this March, I will be entering my fourth year of living with AIDS. After my initial shock at being diagnosed, and coming to understand the situation, I decided not to cave in but to stand up and fight.

"For a person diagnosed it is essential that the belief of living longer is strongly established. This is not denial! This is looking forward to the future, fighting on after diagnosis. I've tumbled a few times but the coalition helps me to stand back up."

He added defiantly, "We will show the world the meaning of strength."

Russ's condition was rapidly worsening. Lesions covered his body, and constant diarrhoea was stripping the flesh from his bones. The virus moved to his brain. By late summer Russ had difficulty keeping the foundation records. He simply couldn't remember numbers long enough to write them down accurately.

Jim made it a habit to check everything that Russ did, though he took care that Russ didn't know. Early in September, Jim dropped in to see Russ and found the big man in his dressing gown. As Russ settled back on the couch to talk, his dressing gown fell open. Jim had never seen so many tumours on anyone, not even Allan D. Hundreds, he thought, literally hundreds.

Russ saw the shock on Jim's face and silently covered himself. They were quiet together as Jim's eyes filled with tears. To avoid breaking down in front of his friend, he left quickly.

Russell died in his sleep on September 11, his forty-third birthday.

The regulars, going to a funeral that week, simply remained in the chapel when it was over. A second PWA funeral was scheduled for a few minutes later.

Each closed casket had on the lid a single long-stemmed scarlet rose, with a black stem and leaves, tied with a black ribbon. In the beginning the foundation had always sent bouquets to the funerals of people who died of AIDS, but that had become too costly: there were so many funerals. Jim thought of economizing with a single rose dipped in black except for the petals. The flower from the PWA Foundation came to be known as "the black rose". Attached to each black rose is a card that says, *We understand* .

One Sunday morning Jim went out to a restaurant for brunch. Sunday brunches are a favourite indulgence with him. As he set out alone, he was struck by the oddness of it.

293

"I never used to go to brunches alone," he mused. "Why am I going to Sunday brunch by myself?"

Then he realized that everyone who used to go to Sunday brunches with him was dead.

The third memorial service for people who had died of AIDS was held on November 1, 1987, in St. Andrew's Presbyterian Church. ACT's veteran counsellors Theresa Dobko and Yvette Perreault, women who had befriended more than seventy men who had died, stood arm in arm to describe one of them, a funny, outrageous man. They laughed as they told stories about him, but tears ran down their cheeks.

14

Jim moved through the carnage like a sleepwalker. His past was dying. The men who had known him in his twenties, those who had seen him through his collapses and triumphs, the people who shared his memories of good times, all were being wiped out. Almost the only people he had left were those he had known only a year or two. Who was left who had known him as a well man, really knew him at all?

Rodney Polich was too ill to chair the September 23 meeting that would resolve the controversy within the PWA Foundation. Jim said he couldn't attend. He had to make a speech in Orillia that night. Ray Barnard, one of the few survivors of the founding group still on his feet, prepared glumly to chair it. The gay community was boiling with debate about the foundation, with heated supporters on both sides. Jim withdrew from the turmoil and stopped answering his phone.

Ray was almost too exhausted to care any more how the meeting turned out. Franz H., another of the founders of the foundation, was dying in great misery, paralysed and incontinent. Ray was visiting him almost every day.

Ray came to see Jim one day to vent his rage. Franz's mother had just appeared at the hospital, visiting her son for the first time. She encountered Dave P., a PWA friend of Franz's, who was helping the nurse wash Franz's wasted body. Apparently unconcerned that Franz was conscious and could hear her, she demanded to know about his will. There was a lot of money involved, she said sharply, and it should be coming to her.

Dave took her into the corridor, leaned towards her with his face inches from hers and hissed, "You are a witch."

She hissed back, "You are a faggot."

Franz died on September 21.

Jim made a head count. That made nine people he knew who had died in the past two weeks.

The September 23 meeting of the Persons with AIDS Foundation was chaotic. An hour or so into the proceedings Ray Barnard was asked to leave the room. In his absence a new group, the Interim Committee for PWA Foundation Continuance, was formed to assume control. The committee was instructed to consult widely and draw up a list of recommendations about such matters as membership qualifications and amendments to the by-laws.

A three-person directorate was chosen—one of them, John Hamilton, a man who did not have AIDS. In view of the current rash of deaths among foundation members, it was deemed prudent to have at least one officer who wasn't likely to become too sick to function.

A task force of five people was selected to define services and goals, to pursue the elusive tax registration number, and to find a location for a headquarters. Meanwhile the good news was that the provincial government was likely to fund the organization once it became stable.

Jim arrived back in Toronto too late to attend the meeting but he found a sobbing message on his telephone answering machine from Ray Barnard. Ray said the meeting had been a total disaster.

Jim put his coat back on and went immediately to Ray's place. Ray gave an incoherent account of the part of the meeting he had witnessed. He had hoped to prevail upon people to agree to a freeze to allow the foundation time to reform. Instead he had endured a torrent of abuse about the past. Many people at the meeting were strangers to him, but few had anything good to say about the founding group. Not many criticized Jim, but there were some snide comments.

Ray wept, but Jim was dry-eyed with shock. How had this happened? The foundation was the contribution of his lifetime to his community.

Jim and Ray agreed to fold the foundation. They were weary of the controversy and too many members were dead. Neither had the heart to try to carry on. Word was that Rodney Polich, the man they had picked as Jim's successor, was dying.

Jim went the next day to tell Rodney the decision and found him in a hospital out-patient clinic, his arm attached to an IV drip that was providing his medication. When Jim said gently that it was no use their trying to continue against so much adversity, Rodney began to cry, tears rolling down the sides of his head to soak the pillow.

"Please, Jim," he begged. "Don't give up. I'll get out of this, you'll see. Give me a chance, just a chance."

Jim said, stroking Rodney's hair, "Sure Rod. We'll do that. We'll decide when you're better."

Rodney Polich died the next day, September 24.

Jim was in a foul mood as he walked to Linda Boyd's apartment that day for a meeting of representatives of PWA support groups. The Tuesday night support group had grown so large that it was split into two, meeting on Mondays and Fridays. Linda had decided that a co-ordinating meeting was necessary.

Word in the gay community was that the remarkable Linda Boyd was burning out after almost four years of being a fortress. She indeed was drained from too many bedside vigils and too many funerals, but her more pressing problem was financial.

For four years she had worked for people with AIDS and their support groups as a volunteer, supporting herself for a time on the proceeds of the sale of her home. Early in 1987, that money ran out. Linda's efforts to get employment in the counselling field failed, despite her unusual and compelling experience. Some suspected that her joyful wardrobe was viewed as inappropriate for such a solemn task as counselling. In any event, she had been forced to apply for welfare.

Jim found Linda attired in fuchsia and sapphire silk with eye make-up, hair, and fingernails to match. In her tiny living-room were facilitators from both support groups and some people from ACT. To Jim's dismay, they had criticism about the way he had run the PWA Foundation. They told Jim that the foundation was overdue for change. Most of the founding group had died and those left alive were exhausted so it was time for new blood and fresh ideas.

Jim furiously hurled himself out of Linda's apartment. When he got home, he called her and, getting her telephone machine, ranted an angry message on her tape. He paced his apartment in a rage that didn't subside even when he picked up a table and crashed it against a wall. He swallowed two sleeping pills with a glass of wine, hoping to calm down, but they only made him more excited. He noted that his temperature was soaring.

By two in the morning it had reached a dangerous peak so he checked himself into St. Michael's Hospital. No bed was available on 6A, but his heart rate was greatly accelerated so it was decided to keep him in emergency. He asked to speak to someone from psychiatry and was reminded that it was a Saturday night. The staff would see what could be done but he would have to be patient. He was placed in a cubicle in a corner of the emergency department with curtains drawn around his bed for privacy. When the breakfast tray came he refused to eat.

Towards dawn he was moved to a room on the fourth floor and a young nurse stayed with him, holding his hand tightly.

"You're going through a bad time, aren't you?" she observed. He turned his face to the wall without answering. She persisted, keeping a firm grip on his hand. She chatted idly about some family matters for a while—her mother's peculiar ailment and what people were doing about it. Jim did not respond.

She switched the subject. She said she had seen Jim on television. It was wonderful what he was doing, helping people with AIDS. Such a terrible disease, she went on, but she had noticed what spirit many people with AIDS had, and how gentle they were with one another. Jim remained silent.

As she rose to leave, he relented. "Thank you," he said stiffly. "I know I haven't been easy, but I appreciate what you did."

She smiled warmly at him and he managed a smile in return.

It wasn't until later that he realized she had remained with him an hour after her shift ended.

He asked again to speak to a psychiatrist. "I don't think that what's wrong with me is physical," he explained. "I know Linda Cohen, my social worker, isn't here on Sundays, so would you please get me someone else to talk to?"

Very soon, he was promised.

The next morning he called Linda Boyd to apologize for his unpleasant message on her machine. She gave him a blast about being "a grandstanding AIDS star" and hung up in his ear.

Jim could think of no one left who would care about him. They were all dead—Bruce, Allan, Terry.... Breakfast came but he still was too despondent to eat. He asked again for a psychiatrist. A nurse told him impatiently that he would have to wait, everyone was very busy. His lunch tray came and he pushed it away.

He brooded about the friends and lovers he had buried. The one he most wanted to see, he decided, was Larry W. Larry had been the first person he told about wanting to start an organization for people with AIDS. Larry had appreciated how much the foundation meant to Jim and would understand his hurt. Larry always had something helpful to say when Jim had a problem; Jim had counted on Larry's sympathy and sensible advice many times.

Jim couldn't even remember how long it had been since Larry died. Was it really two years? He could still see Larry's parents, dressed so simply, weeping by the bier as their only son was lowered into his grave.

Jim's imagination played a familiar trick. He pictured the graveside with all his dead friends standing around the grave—Bruce and Allan and Larry and Dennis and Steve and Irv and Ross and Sam and Nathan and Lawrence and Scott and Luc—all of them looking well and happy, smiling at him. He loves conjuring those men up that way. His friends look so contented, standing there smiling at him. The pain and struggle are done with and they are their young selves again.

With no plan in mind, he took a black pen and wrote on the wall beside his bed, "If someone doesn't help me soon, I will die." He sat on the edge of his bed waiting for someone, preferably the psychiatrist, to come. A nurse entered, read it, and said, "Well, I hope it washes off."

He was given a sedative and fell asleep. When he wakened an hour later, he lay a while listening to the familiar sounds of a hospital going about its business. No one came. He decided he had to talk to Larry W. or he would become insane. He dressed and wrote a note, "I've gone to visit Larry. I would have gone to talk to Bruce but he's too far to go." He left it propped on his pillow.

The nurse who found it immediately called a doctor. They found Jim's address book among his possessions and looked for the names Larry and Bruce. When they found them, both had been stroked through. The doctor called the AIDS Committee of Toronto and confirmed that Larry and Bruce were dead.

A hasty conference was called. It seemed evident from the scrawl on the wall and the note on the pillow that Jim was suicidal. The plan to see Larry must mean that Jim was going to join his friend in death. A doctor called the police, who broadcast Jim's description to all officers.

Meanwhile Jim was sitting beside Larry's grave, telling him his troubles. He asked, "Larry, what would you do about the people who are trying to tear the foundation apart? Should I fight them? How can I handle this? I have no one. Why did you leave me? Sometimes I'm really angry at you people who have left me. I need you now, I really need you."

He was beginning to feel more relaxed as his disjointed thoughts tumbled out. He went on in a chatty tone: "I've got some new furniture, Larry. A coffee-table that's a sheet of heavy glass balanced on a stone pillar base. I've arranged some small crystal ornaments on it and I've got track lighting fixed to make them sparkle. Looks great, Larry, you'd love it. And I've painted a huge white-on-white painting for the living-room wall that you haven't seen.

"Larry, have you noticed the people buried around you? I'll introduce you. You should get to know them, they're your neighbours."

Jim looked up from reading the names on nearby graves and saw Theresa Dobko strolling towards him. Theresa was one of the first people hired by ACT as a counsellor. Like Linda Boyd, she's one of the legends in the gay community, a woman of great intelligence and composure. When she heard that Jim had gone to see Larry, she guessed that he would be found at Larry's grave and she knew exactly where it was, Plot 104 in Section 46 of Mount Pleasant Cemetery.

She knelt beside Jim.

"Are you visiting?" she asked tenderly.

Jim nodded, too choked to speak.

She put her arms around him and he cried. After a while he dried his eyes and she led him to a car and drove him to the hospital.

A doctor told Jim there was a young man with AIDS, Jamie S., across the corridor. He was in a bad way, the doctor said. Would Jim talk to him, cheer him up?

Jamie was a youth of only twenty-two whose face was so swollen with cancer that it was like a balloon. When Jim came in, Jamie quickly covered his bloated features with his hands.

"Please, not now," he said with his eyes squeezed shut. "I don't want you to meet me like this."

"Of course," Jim said understandingly. "We'll talk later."

Jim went home. A message on his telephone machine said that Roger, another PWA Foundation member, had died. The next day he had a call that Bill L. was dead. Bill had been a director of ACT and a great friend to the PWA Foundation. Jim stopped answering the phone.

He heard on September 30 that Jamie, the boy with the swollen face, had just died.

The *Toronto Star* of October 8, 1987, carried a banner headline on its front page: 16 AIDS DEATHS IN MONTH CRIPPLE TORONTO PATIENTS' GROUP. The respected journalist Lillian Newbery wrote that the Toronto PWA Foundation had experienced sixteen deaths in the past month.

There was no reference to the group's internal problems. Instead the writer dealt compassionately with the havoc of so many deaths. She quoted Jim St. James of the Persons with AIDS Foundation, who said to her that the group "really got slammed by these 16 deaths, which included some key people." The foundation, he said, would have to "just sit tight for another month or two and see if any new PWAs are interested in helping."

Early in October, the City of Toronto's Board of Health revealed it was withholding a $6,000 loan to the organization until the Public Trustee completed an investigation of the finances. Jim was quoted again. "We're real clean as far as I know." Dr. Jay Browne, head of OPEPA, told Jim informally that the $80,000 the Foundation had requested had been approved. It was being held, pending the foundation's reorganization.

People in the office of the Public Trustee were conferring with the new leadership of the foundation. Better accounting procedures were agreed upon, but the review of the past year's operation was inconclusive. Irregularities had occurred but these seemed to be the consequence of poor advice and insufficient experience in record-keeping, a not uncommon problem in new community-based organizations.

Ray Barnard and Jim met in a lawyer's office at the end of October to sign the papers that officially turned the organization over to a new group. The ceremony was sombre and businesslike, as lawyers shuffled papers and witnessed the signatures, stamping the documents with the foundation's official seal.

It took less than ten minutes and everyone shook hands.

Ray and Jim drove home in silence.

"I feel awful," Ray said, finally.

Jim nodded. "I know. It's like handing over a child to strangers."

On December 15, 1987, Jim and Ray attended the first membership meeting called by the new leaders. The two men sat quietly amazed in the back of the room. They had never seen a Persons with AIDS meeting like it. The lazy camaraderie of the founding group was gone, to be replaced by severe adherence to Robert's Rules of Order. The meeting began crisply with a vote to appoint someone to take minutes. Then the notice of meeting was read and there was instruction that the notice of meeting should accompany the record of the meeting. The chair checked to establish if a quorum was present, following which a motion was made to approve the minutes of the previous meeting.

Jim and Ray were depressed. The old PWA meetings had ignored such formalities, but at least they talked about people who had AIDS and what could be done to help them. Motions, none of them relating directly to PWAs, were made, seconded, and discussed. Votes were called: all in favour? Opposed? *Passed*.

"So formal," Jim whispered to Ray. "Holy smokes. They think this is IBM."

Someone stood and offered a motion congratulating the Interim Committee on its fine work in reconstituting the organization. The motion was approved unanimously with applause.

Ray nudged Jim. They waited expectantly for someone to move a vote of thanks to them, the founders. Instead the next order of business was a financial report; then there was a report on discussions with the Public Trustee, and then a motion to appoint auditors. After more reports there was a motion to adjourn and the meeting was over.

Jim and Ray left feeling they had been stabbed.

Trying to make light of it, Ray said disgustedly, "They might have sent flowers."

The City of Toronto released its promised funds and the Ontario government announced the OPEPA grant of $80,000 to get the new organization started. Staff was hired and spacious premises were quickly located on Yonge Street. Jim did not attend the opening.

On January 12, 1988, Ray and Jim received letters from the new PWA Foundation to inform them that their memberships had been revoked by a vote of the membership. They were advised that they were not eligible to attend meetings ever again. No reason was given, but an explanation emerged a few weeks later when Jim and Ray were summonsed into court to produce PWA Foundation records that had never existed. Bureaucracy was having its sternest day. The development of the foundation had followed a classic pattern of grassroots organizations, all heart and no ledgers. In addition, it was founded and run by dying men using the last precious days of their lives. The reputation of the Public Trustee was not seeing its finest hour.

That was not the only controversy involving Jim in the spring of 1988. A commercial he made for the Canadian Public Health Association (CPHA) and the Canadian Association of Broadcasters was deemed too explicit by some radio and television stations, who refused to run it. The television version showed Jim's strong, hollow-eyed face staring directly at the viewer.

"My name is Jim," he says, "and I have AIDS."

He continues with burning eyes, "And I've seen many people die. You have the advantage. You can get information now that I couldn't...please, learn how to avoid AIDS and protect yourself."

Dr. David Walters, director of CPHA's AIDS Education and Awareness Program, said, "We thought it was worthwhile.... What's built into the message is a sense of hope."

Jim doesn't believe he has AIDS any more. He's puzzled that the handful of longest survivors in North America haven't all been tested for the human immunodeficiency virus. His theory is that none of them has HIV. His theory is that the virus devoured his entire immune system in the first two years and then died for lack of nutrition. He's waiting for his immune system to rebuild itself and takes encouragement from blood tests showing his T-4 cells are in an acceptable range.

"Meanwhile," he says seriously, "all I have to worry about is cancer."

In the spring of 1988 Jim had plenty of time to clean his apartment. He was alone and idle most of the day. His left leg was troubling him. Once he counted the purple boils of Kaposi's sarcoma that had erupted from his thigh to his ankle, with a thick cluster around his knee, and got to sixty-five. Doctors at St. Michael's were treating the biggest and most troublesome ones with radiation. Jim had been seven times for radiation therapy, with the result that fluid from radiated tissue had drained into his foot and ankle, making them swollen and painful.

He hates anyone to know that he's sore. Whenever he feels he is being watched, he tries to walk without a limp.

He had been assured many times that it would never be necessary to remove his leg, but looking at the mess on his leg, he wasn't convinced that it wouldn't happen. He had been warned that there is a limit to the amount of radiation the limb can take, and he wondered what doctors would do when that point was reached.

The appearance of his leg disturbed him. Jim had always been rather vain about his long well-shaped legs, and he owns many pairs of well-tailored summer shorts. He wasn't sure he would have the courage to wear them when the warm weather arrived, but he thought about the example of Russell A., sunbathing that last summer of his life even though he was covered in Kaposi's boils. In May 1988, when Toronto had unseasonably hot weather during a three-day conference on he wasn't convinced, , Jim wore a short-sleeved shirt that revealed the Kaposi's on his left arm while addressing one of the sessions.

Every week or so Jim found new tumours starting. One night in bed he felt wetness around his foot. When he threw back the covers he discovered that he had rubbed the top off of one of the tumours and it was spouting a pulsing jet of blood.

"Talk about springing a leak," he chuckled when he told friends about it, but he didn't laugh at the time.

He worries about occasional headaches that come with blinding intensity, but Dr. Bernadette Garvey assures him they aren't a sign that he's developing a brain tumour.

"Don't worry," she told him. "Slow down. You're not in any trouble. There's nothing to be so worried about."

He and Ray Barnard spend a lot of time together. They are the survivors and they've become experts on the progress of AIDS.

If a man comes to the support group one night and says brightly, "Gee, I've lost ten pounds this past month," that's trouble. If he says, "They've started me on AZT and they think it's working," Jim and Ray aren't impressed. They've noted that AZT slows down the progress of the fungus but also makes the person very sick. All the experimental drugs for AIDS have miserable, and even dangerous, side effects.

Jim and Ray agree that the only way for them to handle themselves responsibly, as people with AIDS, is to do their best to help their bodies fight the disease. That's why Jim is so careful to remember to take his vitamins and drink apple juice and get plenty of exercise and sleep. He doesn't want to be one of those dying people he has seen who pour out regrets that they hadn't given themselves a better chance by quitting smoking, or cutting down on their drinking.

He remembered one man, David, in the PWA support group who said angrily, "If I hadn't been such a slut, I wouldn't be in this mess."

Jim argued with him. "Sure, the law of averages says if you had sex with a hundred people you're more likely to come in contact with AIDS than if you had sex with one. But it won't help any of us if we lambaste ourselves for having sex. I think it's wrong for us to guilt ourselves about this. If we have to die of something, it's better to die of something we got from making love than to die in a war trying to kill someone else."

Throughout the winter of 1987, Ray Barnard gave Jim piano lessons. Ray, thirty-one, is a former pianist with the Royal Hamilton Chamber Ensemble. He told *Toronto Star* reporter Kellie Hudson that he had only two sexual relations in thirteen years. "You wouldn't have thought I was a candidate for AIDS, but obviously one lover passed it on and I have a weak immune system." When he was diagnosed in 1986 he lost sixty pounds and had to quit his job as a Canada Post letter carrier.

The two men, the only survivors of the original Toronto Persons with AIDS Coalition, became close friends.

Sometimes when Jim was in a bar, he would meet someone who seemed interested in sex. If he felt the same, he would ask, "Do you know who I am? I have AIDS."

Often the man would say, "Sure, I know. I have AIDS too."

It was becoming such a common occurrence that Jim was beginning to think, "*Everyone*'s got AIDS."

Jim pulled out his old audition pieces and spent hours working on them. He found an acting coach and set up regular appointments. He was planning to go back to acting as soon as his leg healed, and he wanted to be ready. He found his much-thumbed script of *Man of La Mancha* and refreshed his memory of the lines. Don Quixote is the role he loves most, and he reasoned that in the part of the old man he could get away with the limp.

In 1984 when Allan D. died Jim started a list of names of friends who died of AIDS. In August 1988 there were seventy-four people on it. He was sorry he had started it, but he felt compelled by a sense of obligation to the dead. He has stopped attending funerals.

He told friends he had never known such calm and peace in his whole life. Living for four years with a fatal disease had not instilled in him any fear of death; instead he had developed an intense appreciation of life. He spent his days in a tranquil frame of mind, taking deep pleasure in the fall of sunlight in his rooms or soft music in the night. His boyish, impish sense of humour returned. Always an affectionate man, he paid special attention to friends and family. The progress of the book about his life intrigued him, and he was pleased at the efforts Natalie Wexler and agent Michael Levine were making to turn the book into a film. The point of the book and the possible film, as he told everyone repeatedly, is to send a message of hope to people with AIDS and people afraid of AIDS.

He thinks his AIDS is cured and he's anxious to be tested to see if his theory is correct. He has plenty of cancer to confront but he thinks his immune system is beginning to work again.

On April 7, 1988, the fourth anniversary of Jim's diagnosis with AIDS, Natalie and Bernie Wexler gave a champagne cocktail party to celebrate. All Jim's friends were there, the living and the dead.

Jim's father volunteered to call his mother to see if a reconciliation could be possible. The separation from his mother has been so painful for Jim that he can't bear to hope. He doesn't expect that the matter can be resolved. He knows the Jehovah's Witnesses very well and doesn't expect the elders to relent. He has compassion for his mother's need to follow her faith. He dreads opening wounds that won't heal afterwards.

He prays to Jehovah at funerals, always, and also in hospital when he knows that the test or procedure he faces will be painful. He prays for strength to bear it.

He feels at peace with Jehovah. He'll be resurrected, or he won't. He can't believe that Jehovah will refuse to resurrect him just because he is gay. It doesn't make sense that a loving and fair-minded God would be so cruel.

In the first year of his illness Jim made a tape that he wants played at his funeral. It opens with the song from the musical *West Side Story* that begins: "There's a place for us, somewhere a place for us...."

It is followed by Jim's voice:

"Well, this is Jim.... You know what I'm like. I always like to get the last word.... What you're going to hear now is not a chronicle of the nice times I've had in my life but some of my deepest thoughts and hopes that were taught to me by many of you.... I hope my father made it here. I don't really know if he would.... Dad taught me to stand firm because he always did....

309

Dad, I love you. You never made a servant of me, father, or a child out of me, but you certainly helped in making me a man. Kathryn and Allan, I want to thank you for everything. You've been wonderful. Keep going. Look after your kids....

"Take care of my Natalie. She is the most precious thing that ever happened to me....

"And what can I say of my beloved boys and girls who are here. Thanks for coming guys. Never *never* give up your fight for life.... As long as you have love among yourselves, and love and respect for yourselves, you shall endure....

"I want to take a moment to tell you about my hope. Although I am sleeping in front of you now, I will come back to you through the promise of the resurrection that the God of the Bible made....

"That's all I have to say. Take care, everybody. I'm going to sleep."

Jim doesn't expect the tape will be needed for years and years. "I'm not going to die of AIDS," he said with his cocky grin. "I'm going to die of old age. I promise."